THE RIGHTS OF PEOPLES

The Rights of Peoples

Edited by

JAMES CRAWFORD

CLARENDON PRESS · OXFORD

Oxford University Press, Walton Street, Oxford OX2 6DP
Oxford New York Toronto
Delhi Bombay Calcutta Madras Karachi
Petaling Jaya Singapore Hong Kong Tokyo
Nairobi Dar es Salaam Cape Town
Melbourne Auckland
and associated companies in
Berlin Ibadan

Oxford is a trade mark of Oxford University Press

Published in the United States
by Oxford University Press, New York

First published 1988
Reprinted (new as paperback) 1992

British Library Cataloguing in Publication Data
The Rights of peoples.
1. Human rights. International legal aspects
I. Crawford, James, 1948–
341.4'81
ISBN 0–19–825624–8
ISBN 0–19–825804–6 (pbk.)

Library of Congress Cataloging in Publication Data
The Rights of peoples.
Bibliography: p.
Includes index
1. Human rights. I. Crawford, James, 1948–
K3240.6.R54   1988   342'.085   88–5298   342.285
ISBN 0–19–825624–8
ISBN 0–19–825804–6 (pbk.)

Printed in Great Britain
by Bookcraft Ltd
Midsomer Norton, Avon

Contents

Editor's Preface

Questions of collective or group rights have been contentious questions in international law and politics for a long time—arguably for as long as have individual rights. More recently there have been attempts, in the United Nations and elsewhere, to assert what is perceived as a new category of rights, a so-called 'third generation' of collective or peoples' rights. The variety of these assertions, the often vague and woolly way in which they are described, their relation to established human rights, to the earlier 'group' rights and to other rules of international law—indeed, their identification as human rights properly so-called, as distinct from rights of States—all these are controversial and disputed issues. One focus for the dispute has been UNESCO's Major Program XIII, 'Peace, International Understanding, Human Rights and the Rights of Peoples'. The United States Government gave as one of its reasons for withdrawing from UNESCO in 1984, its distaste at UNESCO's apparent support for 'people's rights', and at the danger that they could create new excuses for the denial of individual human rights. But the issue has not been confined to the UN and its agencies. The African Charter of Human and People's Rights (the Banjul Charter) adopted by the Organization of African Unity in 1981, incorporates statements of 'people's rights' for the first time in a multilateral human rights treaty.[1]

As a contribution to the discussion of these questions, and to help to clarify its position before the 23rd General Conference of UNESCO in October 1985, the Australian National Commission for UNESCO sponsored two symposia in Australia in March and June 1985. Most of the papers in this volume are revised and edited versions of papers given at those symposia. Opportunity has been taken in the revision to incorporate subsequent developments, including the UN General Assembly's approval of a 'Declaration on the Right to Development' in 1986. Two further papers have been added: the first, by David Makinson, discusses some of the logical and philosophical issues raised by the debate; the second is an attempt by the editor to summarize the debate and to suggest some general conclusions. There is also a select bibliography, and a documentary appendix giving appropriate references to (and, in the case of some of the

---

[1] The African Charter entered into force on 21 October 1986, at which time 29 States had ratified or acceded to it.

more recent or inaccessible documents, the text of) the main declarations, treaties, and other instruments referred to.

In addition to the contributors, thanks are due to the staff of the Australian National Commission for UNESCO (especially Eric Meadows and Judy Middlebrook), for their enthusiasm and support in the organization of the symposia, to Tom Musgrave for assistance with the bibliography, and to Professor Alice Tay for making available a special issue of the Bulletin of the Australian Society of Legal Philosophy (vol. 9 no. 33 (1985)) in which four of these essays (those by Brownlie, Rich, Crawford and Kamenka) were first published.

JAMES CRAWFORD

Sydney
1 September 1987

Notes on the Contributors

IAN BROWNLIE QC DCL FBA is Chichele Professor of Public International Law in the University of Oxford. He is a barrister of Gray's Inn, and took silk in 1979. He was counsel for Chile in the Beagle Channel arbitration (1977-9) and in the subsequent Papal Mediation and has been involved as counsel in a number of cases in the International Court of Justice, including the *Gulf of Maine* case (for Canada) and *Nicaragua* v. *United States* and before the European Commission of Human Rights and the Commission of the European Communities. He has advised, among others, organizations of Canadian Indians in respect of the 'patriation' of the Canadian Constitution in 1982. His books include *Principles of Public International Law* (3rd edn, 1979); *International Law and the Use of Force by States* (1963); *African Boundaries: A Legal and Diplomatic Encyclopaedia* (1979); and *System of the Law of Nations: State Responsibility* (1983).

JAMES CRAWFORD is Challis Professor of International Law in the University of Sydney, and an Associé of the Institut de Droit International. He was formerly Professor of Law at the University of Adelaide. As a Commissioner of the Australian Law Reform Commission he was responsible for Reports on *Foreign State Immunity* (1984). *Admiralty Jurisdiction* (1986), and *The Recognition of Aboriginal Customary Laws* (1986). His book *The Creation of States in International Law* (1979) was awarded the American Society of International Law's Certificate of Merit in 1981.

RICHARD FALK is Albert G. Milbank Professor of International Law and Practice, and a fellow of the Center of International Studies, Princeton University. He was counsel for Ethiopia and Liberia in the *South West Africa Cases* before the International Court of Justice. He has written extensively on issues of international law and relations: his principal books include *Human Rights and State Sovereignty* (1982), *The End of World Order* (1983), and *A Study of Future Worlds* (1975). He is on the Executive Council of the American Chapter of the International League for the Rights of Peoples.

EUGENE KAMENKA is Professor and Head of the History of Ideas Unit, Research School of Social Sciences, Australian National University, and a Fellow of the Australian Academy of the Humanities and the Australian Academy of the Social Sciences. He has written widely on Marxism, nationalism, human rights, and the philosophical and social foundations of law.

DAVID MAKINSON was educated in Australia and Britain, and was Professor and Head of the Department of Philosophy at the American University of Beirut. He is currently Program Specialist in the Division of Philosophy and Human Sciences, UNESCO (Paris). Dr Makinson is the author of several books (including *Topics in Modern Logic* (London, Methuen, 1973)) and of numerous articles on modal logic and on the logic of norms and of theory change.

GARTH NETTHEIM is a professor of Law at the University of New South Wales, and chairs the Aboriginal Law Centre within the University. He assisted in the establishment of the first Aboriginal legal service, in Sydney, Sydney, in 1971. He has written extensively on legal issues involving Australian Aboriginal people and the rights of indigenous peoples generally.

LYNDEL V. PROTT in Reader in International Law and Jurisprudence in the Faculty of Law, University of Sydney. She is the author of *The Latent Power of Culture and the International Judge* (1979), and (with P. J. O'Keefe) *Law and the Culture Heritage* (5 vols, in progress).

ROLAND RICH is a graduate of the University of Sydney and the Australian National University (BA, LL B (Syd), M Int L (ANU)). He is currently First Secretary in the Department of Foreign Affairs and Trade, having served in Paris and Rangoon. He has worked on law of the sea issues and is presently in the United Nations Political Section of the Department.

Dr GILLIAN TRIGGS is a senior lecturer in law in the University of Melbourne and a member of the Victorian bar. She has written extensively on international law issues of concern to Australia, including Antarctica, human rights, and extraterritoriality.

1

The Rights of Peoples in Modern International Law

IAN BROWNLIE

THE subject of this article is essentially that of human rights, with particular reference to the rights of groups and indigenous populations. UNESCO, along with other international organizations, universal and regional, has been much concerned with the articulation and elaboration of human rights concepts, and within UNESCO a particular subject of debate has been the Rights of Peoples. It is thus my responsibility to contribute to a process already in being. My position is that of a professional lawyer, not associated with any pressure group, whose role will be that of the chorus in Greek tragedy. That is to say, I shall speak as an 'interested spectator', sympathizing with the fortunes of the characters, and giving expression to the legal and moral critique evoked by the action of the play.

The background, the setting, is the subject of human rights. The term 'human rights' is relatively new, first appearing in documents on post-war organization produced within the United States in the war years. However, the concept is much older than the terminology: it reaches back to secular political concepts, such as the Rights of Man, and religious thinking about natural rights. The more traditional term for human rights would be the Rule of Law. However, in the era of the United Nations the concept of human rights has acquired elements which take matters beyond the original notion of the Rule of Law.

In the first place, the modern concept of human rights places particular emphasis on equality. Thus two of the 'Purposes of the United Nations' set forth in the United Nations Charter adopted at San Francisco in 1945 were as follows:

2. To develop friendly relations among nations based on respect for the principle of equal rights and self-determination of peoples, and to take other appropriate measures to strengthen universal peace;

3. To achieve international co-operation in solving international problems of an economic, social, cultural, or humanitarian character, and in promoting and encouraging respect for human rights and for fundamental freedoms for all without distinction as to race, sex, language, or religion.

Secondly, the idea of human rights involved the checking of the performance of national legal systems against external standards, and the consequent erosion of the reserved domain of the domestic jurisdiction of States.

Thirdly, whilst the Rule of Law in its classical form involved a static model of equality before the law, with the accent on procedural justice and civil rights, the concept of human rights has been at least equally and perhaps more concerned with equal access to resources and education, that is to say, with a more dynamic concept of economic justice and substantial equality. This change of content was signalled by the appearance of the International Covenant on Economic, Social and Cultural Rights alongside the International Covenant on Civil and Political Rights in 1966.

In the years since 1945 the propagation and elaboration of human rights concepts has proceeded at an impressive pace. Not least among the developments has been the appearance of a rich body of case law produced by the national courts of some States, including India and the United States, and also by the European Commission and European Court of Human Rights. In particular, the concepts of equality and discrimination have been, and are being, articulated and refined in the process of application.

Inherent in the concepts of equality and of human rights is the idea that groups as such may have rights. The classical human rights instruments say little or nothing about the rights of groups as such, apart from the right of self-determination. However, in the Covenant on Civil and Political Rights the family is stated to be 'the natural and fundamental group unit of society' (Art. 23) and Art. 27 provides as follows:

In those States in which ethnic, religious or linguistic minorities exist, persons belonging to such minorities shall not be denied the right, in community with the other members of their group, to enjoy their own culture, to profess and practise their own religion, or to use their own language.

In a general way, the assumption lying behind the classical formulations of standards of human rights, including the Universal Declaration of 1948 and the two Covenants of 1966, has been that group rights would be taken care of automatically as the result of the protection of the rights of individuals. Thus if it is provided that 'everyone shall have the right to freedom of thought, conscience, and religion', then it is to be assumed that the rights of members of a religious community are adequately protected. Moreover, the Covenant on Civil and Political Rights contains a strong guarantee of equality before the law. Article 26 provides that 'the law shall prohibit any discrimination and guarantee to all persons equal and effective protection against discrimination on any ground such as race, colour, sex, language, religion, political or other opinion, national or social origin, property, birth or other status'.

However, it is not the case that the rights of groups are taken care of in all respects by the protection of the rights of individuals. Certain claims by groups which are not on their face unreasonable have involved subject matters not adequately covered by the usual prescriptions for individuals. Three types of such claims may be identified, although there may be others.

First, the classical formulations do not cope with claims to positive action to maintain the cultural and linguistic identity of communities, especially when the members of the community concerned are to some extent territorially scattered. It is to be recalled that Art. 27 of the Civil and Political Rights Covenant, in dealing with the protection of ethnic, religious, or linguistic minorities, formulates a classical static guarantee, namely, that such persons 'shall not be denied the right' to enjoy their own culture, and so forth.

The question of positive action was highlighted by the decision of the European Court of Human Rights in the *Belgian Linguistics* case of 1968.[1] In that case six groups of applicants from communities of French-speaking residents of the Flemish part of Belgium were seeking to use Art. 2 of the First Protocol to the European Convention in order to increase opportunities for their children to be educated in French, the language of the family. Article 2 provides that:

No person shall be denied the right to education. In the exercise of any functions which it assumes in relation to education and to teaching the State shall respect the right of parents to ensure such education and teaching in conformity with their own religious and philosophical convictions.

One of the complaints presented by the applicants was that the absence of positive action to maintain education in French in the municipalities in which they lived obliged the applicants either to enrol their children in the local Flemish schools or to send their children elsewhere, a cause of hardship and expense.

The Court considered that the facts complained of did not involve a violation of Art. 2, or of Art. 8 of the Convention itself, which is concerned with the protection of private and family life. The reasoning rested upon the premiss that the legislative history of the Convention did not support the view that positive action was necessary on the part of the State to provide subsidies and other material underpinning to the rights protected. In particular the Court observed:[2]

The legal provisions in issue . . . do not violate Art. 8 of the Convention. It is true that one result of the Acts of 1932 and 1963 has been the disappearance in the Dutch unilingual region of the majority of schools providing education in French. Consequently French-speaking children living in this region can now obtain there only education in Dutch, unless their parents have the financial resources to send them to private French-language schools. This clearly has a certain impact upon family life when parents do not have sufficient means to enrol their children in a

---

[1] European Court of Human Rights Ser A No 6 (1968).

[2] id., 43.

private school, or prefer that their children should avoid the inconvenience...
which the application of the law entails as regards education received in a private
school which is not in conformity with the linguistic requirements of the laws on
education. Such children will complete their studies in Dutch in the locality, unless
their parents send them to school in Brussels, Wallonia, or abroad. Harsh though
such consequences may be in individual cases, they do not involve any breach of
Art. 8. This provision in no way guarantees the right to be educated in the language
of one's parents by the public authorities or with their aid. Furthermore, in so far
as the legislation leads certain parents to separate themselves from their children,
such a separation is not imposed by this legislation: it results from the choice of
the parents who place their children in schools situated outside the Dutch unilingual region with the sole purpose of avoiding their being taught in Dutch, that
is to say in one of Belgium's national languages.

So that is the first special aspect of group rights, the claim to positive
action. It is not suggested that the problem of positive action is only
associated with the rights of groups, but the claim is more likely to be made
in this context.

The second type of claim involving group rights is the claim to have
adequate protection of land rights in traditional territories. The view that
in certain societies there is a special connection between the indigenous
people and the lands and waters of a region was articulated in the course of
the Mackenzie Valley Pipeline Inquiry by the communities affected, and
accepted in the Report compiled by the Commissioner, Mr Justice Thomas
Berger.[3] That is not, of course, the end of the matter, since the land rights
question may, and usually does, involve issues of title, historic justice, and
restitution. The central point, however, is the claim to exclusive rights in
respect of specific areas. This sets the land rights issue, and the concept of
traditional ownership of a group, apart from the usual prescription of
human rights on the basis of individual protection.

The third type of claim specific to groups is based upon the political and
legal principle of self-determination, the exercise of which involves a range
of political models, including the choice of independent statehood or some
form of autonomy or associated statehood.

It follows that in certain important respects the classical approach via
the protection of individuals is too limited, and additional concepts and
principles must be applied. The problems of application are considerable
in practice and I shall not, for the moment, follow them up. For the while
my focus will be the principle of the equal rights and self-determination of
peoples which receives recognition in principle in the text of the United
Nations Charter (Art. 1, para. 2; Art. 55).

The historic roots of the principle of self-determination include the
American Declaration of Independence and the decree of the French Con-
stitutent Assembly of May 1790, which refers both to the Rights of Man

[3] *Northern Frontier, Northern Homeland: Report of the Mackenzie Valley Pipeline Inquiry*
(Ottawa, 1977).

and to the rights of peoples. In the course of nineteenth-century European history the principle of nationality was influential and it was the *alter ego* of the principle of self-determination. These concepts, together with the concept of the protection of national minorities, were prominent in the deliberations of the Allied Supreme Council at Versailles in 1919. It is obvious that the concept of self-determination was not as yet accepted as a general principle. Thus the concept of racial equality was excluded from the Covenant of the League of Nations. Moreover, the Mandates System and the famous Minorities Treaties were conspicuous in their application only in certain cases. The special application of such institutions to defeated or newly established States only testified to the absence of a *general* recognition of the 'principle of equal rights and self-determination of peoples'. However, once the *principle* had been recognized as such, it was in the long run difficult—in terms both of morality and logic—to maintain that it only applied within the Americas and Europe. Thus, during and after the Second World War it was more and more accepted that self-determination was a universally applicable standard.

No doubt there has been continuing doubt and difficulty over the definition of what is a 'people' for the purpose of applying the principle of self-determination. None the less, the principle appears to have a core of reasonable certainty. This core consists in the right of a community which has a distinct character to have this character reflected in the institutions of government under which it lives. The concept of distinct character depends on a number of criteria which may appear in combination. Race (or nationality) is one of the more important of the relevant criteria, but the concept of race can only be expressed scientifically in terms of more specific features, in which matters of culture, language, religion, and group psychology predominate. The physical indicia of race and nationality may evidence the cultural distinctiveness of a group but they certainly do not inevitably condition it. Indeed, if the purely ethnic criteria are applied exclusively many long-existing national identities would be negated on academic grounds—such as, for example, the United States. In any case the community of States has been prepared to recognize both new States and the existence of legitimate claims by units of self-determination either by institutional procedures within the United Nations or on the basis of general recognition. Bangladesh, for example, was recognized as a State on the basis of general recognition by existing States. Provisions in written constitutions may acknowledge the relevance of self-determination to the affairs of multinational societies.

It is my opinion that the heterogeneous terminology which has been used over the years—the references to 'nationalities', 'peoples', 'minorities', and 'indigenous populations'—involves essentially the same idea. Nor is this view based upon a theoretical construction. Once a member of a people or community is expressing political claims in public discourse in Geneva,

New York, Ottawa, or Canberra, and using the available stock of concepts so to do, it seems to me that the type of political consciousness involved is broadly the same. The external participation of culturally distinct groups in the political process is essentially the same as that of individual States in respect of the Law of Nations. By this I mean that in order to obtain recognition of the claim to cultural identity, or to statehood, the claimant must accept the terms of the dialogue. This may sound rather obvious but it is in this context that I want to make the point that the opposition which appears in the sources between the definition of indigenous populations 'by themselves' and their definition 'by others' is a false dichotomy.

At this point I would like to stress that in practice the claim to self-determination does not necessarily involve a claim to statehood and secession. There are various models of 'self-government' or 'autonomy' but neither of these is a term of art. It is true that some models, such as Trusteeship, are related to the purpose of an ultimate transition to independence. However, there are a variety of other models, including that of 'Associated State' (as in the case of the Cook Islands and New Zealand), the regional autonomy of Austrians in the South Tyrol, the Cyprus Constitution of 1960, and the various arrangements within the Swiss and other federal constitutions. There can be little doubt that federalism as a system provides a special capacity and a flexibility in facing cultural diversity. Federalism is probably better able than any other system to provide a regime of stable autonomy which provides group freedoms within a wider political cosmos and keeps the principle of nationality in line with ideas of mutuality and genuine coexistence of peoples.

In fact, there is a sort of synthesis between the question of group rights as a human rights matter and the principle of self-determination. The recognition of group rights, more especially when this is related to territorial rights and regional autonomy, represents the practical and internal working out of the concept of self-determination. Such recognition is therefore the internal application of the concept of self-determination.

In practical terms the recognition of group rights usually takes two forms. In the first place, there is the prescription of a basic standard of equality or non-discrimination. The general standard of non-discrimination is prescribed in both the Covenant on Economic, Social and Cultural Rights and the Covenant on Civil and Political Rights of 1966. The issue of racial discrimination is dealt with more comprehensively in the International Convention on the Elimination of All Forms of Racial Discrimination of 1965.

The second form which recognition of group rights takes is the guarantee of the maintenance of group identity. This is the underlying issue addressed by Art. 27 of the Covenant on Civil and Political Rights. But in many countries the lack of adequate resources, the feebleness of the administrative system, and the absence of the rule of law mean that the protection of human rights gets off to a bad start.

In the case of the protection of group rights, precisely because a very delicate balance of interests is called for, the existence of an efficient and sensitive legal system is immensely important. When the problems themselves are approached they are seen to be in many cases essentially difficult. The legal preservation, especially by positive action, of cultural identity may run the risk of appearing to erect principles of discrimination and the problem then becomes, when is discrimination tolerable on grounds of special need?

The difficulties may be compounded by the fact that one set of principles may come into conflict with another. I shall give two examples of such conflicts. The environmental or conservationist ethic may conflict with the life-style of indigenous peoples. The Dogrib Indians of the North West Territory of Canada, whose normal avocation is fur trapping, are concerned about the activities of conservationist groups. Again, the life-style of indigenous peoples, like that of other groups, may in particular respects be incompatible with contemporary standards of human rights. The status of women and resort to traditional punishments are controversial areas in this respect.

Particular problems arise from the existence of legal institutions which identify and protect the group concerned. The establishment of a definition of membership, the analogue of nationality, is a delicate matter. Moreover, the question which must be faced is whether expatriation is to be permitted. Some of the proponents of the rights of indigenous peoples would erect constraints which, whatever the motivation, would be in effect a form of apartheid enforced by the law, with constraints upon assimilation and movement.

The practical difficulties involved may be illustrated by two recent episodes, the first from Canada, the second from Australia.

The first took the form of a decision by the Human Rights Committee which has supervisory powers in respect of the International Covenant on Civil and Political Rights in accordance with the Optional Protocol to that Covenant. Canada is a party to the Optional Protocol. The decision resulted from a communication from a Canadian Indian which put in issue the interpretation of Art. 27 of the Covenant. Sandra Lovelace, a registered Maliseet Indian, lost her status as an Indian under the Indian Act 1970 (Canada) when she married a non-Indian. An Indian man who married a non-Indian woman would not have lost his status in this way. Subsequently her marriage broke up and she returned to live on the reserve, contrary to the Act. She was only saved from eviction from the reserve by threats made on her behalf against anyone attempting to remove her. She claimed violation of her rights under Art. 2 of the Convention (on the basis of the sexually discriminatory rules defining Indian status), and under Art. 27 (on the basis that the Indian Act prevented her from enjoying her own culture in common with other members of the tribe). The Human Rights

Committee took the view that, at least after she ceased to live with her husband and returned to the reserve, the provisions of the Indian Act violated Art. 27. It was not necessary, therefore, to decide on the application of Art. 2 in this case.[4] The Australian Law Reform Commission drew the following conclusion from the decision, as to the scope of Art. 27:[5]

One effect of Art. 27 ... is to oblige a State to allow someone who is in fact a member of an ethnic minority group to associate with that group, even on reserve land. At the least, legal impediments must not be placed in the way of the exercise of rights under Art. 27, unless these have a 'reasonable and objective justification and [are] consistent with the other provisions of the Covenant'. It is also arguable that the failure to make equivalent legal provision for members of minority groups could contravene Art. 27 in particular cases.

The second episode, from Australia, illustrates the way in which protective land rights legislation may be in danger of falling foul of human rights obligations arising under major international conventions, at least as these are interpreted by national courts. *Gerhardy* v. *Brown*,[6] a decision of the High Court of Australia in 1985, involved the meaning of discrimination under the Racial Discrimination Act 1975, the Australian legislation which implements the International Convention on the Elimination of All Forms of Racial Discrimination of 1966. The key provision of the Act, s. 8(1), provides as follows:

This Part does not apply to, or in relation to the application of, special measures to which paragraph 4 of Art. 1 of the Convention applies except measures in relation to which subsection 10(1) applies by virtue of sub-section 10(3).

By paragraph 4 of Art. 1 of the Convention it is provided:

Special measures taken for the sole purpose of securing adequate advancement of certain racial or ethnic groups or individuals requiring such protection as may be necessary in order to ensure such groups or individuals equal enjoyment or exercise of human rights and fundamental freedoms shall not be deemed racial discrimination, provided, however, that such measures do not, as a consequence, lead to the maintenance of separate rights for different racial groups and that they shall not be continued after the objectives for which they were taken have been achieved.

The issue was whether the access to land provisions of the Pitjantjatjara Land Rights Act 1978 (SA) were racially discriminatory under the Commonwealth Act and the Convention. Their effect was to prevent any person other than a Ptijantjatjara (or a police officer, etc., in the course of official duties) entering the Pitjantjatjara land in the north-west of South Australia

[4] Views of the Human Rights Committee under Art. 5(4) of the Optional Protocol concerning Communication No R6/24, 30 July 1981: *Report of the Human Rights Committee*, GAOR 36th Sess, Supp. No 40 (A/36/40), Annex XVIII, 166.
[5] See Australian Law Reform Commission, Report 31, *The Recognition of Aboriginal Customary Laws* (Australian Government Publishing Service, Canberra, 1986) para. 176.
[6] (1985) 57 ALR 472.

without a permit from the corporate body of the Pitjantjatjara. Brown, the defendant in the case, was himself an Aborigine, though not a Pitjantjatjara. The High Court held unanimously that there was no conflict between the South Australian provisions and the Commonwealth Act, on the ground that the South Australian Act (including its permit provisions) was a 'special measure' within the meaning of Art. 1(4) of the Convention, and s. 8(1) of the Act. However, five of the seven judges (Wilson & Dawson JJ not deciding) held that, in the absence of Art. 1 para. 4, the provisions would have been discriminatory, because they made a distinction between Pitjantjatjara and non-Pitjantjatjara, one element of which was the proposition that to be a Pitjantjatjara was to be a member of a race. All the judges rejected the argument that the Act merely recognized traditional ownership and gave it effect within the general legal system, and that it was therefore not a discrimination based on race but a reasonable response to a traditional relationship with land. Accordingly, they treated Art. 1 para. 1 of the Racial Discrimination Convention, as implemented by ss. 9 and 10 of the Act, as being very much a prohibition on any formal discrimination by reference to a criterion containing any element of race irrespective of its 'legitimacy'. It follows that any provision containing notions of Aboriginality will be prima facie discriminatory unless it can be saved under Art. 1 para. 4.

The issues raised by *Gerhardy* v. *Brown* are familiar to the international lawyer and the international law materials have a particular value. No doubt the problems are to be examined very much in terms of their own time and social setting. However, the international experience indicates certain points of general technique. The experience of international tribunals and other national jurisdictions justifies the following as points of general approach or technique.

The most important point is this. The fact that a primary criterion involves a reference to race does not make the rule discriminatory in law, provided the reference to race has an objective basis and a reasonable cause. It is only when the reference to race lacks a reasonable cause and is arbitrary that the rule concerned becomes discriminatory in the legal sense.

Some examples can be given. Suppose that in a particular country, in an area of mixed population, special arrangements were made in State hospitals, prisons, and so forth to meet the particular dietary requirements of a racial or religious group. Two criteria would be relevant here: the membership of the racial or religious group and the dietary requirements. Again, in the context of sexual discrimination, it is obviously not discriminatory to make arrangements which are necessary to make allowance for the needs of women who are pregnant. The reference to the sex of the subject of the special provision is coupled with the second criterion, which is pregnancy.

Thus the question of discrimination is that of the relevance of the reference to race, or religion, or sex. Only women can become pregnant, but that does not mean that making special arrangements for pregnant women is in legal terms discrimination on grounds of sex. In the case of the recognition of the traditional ownership rights of the Pitjantjatjara the reference is similarly to a double criterion: that of tribal origin and that of traditional ownership. The fact that traditional ownership is peculiar to Aborigines does not make recognition of such land rights discriminatory in law. The legal recognition has an objective basis; it is not arbitrary and is discriminatory only in the sense that a reasonable and legitimate policy coincides with racial origin, in the same way as pregnancy coincides with womanhood.

Thus the first principle to apply is to ask whether the differentiation in the legal sense has a reasonable cause and relates to a legally relevant basis for different treatment.

The second principle is that the modalities of the different treatment must not be disproportionate in effect or involve unfairness to other racial groups. What is 'disproportionate' is very much a matter of assessment in relation to the particular facts, and there may be some delicate nuances as to what is in local terms reasonable. In the case of the recognition of land rights, the restriction on freedom of movement, linked with such recognition, raises the issue of proportionality. In other words, even when the different treatment is not discriminatory in a legal sense, the modalities, the method of implementation may be unreasonable and hence discriminatory at the second level.

It is in the context of the principle of proportionality that the concept of affirmative action or reverse discrimination is to be seen. When a law prescribes for affirmative action, in effect the principle of proportionality is being explicitly set aside: normally this will only be done on carefully defined terms, one of which will be a time-limit or other condition subsequently placed on the measures concerned. Art. 1 para. 4 of the Convention on Racial Discrimination provides a justification for 'special measures' and stipulates that such measures 'shall not be continued after the objectives for which they were taken have been achieved'.

It was this clause in the Convention, as reflected in the Act of 1975, which was the basis of the reasoning of the High Court in *Gerhardy* v. *Brown*.[7] The difficulty is that the High Court appeared to treat the 'special measures' clause as legitimating what would otherwise be discriminatory in law, since they viewed the legislation without that clause as being discriminatory. This approach is a further development of the original faulty premiss, which is the assumption by the High Court that the protection of traditional land rights is discriminatory in the first place.

[7] (1985) 57 ALR 472.

There are many reasons, both legal and non-legal, for not conducting the inquiry in terms of the category of discrimination but rather in terms of the reasonableness of the objectives, the proportionality of the means employed, and the question whether a special measure involves unfairness as between one group and another. The term 'discrimination' should only be applicable when the measure either favours or discriminates against a racial group without reasonable cause.

I have completed the survey of what I have chosen to call group rights, and can now move on to the concept of the Rights of Peoples which is the object of study under the sponsorship of UNESCO. The concept is not intended to be simply a rerun of notions of human rights, but represents a desire to provide reinforcement and further development of the existing stock of concepts of human rights. The origin of the Rights of Peoples could be said to be the United Nations Charter, which makes prominent reference to 'peoples'. Indeed, the preamble is actually formulated in the name of 'the peoples of the United Nations'. A more recent expression of the idea is to be found in the Universal Declaration of the Rights of Peoples adopted during a conference at Algiers in 1976. The meeting was not a diplomatic conference but an *ad hoc* gathering of lawyers, political scientists, politicians, and others. The document produced by that Conference, known as the Algiers Declaration, is a work of high idealism and a fairly high level of abstraction.[8] It was the product of a conference which did not reflect the views of governments and which was not composed of legal experts, but it has had a certain influence. This influence (or at least the influence of the ideas or aspirations contained in the Algiers Declaration) can be seen in the multilateral agreement adopted by the Organization of African Unity in 1981 and entitled the Banjul Charter on Human and Peoples' Rights.[9]

Of course, any group of persons has a right to get together and produce a statement of moral or political principles said to govern a certain subject matter. But the difficulty with documents like the Algiers Declaration is that they are offered in the language of law. Indeed, the Declaration contains a section devoted to 'Guarantees and Sanctions'.

I find the Algiers Declaration odd from a legal point of view. It confuses peoples with States, and in doing so collides with a large number of instruments, subscribed to by Third World States, in which it is clear that, apart from the cases of illegal occupation resulting from aggression or other usurpation of rights and unfulfilled claims to self-determination, international law applies as between States and the principle of non-intervention forbids going over the heads of States to their populations. Moreover, the plea of assisting oppressed minorities has been used in

---

[8] For the text of the Declaration see A. Cassese & E. Jouve (eds), Pour un Droit des Peuples (1978) 27–30.
[9] Text in: (1981) 21 *International Legal Materials* 58.

attempts to legitimate policies of intervention. Recognition of governments has not hitherto been contingent upon their democratic character.

If the Algiers Declaration is assumed to apply to States, and to peoples as such only in the exceptional cases I have indicated, then it does not add very much to existing positions. If it is intended to refer to 'peoples' and not to States (as representing their peoples), then it refers to a series of principles not recognized by the international community as applicable to peoples as opposed to the recognized governments of those States.

Finally, it is characteristic of the appallingly abstract nature of such exercises that those of us who are engaged in the practical solution of problems relating to group rights can find no assistance in their provisions. In particular, no attempt is made to define peoples or, in the case of the Algiers Declaration, to define 'minorities', to which some of its articles refer. The very problems which stand in need of careful study are left blandly on one side.

The reference to the Rights of Peoples in the Algiers Declaration and the Banjul Charter is in truth simply a part of the proliferation of academic inventions of new human rights and the launching of new normative candidates by anyone who can find an audience. In this context Philip Alston's 'proposal for quality control' in the human rights context is a very therapeutic one. Alston has this to say:[10]

Writing in 1968, the year of the 20th anniversary of the adoption of the Universal Declaration of Human Rights, Richard Bilder concluded that 'in practice, a claim is an international human right if the United Nations General Assembly said it is'. Fifteen years later, as the 35th anniversary is celebrated, the authoritative role that Bilder correctly attributed to the General Assembly is in serious danger of being undermined. The problem has manifested itself in three ways. First, the General Assembly has, on several occasions in recent years, proclaimed new rights (i.e. rights which do not find explicit recognition in the Universal Declaration of Human Rights or the two International Human Rights Conventions) without explicitly acknowledging its intention of doing so and without insisting that the claims in question should satisfy any particular criteria before qualifying as human rights. Second, there has been a growing tendency on the part of a range of United Nations and other international bodies, including in particular the UN Commission on Human Rights, to proceed to the proclamation of new human rights without reference to the Assembly. Third, the ease with which such innovation has been accomplished in these bodies has in turn encouraged or provoked the nomination of additional candidates, ranging from the right to tourism to the right to disarmament, at such a rate that the integrity of the entire process of recognising human rights is threatened.

In rather sharp contrast is the study by Marks entitled 'Emerging Human Rights: A New Generation for the 1980s?'[11] Marks seeks early to disarm

---

[10] P. Alston, 'Conjuring up New Human Rights: A Proposal for Quality Control' (1984) 78 AJIL 607.
[11] (1981) 33 *Rutgers* LR 435.

the reader by announcing that he is only offering a prospectus of the 'good bets' for the 1980s, that is, the newly 'emerging' human rights. This set of 'new runners' is described as the 'third generation of human rights', the first two generations consisting of the civil and political rights and, subsequently, the economic and social rights. Programmatic though it may be, the Marks prospectus of emerging human rights is interesting and comprehensive and, unlike the Algiers Declaration, it is not offered as though it were *lex lata*. His candidate rights are as follows.

First, there is the right to food. Marks refers in this connection to Art. 25 of the Universal Declaration of Human Rights, and in his recent stimulating essay on the subject,[12] Alston refers to Art. 11 of the International Covenant on Economic, Social and Cultural Rights, which provides as follows:

1. The States Parties to the present Covenant recognise the right of everyone to an adequate standard of living for himself and his family, including adequate food, clothing and housing, and to the continuous improvement of living conditions. The States Parties will take appropriate steps to ensure the realisation of this right, recognising to this effect the essential importance of international cooperation based on free consent.

2. The States Parties to the present Covenant, recognising the fundamental right of everyone to be free from hunger, shall take, individually and through international co-operation, the measures, including specific programmes, which are needed:

(a) To improve methods of production, conservation and distribution of food by making full use of technical and scientific knowledge, by disseminating knowledge of the principles of nutrition and by developing or reforming agrarian systems in such a way as to achieve the most efficient development and utilisation of natural resources;

(b) Taking into account the problems of both food-importing and food-exporting countries, to ensure an equitable distribution of world food supplies in relation to need.

Secondly, there is the right to a decent environment, in which connection Marks invokes the Stockholm Declaration of 1972. Thirdly, Marks states that 'the right to development as a human right has been the subject of extensive reflection and proposed formulations for nearly a decade and is well advanced in acquiring the status of an internationally recognized human right'.[13] Fourthly, the author announces the right to peace which, he says, 'is not difficult to deduce from the UN Charter, the Kellogg-Briand Pact, the Declaration on Principles of Friendly Relations, and many other basic documents'.[14] The nature of the law-seeking and law-finding involved is exemplified by the following passage which is remarkable in various

[12] In P. Alston & K. Tomaskevi (eds), *The Right to Food* (Nijhoff, The Hague, 1984).
[13] Marks, 444.
[14] id., 445.

ways. Having asserted the existence of the right to peace, Marks has this to say:[15]

A brief word about the content of the right to peace: it is the right of every individual to contribute to efforts for peace, including refusal to participate in the military effort, and the collective right of every state to benefit from the full respect by other states of the principle of non-use of force, of non-aggression, of peaceful settlement of disputes, of the Geneva Conventions and Additional Protocols and similar standards, as well as from the implementation of policies aimed at general and complete disarmament under effective international control. What I have just said is no more than an illustration of the sort of considerations that should go into the definition of this right. No authorised formulation exists, but I am convinced that this right will be increasingly refined in the coming years.

This type of thinking is completely unhelpful. It overlays existing and generally accepted principles with a layer of novelty. It confuses several distinct areas of law and it suggests that the writer is unaware that the items he refers to have received very considerable refinement already.

It is, of course, easy to be sceptical about experimental views and forward thinking. However, the type of reasoning deployed in some of the 'forward thinking' literature may have results which are negative in terms of the practical advancement of good purposes. As policy goals, as standards of morality, the so-called new generation of human rights would be acceptable and one could sit round a table with non-lawyers and agree on practical programmes for attaining these good ends. What concerns me as a lawyer is the casual introduction of serious confusions of thought, and this in the course of seeking to give the new rights an actual legal context. Many points could be made, one of which would be the tendency of what may be called the enthusiastic legal literature to develop as an isolated genre, with the select few repetitiously citing one another and the same materials, completely outside the main stream of diplomacy and international law.

It will be said that we always have to start somewhere, and that pioneers are by definition isolated. But that is not what is happening here. The type of law invention about which I have reservations involves a tendency to cut out the real pioneering—the process of persuasion and diplomacy—and to put in its place the premature announcement that the new settlement is built. The article by Roland Rich on the right to development is an example of this process.[16] The article is, if I may say so, a strong and fluent statement of the case for the recognition of the right to development, and it is supported by much documentation. However, while citing writers, such as Maurice Flory, and judges, such as Judge Bedjaoui, who assert the

[15] id, 446. The other new human rights chronicled by Marks are the right to benefit from the common heritage of mankind, the right to communicate, and the right to humanitarian assistance.

[16] R. Y. Rich, 'The Right to Development as an Emerging Human Right' (1983) 23 *Virginia* JIL 287.

existence of a right to development, Rich omits to warn the reader that the major texts of international law as yet contain no recognition of such a right. Moreover, he takes a wholly unacceptable view of what is State practice and invokes material which cannot be said to provide any evidence of a sense of legal obligation in this context.

This kind of approach is, in my view, inimical to the recognition of the right of development. It is rather like a commander in the field who announces victory on the basis that the enemy has made a partial withdrawal. For, if Rich and others are correct in their legal assessments, we can now rest, since the battle is won. Much more rigour is called for in the handling of legal materials. The elements of the formation of rules of general international law—international custom—are not some esoteric invention; rather they provide criteria by which the actual expectations and commitments of States can be tested. International law is about the real policies and commitments of governments, it is not about the incantations of secular or religious morality.

A related problem is the tendency to fragmentation of the law which characterizes the enthusiastic legal literature. The assumption is made that there are discrete subjects, such as 'international human rights law' or an 'international law on development'. As a consequence the quality and coherence of international law as a whole are threatened. Thus, for example, points are made as though they are novel propositions of human rights law when in fact the point concerned had long been recognized in general international law.

A further set of problems arises from the tendency to separate the law into compartments. Various programmes or principles are pursued without any attempt at co-ordination. After all, enthusiasts tend to be single-minded. Yet there may be serious conflicts and tensions between the various programmes or principles concerned. It may happen that the life-style of indigenous peoples, like that of any other group, may conflict with human rights principles. Thus the 'preservation' or 'autonomist' ethic in respect of indigenous people may conflict with current standards of human rights. It is typical of the low quality of debate in this field that observations of this kind are likely to be met with accusations of paternalism. But it is obvious that it may be really paternalist to assume that indigenous populations cannot adapt to standards of human rights. Many other examples of potential conflict could be given, amongst which is the tension between human rights and the development concept itself.

I have been speaking of dividing the law, and the debate, into compartments. This process is visible also in the institutional structuring of the debate about the rights of groups. Thus the United Nations Commission on Human Rights has commissioned separate studies, with different special rapporteurs, on the rights of persons belonging to ethnic, religious and linguistic minorities (Capotorti), the problem of discrimination against indigenous populations (Martinez Cobo and Asbjorn Eide), the implementation of United Nations resolutions relating to the right of peoples under colonial and alien domination to self-determination (Gros Espiell), and the right of self-determination (Cristescu).

As I have stated already, the issues of self-determination, the treatment of minorities, and the status of indigenous populations, are the same, and the segregation of topics is an impediment to fruitful work. The rights and claims of groups with their own cultural histories and identities are in principle the same—they must be. It is the problems of implementation of principles and standards which vary, simply because the facts will vary. The point can be expressed by saying that the problems of the Lapps, the Inuit, Australian Aboriginals, the Welsh, the Quebecois, the Armenians, the Palestinians, and so forth, are the same in principle but different in practice. This association of categories is not generally accepted, and the separation of categories is one reason for the hesitant approach to the definition of 'peoples' or 'minorities' or 'indigenous populations'. It is unsatisfactory but nonetheless significant to see, in Cristescu's report on self-determination, the dogmatic assertion that the concept of 'people' is not to be confused with 'ethnic, religious or linguistic minorities'.[17]

In concluding, I would like to stress two points. On technical grounds I have been critical of those I have called enthusiastic. It is necessary to be hard-headed and practical: on the other hand the enthusiasts often succeed in raising the level of consciousness, and in generating widespread interest in the questions which it is necessary to be hard-headed and practical about. The second point is to stress, once more, the need to advance by means of studies which are not conducted at a high level of abstraction and which are not isolated from other areas of legal development which are substantially relevant. The areas on which empirical studies are called for are easily defined. They are:

- First, the identification of those group rights not adequately recognized or protected in the context of existing principles and standards of human rights.
- Secondly, the study of the concept of discrimination in the light of the wealth of material available.
- Thirdly, the study of the concept of a 'people' or group with a cultural identity of its own.

In this perspective the separation of the topic of indigenous populations from the questions of self-determination and the treatment of minorities is not justified either as a matter of principle or by practical considerations. Whilst the term 'minority' is an unhappy one, the experience which has been gathered under the heading is highly relevant.

---

[17] E/CN 4/Sub 2/404/Rev 1, para. 279.

2

The Rights of Peoples
(In Particular Indigenous Peoples)

RICHARD FALK

1. The Statist Conception of Human Rights

One of the earliest tensions in classical international law is between the
territorial sovereignty of governments and the status of individuals and
groups as beneficiaries of human rights. As the emphasis on natural law
rights was superseded by the mid-nineteenth century by a stress upon the
consent of governments, the tension tended to be resolved in favour of the
State. To some extent, the growth of an international human rights law in
recent decades has challenged this deference to governmental supremacy.
Since World War II there has been a steady growth of legal standards
applicable to governmental conduct toward its own permanent residents,
whether citizens or not, and a clamour by human rights organizations and
by an array of international organs for their implementation.

And yet there persists a statist conception of rights. Their content and
character is specified by governments, and those who are targets of governmental abuse have little international recourse to relief. Governments
have some shared interests in keeping certain skeletons in the closet.

2. The Statist Conception of Rights and the Rights of Peoples
(especially Indigenous Peoples)

The evolution of the rights of peoples, in its various dimensions, is a
response, or more accurately, a series of responses, to this 'structural'
inhibition upon the definition, protection, and promotion of rights. It
represents societal initiatives to project normative energy on behalf of those
victimized by current political, economic, and cultural arrangements as
administered by States. In this essay, I concentrate upon one illuminating
type of victimization, that of indigenous peoples denied the basis to per-
petuate in dignity their separate ethnic and national identity. As Rodolfo
Stavenhagen proposes:[1]

[1] 'The Indigenous Problèmatique' (1985) 50 *IFDA Dossier* 4, 4. (IFDA stands for the
International Foundation for Development Alternatives, Nyon, Switzerland.)

Indigenous populations may be defined as the original inhabitants of a territory who, because of historical circumstances (generally conquest and/or colonization by another people), have lost their sovereignty and have become subordinated to the wider society and the state over which they do not exercise any control.

Note that in Stavenhagen's definition the stress is upon the status of an indigenous people as an actor deprived of sovereign rights, without participation or representation in prevailing political arrangements, and thereby victimized in fundamental senses. From this subordinated status arise a variety of encroachments, including deficient social services and constant pressure to take over lands and resources retained by indigenous peoples.

(1) The Impact of the Statist Framework of Rights

It is not surprising that indigenous peoples are victimized by traditional procedures and frameworks. For one thing, indigenous peoples, to the extent that they centre their grievances around encroachments upon their collective identity, represent a competing nationalism within the boundaries of the State. Such claims, posited in a variety of forms, challenge two fundamental statist notions—that of territorial sovereignty, and that of a unified 'nationality' juridically administered by governmental organs. Characteristically, indigenous peoples claim to possess sovereign rights of their own and a nationality that is based on history, tradition, and self-identification. The practical consequences for rights of property, for obligations to pay taxes or serve in the military, for governmental allegiance and education, are manifest and manifold. Controversy, even resistance, is the unavoidable result.

An aggravating feature arises from the normative assumptions implicit in the association by dominant social forces of progress with modernization and of backwardness with indigenous patterns of living. The nationalism of an indigenous people is viewed from the dominant perspective as a primitive stage of human society appropriately extinguished in the course of the modernizing process of development (increasing productivity of labour, first by substituting machines for muscles, more recently, by electronic and automated extensions of mechanization). In this regard, the nationalism of indigenous peoples is not entitled to any greater respect than is granted to it within the domestic legal system; its protection is conferred as a matter of discretion, not as a matter of obligation binding on governments of States recognized as such in international life.

The rights of peoples challenges the competence of an inter-governmental system to resolve these issues. It seeks to enlarge upon the traditional conceptions, and even institutional capabilities, of international law, by providing a perspective, and some institutional support, for a non-

statist approach to inter-group and inter-societal conflict. This development of the rights of people is as yet fragmented and weak, posing
mainly a moral challenge to the State system at the present time, and
possibly augmenting political pressures on governments to be more protective of this category of human claims.

As might be expected the jurisprudential foundation of this moral challenge is often misunderstood or contested, and is at best elusive, as it fails
to flow smoothly out from the familiar and generally accepted sources of
international law. The jurisprudential starting-point of the rights of
peoples is a direct assault upon positivist and neo-positivist views of international law as dependent upon State practice and acknowledgement.
In this regard, the rights of peoples can be associated with pre-positivist
conceptions of natural law which at the very birth of international law were
invoked by Vitoria and others on behalf of Indians being cruelly victimized
by Spanish *conquistadores*.

Perhaps ironically, the growth of modern communications and trans-
portation has internationalized the struggle of indigenous peoples in the
last decade or so. Earlier these conflicts were carried on by the afflicted
peoples within the confines of the State largely by appeal to domestic
courts. It is hardly surprising that the cumulative weight of the legal
response, although there were significant variations from country to country and through time, was a steady erosion of the position of indigenous
peoples. The resort to international arenas was part of a continuing effort
to achieve reforms in State–indigenous society relations by going outside
the State, but operating within the wider confines of the State system
that includes those international institutions in which membership and
participation is confined to States by way of governmental representation.
This process of internationalization in the arenas of the United Nations
(especially the Sub-Commission on Indigenous Populations in Geneva as
an undertaking of the Human Rights Commission) has achieved results,
especially in the form of consciousness-raising and network-building.
Overall, however, indigenous peoples and their leadership have become
disillusioned with their efforts to obtain positive results by way of formal
actions at the international level. The statist character of these international
arenas means that those who are being challenged exert comprehensive
control over such matters as agenda and budget, thereby impairing even
the claiming process. Such control is indeed embodied in the procedural
framework of the international political system. For instance, the International Court of Justice allows access only to its members, and only
States are eligible for membership, and only then, generally, if specific
consent to such a judicial submission has been given by the defendant
government. As a result, indigenous peoples cannot under any likely set of
circumstances have their claims of abuse resolved under international law
as assessed by the International Court, or even by some special tribunal

with any authority to assess claims put forward on behalf of indigenous peoples.

The problems associated with either domestic procedures or with internationalization encourage transnationalization, especially efforts to build strength by co-operative ventures and voluntary associations linking indigenous peoples as a kind of transnational pressure group that is not a creature of governmental or inter-governmental activities. The focus on the rights of peoples as a new normative foundation for rights flows directly from this realization of the oppressiveness of a State system based on deference to territorial supremacy. The circumstances of indigenous peoples present an acute instance of this wider phenomenon, as many indigenous nations have been dispersed culturally and physically, or are threatened with extinction. The new assertion of claims to self-determination as validated by more supportive procedures and institutions is literally experienced as a matter of life and death for the ethnic entity as well as for constituent individuals and groups. A call for the rights of peoples is in many instances a cry of help to those confronted by the terrifying prospect of genocide.

(2) Attempts to Develop Indigenous Rights within the Traditional Framework

A certain salience for these claims of indigenous people has been achieved in recent years. This salience has partly resulted from the new efforts at linking the struggles of indigenous peoples in common regional and global enterprises. As might be expected, imperial centres of State power have been especially hostile to this new effort to press forward the indigenous case in non-governmental channels.

Reflecting this political activity, the status of indigenous peoples is a topic of growing academic concern and dispute. Traditionalist approaches seek to sweep the surge of concern beneath the statist rug, arguing both the adequacy and appropriateness of the available repertoire of international law concepts, procedures, and institutions to assess claims asserted on behalf of indigenous peoples as they arise. More progressive approaches are groping toward the specification of a framework that exerts leverage on the State system, that is relevant to its operations without being of it. The whole orientation of the rights of peoples arises in support of the claims of those with little prospect of justice within statist arenas, so as to exert moral, legal, and political pressure on institutions of statist character and thus to make them more responsive.

It is a challenge to find a way of being constructive about the rights of peoples (including indigenous peoples) without being either sentimental or self-indulgent. It is also important to acknowledge that the reality of the indigenous peoples' experience is part of the story of all parts of the world.

There is no basis anywhere for a sense of cultural superiority, or cultural indifference. The scale of concern here is planetary in scope, although regional, civilizational, and state-by-state variations of importance exist. Professor Brownlie's paper develops with great clarity a perspective in which the emergent demands for the protection of indigenous peoples are better treated as part of the larger framework of human rights, and particularly as part of the framework developed for group rights, for the protection of minorities and the promotion of self-determination. In his view, 'the point can be made by saying that the problems of the Lapps, the Inuit, Australian Aborigines, the Welsh, the Quebecois, the Armenians, the Palestinians, and so forth, are the same in principle, but different in practice'. He concludes 'that the separation of the topic of indigenous populations from the questions of self-determination and the treatment of minorities is not justified, either as a matter of principle or by practical considerations'.[2] His analysis is in effect an attempt to assert constructive, and from this point of view normative, reasons to deny that it is helpful or valid to assert distinct rights of peoples.

(3) Alternative Approaches

The President of West Germany, Richard Von Weisacker, gave a remarkable address to the Bundestag, on the fortieth anniversary of the ending of World War II. He said: 'we seek reconciliation for precisely this reason. We must understand that there can be no reconciliation without remembrance. Seeking to forget makes exile all the longer. The secret of redemption lies in remembrance.'[3] Similarly we cannot approach the challenge of the relationship with indigenous people as long as it remains an abstraction that can be lumped with other categories of injustice. Instead it has a specific history or series of histories, that is bound up with our modernizing, developing civilization. Unless that history is acknowledged and understood, it will be very difficult to make an appropriate response. We need, in other words, a perspective that comes to terms with the entire relationship between modern civilization and the pre-modern societies and peoples that we group under the term indigenous peoples.

In some countries (New Zealand, and possibly Australia, at least in recent years, may be among them) consciousness of these issues seems more advanced than it is in other parts of the world. For that reason to advance the case for remembering, by separating this form of injustice from others, may seem less necessary. But even in the context of the Australian experience, to take one example, there seems ample grounds to continue the search for a just relationship with the indigenous people. I doubt whether there is, in other major countries in the world, a comparable

---

[2] Above, p.16.
[3] Text of speech reprinted in *New York Times*, 9 May 1985, A20.

degree of sensitivity and awareness of Aboriginal antecedents.[4] This suggests a very special set of circumstances, circumstances that may not exist to this degree or in this way elsewhere.[5] Admittedly, such judgements tend to be formed on the basis of a reading of the literature of or about a country, and quite apart from empathy for indigenous peoples, writers and intellectuals are increasingly at odds with the dominant tendencies toward urban development and a continuous rape of nature to gain quick profits. From this viewpoint, the destruction of the cultural identity and folkways of indigenous peoples is understood as a form of civilizational 'strip mining', impoverishing the environment by expropriating and wasting irreplaceable cultural resources that were present when settlement commenced.

These issues are complex and profound, for the cultural commentator is usually a consequence and beneficiary of settlement, and to render complete satisfaction to indigenous claims is virtually to relinquish the basis on which non-indigenous peoples rest their rights. The historian, Geoffrey Blainey, comments that if you divided the human history of Australia into a twelve-hour clock face then the Aborigines reigned during all but the last few minutes of the clock's twelve-hour spectrum.[6] That realization of the recentness of the displacement of indigenous peoples seems to me to be a very important part of trying to grasp the largely unconscious significance of the indigenous elements in one's own identity, that it forms so large a part of the human past in this, and indeed in most regions of the world. The Australian poet, A. D. Hope, said of Australia, 'they call her a young country, but they lie'.[7] It is not principally the matter of the recent advent of modernity compared to the long period of development within the frame of indigenous civilization. What is most important here is the continuing claim on resources and imagination appropriate to make on behalf of indigenous peoples.

The Australian circumstance is notable for the extent to which these pre-modern antecedents remain visible in contemporary cultural consciousness. For most societies, the relationship with indigenous peoples is virtually ignored or treated in some sentimental or distorted manner as a concluded aspect of the past. To the extent our concern is with the normative quality of life, the focus is upon the present, and the degree to which it actively represses the surviving aspects of earlier indigenous experiences, that is, the unassimilated portions of the contemporary civilization that are

---

[4] See e.g. the collection of essays, 'Australia—Terra Incognita' (1985) 114 *Daedalus* No 1, in which a remarkable prominence is given to the Aboriginal heritage and the Aboriginal dimension of Australian reality. (The essays were reprinted in book form: S. R. Graubard (ed.), *Australia: The Daedalus Symposium* (1985).)

[5] Subsequently I have come to appreciate the far greater overall significance accorded to the Maori heritage and presence in New Zealand.

[6] 'Australia—A Bird's Eye View' (1985) 114 *Daedalus* 1, 9.

[7] 'Australia' in H. Heseltine (ed.) *The Penguin Book of Australian Verse* (1972) 190.

asserting a variety of claims to uphold and nourish indigenous identity as a positive end in itself. This nourishment may take the form of an array of claims by an indigenous people to establish or re-establish cultural, social, economic, and even political autonomy as a group and of claims protecting or facilitating individuals who seek to withdraw from the dominant society, and seek relief from its burdens.

There is also the substantive matter of cross-cultural learning. Judith Wright, also a poet and naturalist, said: 'the gulf between the aboriginal way of seeing the landscape and that of Europeans is clearly almost un-bridgeable, yet it has only been in quite recent decades that any attempt to understand the aboriginal viewpoint has been made. Few of us can say that we have succeeded.'[8] The issue posed here is one relating to the survival and well-being of the human species, as well as to the rights of individuals and groups living within the modern, dominant civilization in control of State apparatus. In a fundamental sense, indigenous peoples preserve and embody alternate life-styles that may provide models, inspiration, guidance in the essential work of world order redesign, an undertaking now primarily associated with overcoming self-destructive tendencies in the behaviour of modern societies. The gulf to which Judith Wright refers arises especially in attitudes toward the appropriation of nature. The Aboriginal viewpoint corresponds closely with the ecological perspective, and is at odds with developmental and growth perspectives of modern industrializing societies. The importance for all of us to maintain these societal models of ecological success, tested over a long stretch of time, provides a pragmatic rationale for safeguarding Aboriginal peoples. Beyond this, societal diversity en-hances the quality of life, by enriching our experience, expanding cultural resources. In essence, protecting the Aboriginal viewpoint is not a pa-ternalistic undertaking, it is increasingly recognized to be an expression of overall enlightened self-interest.

Although this rationale for protection is a positive one, focusing not merely on the past for its own sake but on present needs, the prospects for protection depend on containing the State, or on inducing its institutions to act in a protective manner. In this regard, the underlying concern with protection against abuse can be connected with group rights, but the ad-ditional dimension arising out of claims for varying degrees of political and cultural autonomy falls outside the natural capacities and tendencies of a world order system administered by and for sovereign States. Part of the impetus for 'the rights of peoples' is to provide normative co-ordinates to assess claims on the basis of a world order logic that is mindful of statist claims, but also receptive to societal claims of an anti-statist character, including those of 'captive nations' caught within the confines of these juristic entities often established and maintained by coercion, not consent,

---

[8] 'Landscape and Dreaming' (1985) 114 *Daedalus* 29, 31-2.

that we identify as States. In this regard, upholding the Aboriginal view-point in a legally serious manner involves a commitment to the process of drastic global reform, that is, the design and embodiment of a world order system in which societal and ethnic co-ordinates play more significant law-shaping and boundary-delimiting roles, possibly by way of supra-national arenas and actors.

Of course, the scope and scale of global reform is far broader than these issues posed by the claims of indigenous peoples. Indeed, most of the world order literature is deficient in its tendency to overlook these claims altogether, focusing much more characteristically on a strengthening of global institutions, on mechanisms for the formation and functioning of a more equitable international economic order, the promotion of traditional menus of human rights, and of achieving a sustainable ecological balance. At most, there are questions raised by ethnic groups that seek a separate State, yet find themselves entrapped in a political arrangement that is somehow hostile to their sense of status and aspiration (e.g. Sikhs in India, Basques in Spain).

The degree of insensitivity toward these concerns is suggested by the failure of even the Algiers Declaration on the Rights of Peoples of 1976,[9] the prime juridical assertion of this non-statist conception of rights, to take explicit account of the plight of indigenous peoples. To stress the place of indigenous peoples in the emerging conception of 'the rights of peoples' is to insist that the plight of indigenous peoples, with their history (too often a modern history) of persecution, degradation, genocide and ethnocide, be placed on the normative agenda. There is nothing to prevent the upgrading of the claims for redress by indigenous peoples on statist agendas, as well. But there is little reason to regard statist forums as likely to be responsive, especially in the absence of intense political pressure from anti-statist, or non-statist, forums. In other words, whether the concern here is expressed in an antagonistic or conciliatory spirit *vis-à-vis* the reform capabilities of the State system, there is ample justification for treating this subject matter as distinct from the mainstream international law tradition of human rights, and as urgently requiring attention in its own right.

3. Three Versions of 'Peoples' Rights'

It is against this background that I want to examine the broader com-mitment to establish the 'rights of peoples' at this time. In this context it is important to distinguish three different ways in which the term the 'rights of peoples' is used. These distinct usages are connected, but they tend also to be rather confusingly lumped together.

[9] For text see B. Weston, R. Falk, A. d'Amato (eds), Basic Documents in International and World Order (West, St Paul, 1980) 413-15.

(1) The Role of 'Peoples' in Formal International Instruments

First of all there are references to peoples in some important international documents that have been blessed by governmental assent. The Preamble of the United Nations Charter begins by asserting that: 'we the peoples are determined to eliminate the scourge of war'. According to Art. 1(1) of the two principal Human Rights Covenants, 'All peoples have the right of self-determination.' In both these settings what is really being expressed, or assumed, is that governments are the authoritative representatives of people, that they act in international institutions in a fundamental representational role, and that it is ultimately the legitimacy of the peoples that they represent, not their own expression of State interests, that is the underlying ground of their validity. On this view, it is the legitimacy of peoples, not the transient and potentially dubious legitimacy of governments, that constitutes the purpose and rationale for the instruments protecting human rights and for the whole idea of international solidarity. That is, States in this sense are an artificial and derivative political reality as compared to peoples.

This argument is obscured by the reality of state-society relations around the world. It is obvious that many governmental actors with the authority to represent States can govern only by reliance on coercion and intimidation. That is, the apparatus of the State has quite often been captured by small élites, even individual tyrants, who rule on behalf of only a fragment of the population within the boundaries of the State. Thus, to assume a correspondence between State and society would be grossly distorting in many cases, even if distinct classes, races, ethnic groupings and regional orientations did not exist. Typically, patterns of rule embody societal hierarchies or constellations of power groupings in a manner that is abusive to those in subordinate positions. In some respect, the circumstance of indigenous peoples is at the extreme, as these peoples have been marginalized by virtually every modern government, endangering their very survival as distinct cultural, political, and social realities.

This view has been most specifically discussed in the decolonization context and in relation to various disputes about the right of self-determination. The tension in the celebrated General Assembly Resolution 1514 illustrates one of the central ambiguities and problems with this formulation of self-determination as a right of peoples, as it has been understood in the United Nations. The first declaratory paragraph of Resolution 1514 states that 'the subjection of peoples to alien subjugation and domination and exploitation constitutes a denial of fundamental human rights'. Article 1 states that 'all peoples have the right to self-determination. By virtue of that right they freely determine their political status and freely pursue their economic, social and cultural development.'

But these two provisions have to be read in conjunction with especially the sixth and seventh paragraphs of Resolution 1514. According to para. 6:

Any attempt at the partial or total disruption of the national unity and the territorial integrity of the country is incompatible with the purposes and principles of the Charter of the United Nations.

In other words, self-determination for peoples must be reconciled in practice with the existing geographical delimitation of territorial boundaries of sovereign States. According to para. 7:

all States uphold the obligation to enforce the Charter of the United Nations and the Universal Declaration of Human Rights and this Declaration, on the basis of equality, non-interference in the internal affairs of all States and respect for the sovereign rights of all peoples and their territorial integrity.

This is an affirmation of the rights of peoples, but as qualified by the fiction that a people and a state are virtually interchangeable ideas. Furthermore, the notion of self-determination itself is subordinated to an overriding conception of the unity and integrity of the State. This obviously deals with the situation of peoples in a very artificial and contradictory way, because in many territorial units there are distinct, often antagonistic nationalities, even aside from the characteristic exclusion of indigenous peoples from government. One of the most severe sources of injustice and denial of human rights today is that the apparatus of State power has been captured by one of those fragments of a people, defined as the totality of persons within a given State, while the other elements are subjugated to varying degrees. This situation exists in many territorial States where there are distinct peoples. In that sense the notion of human rights to be enjoyed by a particular national identity is subordinated to and administered through the organs of the State. This underscores the vulnerability of 'peoples', even if their status seems to be acknowledged in the basic instruments of the United Nations.

There is also implicit in much international practice the idea that State boundaries are coterminous with the boundaries of national identity. The primacy accorded those boundaries is in many instances quite incompatible with the realization of self-determination by distinct 'peoples'. Respect for the integrity of existing political units is as strong as the inhibiting spectre of their fragmentation, and consequent chaos. It confines the operation of principles of self-determination to the limited category of instances of 'captive States' (that is, States held captive by an extra-territorial governmental actor), an important focus during the decolonization struggle where the political goal was one of independence from the mother country, but increasingly less so in light of the collapse of the main colonial systems.

But according priority to this kind of statist view of self-determination means that the promise of self-determination is for many subject peoples an empty and irrelevant one, and has made these peoples fully dependent on the domestic legal system, which has been demonstrated to be so inadequate that it has eventually given rise to urgent appeals from victim peoples for some form of 'legal' intervention to assure greater protection. The Kurds, as subordinated 'nations' within the States of Iraq, Iran, and Turkey, have no right of self-determination at the international level given this understanding of the United Nations approach to these questions. The situation of indigenous peoples is even more extreme, more neglected, from this point of view. Indigenous peoples, by and large, have not even participated in the 'self' that is being accorded the right to determine its destiny. They have overwhelmingly been marginalized as outside the framework of normal political behaviour. The promises associated with the mainstream right of self-determination have almost no relevance to them: this creates a high degree of normative confusion as a fundamental as-piration of these peoples is inevitably some form of self-determination, but not the prevailing one. In other words, the semantic confusion that is implicit in statist views of self-determination has been used to avoid con-fronting the actual situations of either captive nations and even more in-sistently, the various lamentable situations of indigenous peoples.

(2) International Civil Society as a Challenge to Statist International Law

The second dimension of the rights of peoples has to do with the emerging internal tension between civil society and the State, with the State being challenged in an increasing number of ways with regard to its claim as the sole legitimate source of law-making and law-applying. We have absorbed an ideology of statism that is so strong, not only internationally but also domestically, that we regard States as the only actors with the legitimate authority to establish normative order on an international level. What has been increasingly happening is that governments of States have failed to carry out some of the fundamental normative tasks that citizens and peoples of various societies regard as imperative.

Let me illustrate this in three ways. The MacBride Commission was set up by a group of prominent British citizens to establish an international commission to investigate allegations that Israel violated international law by the manner in which it conducted the 1982 Lebanon War. The Com-mission itself was mainly composed of international law experts, but it had no authority to undertake its mission either from governments or international institutions. At the same time it was created in a normative vacuum. No constituted organization of the State system was investigating what appeared to many private observers of that war as clear patterns of flagrant violations of the laws of war. This societal or populist initiative responded to the failure of constitutional governments and international institutions, for a variety of political reasons, to undertake an appropriate investigation of the charges against Israel. The MacBride Commission and its Report[10] seem to me to establish a certain kind of legal judgment on the issues, and to constitute an appeal to public opinion and, particularly, the legal community to assess the conduct of Israel in the Lebanon War in light of its findings. It is an appeal, in other words, to civil society and an attempt to bring to bear on governments certain pressures of public opinion otherwise inadequately reflected by States and their governments. Such a proceeding intends to rise above partisan propaganda, although the side criticized, in this instance, the State of Israel, will tend to reject such a report as biased or a species of hostile propaganda.

Another initiative of a comparable sort is the Permanent People's Tribunal, a judicial process established in Italy in the late 1970s and constituted by a loose assemblage of designated private citizens of high moral authority, Nobel Prize winners and well-known cultural, legal, and religious figures. The Tribunal has carried on its activities within a constitutional framework, established by the 1976 Algiers Declaration of the Rights of Peoples, a declaration drafted by a group of jurists acting as volunteers but which attempts to address the concerns of the global society. The Algiers Declaration has provided a framework in which the Permanent People's Tribunal has examined a series of human grievances that have not been treated, or not sufficiently, by established institutions. A session was devoted to allegations against Turkey of genocide against the Armenian people, especially in the 1915 period.[11] The tribunal has also investigated the Soviet military role in Afghanistan,[12] the Indonesian use of force in East Timor,[13] the alleged US intervention in Central America,[14] the repression of human rights in the Philippines during the period of the Marcos Government.[15] In each case the tribunal heard a variety of witnesses, invited the defendant government to participate, set itself up like a tribunal, and issued a judgment on the basis of an appraisal of the evidence and the testimony that it heard. In recent sessions, the Tribunal has appointed an international lawyer of repute, to set forth the facts and arguments favourable to the defence as well as possible.[16] It has published the indi-

[10] *Israel in Lebanon. The Report of the International Commission to enquire into reported violations of International Law by Israel during its Invasion of the Lebanon* (Ithaca, London, 1983).

[11] Permanent People's Tribunal, *A Crime of Silence. The Armenian Genocide* (Zed Books, London, 1984).

[12] 'The Investigation of the Soviet Role in Afghanistan' (Judgment of the Permanent People's Tribunal, Stockholm Session, 1–3 May 1981).

[13] 'Consultative Advice on East Timor' (Judgment of the Permanent People's Tribunal, Rome, 1979).

[14] M. Dixon (ed.), *On Trial. Reagan's war against Nicaragua. Testimony of the Permanent People's Tribunal* (Synthesis Publications, San Francisco, 1985).

[15] *Philippines: Repression and Resistance* (Permanent People's Tribunal, Session on the Philippines, distributed by Meriam Books, London, 1981).

[16] In the 1984 session on US involvement in Nicaragua the tribunal requested Professor Francis Boyle of the University of Illinois (Urbana) to present Washington's position, and he did so with clarity and forcefulness. See F. A. Boyle,'Statement on Behalf of the United States of America' in Dixon (ed.) (1985) 153–71.

vidual judgments, together with the main presentations of evidence, in a series of book-length volumes.[17] In several instances the Tribunal, despite limited resources, has produced the most cogent and compelling legal documentation of injustice experienced by the particular victims. It has been of some political significance, varying from case to case, in struggles against the policies at stake, but its main impact has been one of political education.

What is radical in a constitutional or legal sense is that this is an initiative by civil society without any authorization, directly or indirectly, from government or the State. At most, the State allows the Tribunal to operate on its territory and does not interfere with the proceedings by denying witnesses visas or by limiting operations through police interference. It has not been possible to organize sessions in States whose government is directly or indirectly implicated in the allegations being considered. As might be expected, the most favourable political environments have been in Western Europe where democratic liberalism supports the initiatives. Also, Europe provides a more convenient *locus* for many inquiries than could be provided by other possible sites—including, for instance, some in the Pacific region. Such a view of convenience is partly a reflection of the Italian organizational base and partly a more general clustering of global policy activities in Western Europe.

Other *ad hoc* and more enduring tribunals have been organized under a variety of auspices. For instance, the Green Party in West Germany held a tribunal at Nuremberg on the nuclear arms race in 1982, a group of lawyers in England organized a tribunal on the legality of nuclear weapons in 1984,[18] and a group of Japanese people put together in 1983 a tribunal on the legalities surrounding Israel's invasion of the Lebanon. These initiatives grounded their claims of validity on the rights of peoples to apply law and render a judgment entitled to respect. Since these tribunals did not issue a subsequent publication their importance needs to be assessed in relation to the event itself.

A basic postulate of political theory is at issue here, that is, the notion of a democratic polity and the character of the social contract binding State and society. Law is an instrument of civil society in the first instance, and not exclusively an instrument of the government of the State. These initiatives by way of societal assessments of legal allegations also respond especially to certain failures on the part of the State to protect the interests of human well-being, as perceived by those who feel victimized by State structures and policies.

[17] A summary of the first series of opinions and decisions of the Permanent People's Tribunal is contained in E. Jouve (ed.), *Un Tribunal pour les Peuples* (Berger-Levrault, Paris, 1983).
[18] 'An Examination of the Legality of Nuclear Weapons' (Nuclear Warfare Tribunal, London, 3–6 January 1985).

The third illustration of this attempt by civil society to contain the encroachment by organized State power have been efforts, particularly in the United States, of citizens to use domestic courts in litigation to challenge governmental policy in the war/peace and human rights areas by reference to international law, including especially the Nuremberg Principles. These cases arise from acts of conscience by citizens who engage in symbolic disobedience of domestic law and then invoke international law by way of justification or necessity defences. For instance, defendants might enter a prohibited area (e.g. a military base), or block transit of challenged weapons systems (e.g. first-strike missiles and submarines) or attempt to dismantle or damage weapons (e.g. nose-cones of first-strike missiles). They will then be charged with criminal trespass and/or malicious destruction of government property. Defendants argue, in effect, for a doctrine of lawful civil disobedience (sometimes called a 'Nuremberg action'), that it is permissible and reasonable to violate domestic law so as to implement applicable rules of international law that are being violated by the government. Such an analysis is reinforced by what has come to be called 'the Nuremberg obligation', the notion that citizens since the Nuremberg war crimes trials have an obligation to uphold international law in the area of war and peace by taking action even if it violates applicable domestic law.

This type of judicial challenge of official policy originated in the United States during the Vietnam War, and took the main forms of resistance to military service and tax refusal. In the more recent period international law challenges in domestic courts have dealt with interventionary diplomacy, relations with South Africa, and the exclusion of refugees seeking protection.[19]

The shared basis of these challenges is the assertion that citizens have an enforceable right under the US Constitution to a lawful foreign policy. Every citizen, and every person, has the right to be governed not only internally by a constitutional legal framework, but as well has a direct legal interest in a lawful foreign policy, in the conduct of foreign policy in accordance with international law, and this is not an issue that can be exempted from substantive resolution by domestic courts. In effect, domestic courts are made into agents of interpretation and implementation of critical norms in the war/peace and human rights area of the international legal order.

The initiative of citizens as an expression of the right of peoples to a lawful foreign policy is a daring challenge directed at the State system through recourse to governmental institutions. It flows from the wider logic of individual accountability that was enforced against leaders of the

---

[19] Many of these are discussed, along with the text of international law testimony, in F. A. Boyle, *Defending Civil Resistance against the Reagan Administration under International Law* (Transnational Publishers, New York, 1987).

defeated countries in World War II by the joint action of the main vic-
torious governments. The extension of this logic to the empowerment of
the citizenry exposes the tension between statism and legality in the context
of foreign policy. As might be expected, this tension, to date, with several
notable exceptions, has been resolved by domestic courts in favour of the
State, mainly on procedural grounds—that the international law argument
is inadmissible or that the issues posed are non-justiciable or not relevant
to a defence against the crime charged.[20] But the importance of these
initiatives cannot be measured by formal outcomes. These cases facilitate
political education, as well as encourage debate on the proper relation
between State and society with respect to challenged elements of international policy.

I mention these conflicts between civil society and the State, and the
new and important tendency for civil society to assert some normative
prerogatives of its own, alongside those of the government, as the second
dimension of the rights of peoples.

(3) Indigenous Peoples and the Rights of Peoples

The third aspect, already anticipated, is the aspiration for a special regime
expressing the rights of indigenous peoples, both the individual and group
rights that pertain to the special circumstances of indigenous peoples. This
set of initiatives taken together is a move toward a specific regime to be
established within international law for the protection of indigenous
peoples. Such a movement acknowledges the impact of past experience, in
particular, the appreciation that to grant mere autonomy to indigenous
people, or to assure their participation in the dominant society on the basis
of equality and non-discrimination, is insufficient. That is, there is a special
set of demands and grievances that cannot be easily understood, much
less accommodated, by existing international law rules, procedures, and
structures for ascertaining and protecting human rights. The present international legal framework does not give access to the main political arenas
to the representatives of indigenous peoples themselves, nor does it seem
to deal with their specific historic identity, their special claims, nor with
their special value to human society as a whole.

This third dimension of the rights of peoples has to be understood as a
qualitative extension of human rights and self-determination that poses
new challenges. It has always been the case that one of the impulses to
create a distinct category of human rights has been to protect those who

---

[20] See the cases and references cited in Boyle (1987) chs. 1–2. In other jurisdictions similar
technical obstacles have also been raised: e.g. *Ingram* v. *Commonwealth of Australia* (1980) 54
ALJR 395 (held: private plaintiff had no standing to challenge legality of Australian support
for the SALT II treaty. For a summary of the plaintiff's substantive arguments see (1980) 54
ALJ 615).

have been particularly victimized by existing policies and arrangements or who represent the most vulnerable sectors of humanity, especially if the maltreatment is a consequence of ignorance and misunderstanding. If we look back at the circumstances surrounding the formulation of the Genocide Convention or of the Convention on the Rights of Women, the Prohibition of all Forms of Racial Discrimination or the Prohibition of Crime of Apartheid, a pattern is evident. Each of these undertakings represented the crystallization of particularly intense demands that took shape at a given time for an acknowledgment of rights, as a collective and formal expression of the urgency and seriousness of the claim and the grossness of the abuse. In each instance the prohibited behaviour could analytically have been subsumed under a broader group of pre-existing rights or demands. The insistence on a distinct category is a matter of policy, not logic. A social movement has decided to express its priorities by making a particular specification of a human rights concern in a detailed form and by way of a new and separate document. Indigenous peoples are in a situation where their claims for protection cannot be coherently understood except when treated separately. Besides, activism on behalf of indigenous peoples has brought past injustices and current dangers to the attention of a wider public, thereby creating a political and moral climate that would support the formulation of a special regime. At this stage, pressure on government is unlikely to achieve legal results. Unlike genocide or apartheid, many governments are sensitive to their own vulnerability to charges of past and present abuses with respect to indigenous peoples. Therefore, the most appropriate response to the growing movement on behalf of indigenous peoples is the elaboration of a special regime that enjoys the kind of distinctive validity that arises from non-governmental law-making endeavours. In this crucial respect, the law-making dimension of the rights of people is a precondition for the elaboration of a special regime that will clarify to a degree the substantive extent of the rights of indigenous peoples as an instance of the rights of peoples more broadly conceived, and do so with the full participation of authentic representatives of various indigenous peoples. One problem has been that indigenous peoples have been judged and their claims assessed in the setting of alien assumptions and institutional arrangements.

An additional justification for distinct treatment is that existing efforts by international institutions to take account of the circumstances of indigenous peoples are woefully inadequate. The International Labour Organization's Convention 107, adopted in 1957, remains the only specific intergovernmental document in the human rights context that deals with what it calls indigenous tribal and semi-tribal peoples. It is pervaded by an implicit deference to assimilation as the natural sequel for those who retain an indigenous identity. In effect, ILO Convention 107 says that equality and non-discrimination must be granted to these peoples who are mainly victimized, in its view, because they have not yet been allowed or enabled to join the dominant society quickly enough. The major normative demand is to facilitate what is called progressive integration into their respective national communities (in other words, assimilation). A fundamental deficiency of this approach is that it directly contradicts the definite preferences of indigenous peoples themselves. It has also produced a record of demoralization, where assimilation occurs only partially, leading to a loss of traditional identity without any inner adjustment to the modern circumstance. Indigenous peoples increasingly resist integration and assimilation and seek above all to re-establish connections with their traditional lands and their traditional ways of life, so as to live with dignity and in a manner that reflects their own world view. In that sense they are not prepared as a whole to accept the paternalistic judgement of the dominant civilization that what is important is to enable them to participate equally in and gain access to the modern world of industrialism, electronics, and nuclearism—a judgement more often dishonoured in practice.

Of course, norms of non-discrimination and equality of treatment are by no means superfluous. Indigenous peoples have been persistently exploited by the dominant modern society, especially in relation to land and water rights and beneficial ownership of resources. In this respect, the ILO approach should not be entirely repudiated, especially in the absence of an effective substitute. The ILO initiative expressed, at the very least, a growing international concern about the welter of evidence that abusive practices harmful to indigenous peoples are widespread in all parts of the world.

Finally, it is clear from experiences with such undertakings as the anti-apartheid campaign, and with the efforts to proscribe genocide as a distinct crime, that the very process of formulating a coherent legal regime on behalf of an emergent category of human rights itself possesses enormous educative benefit by raising political and social consciousness. The preparation to take part in such a process compels those that represent governments or other institutions, and indigenous peoples themselves, towards a greater appreciation of policies and problems. The dynamics of law-making in this area are themselves a positive gain, particularly if it is accepted, as I have argued from the outset, that indigenous peoples play a central role in the specification of a legal regime of their own. It is not something that can be given, it is not a gift. It needs to be a joint creation, something that is the product of participation at all stages. Ideally, indigenous peoples would have a central role in defining the framework of the rights of indigenous peoples, because in one sense the content of rights is the projection of human needs in relation to a particular circumstance in society.

There are some complexities here that need to be admitted. The preferred regime on behalf of indigenous peoples is likely to challenge the sense of settled rights of existing sovereign States, threatening in some instances, at least, a reduction of control by the central government, or even dismemberment of the State. As well, problems of title to land and the character of land use are certain to arise expressive of conflicts between indigenous peoples and post-indigenous developments. How to resolve these conflicts is a very difficult issue. It suggests the need for a kind of meta-law and meta-framework that takes account of conflicting viewpoints, claims, traditions. At this stage it is not realistic, or even necessarily ethical and equitable, to formulate a special regime for the sake of indigenous peoples in a historical vacuum. The rights of non-indigenous peoples, and the relations between communities with distinct national and cultural identities, must be considered. Little effort in this direction of mutual reconciliation of group rights has so far been attempted.

There is also the question whether a special regime for indigenous peoples should be conceived of as a reform of the State system or a body of claims advanced against its practices and approach. The choice of reform has the advantage of invoking the capabilities of prevailing power structures if once accepted as authoritative. The disadvantage is that there is virtually no prospect that a statist framework with an outlook hostile to indigenous peoples is going to endorse a legal regime that is anti-statist in its basic character. In the near term, the positing of an adequate special regime to preserve indigenous peoples is only likely to be achieved in informal or populist arenas that are not accepted as valid on the basis of statist criteria. What the behavioural effects of such a regime could be is a difficult matter about which to conjecture.

A further point concerns the absence of any assured consensus among indigenous peoples. There are conflicts among indigenous peoples whose claims to antecedent lands and rights overlap. There are also differences in tactical assessments. Some indigenous peoples seek to assert modest claims to preserve and augment what they possess, others associate their survival as an entity with a full and radical restoration of traditional rights. There are also important differences in styles of leadership among indigenous peoples. Some leaders are assimilationist, or have stakes in an accommodation with the dominant civilization, while others are separatist and want to base the revival of the vitality of indigenous peoples upon a radical encounter.

To provide some sense of the contours for a special regime, I would suggest, subject to the preceding discussion, that it possess the following six features:

First, there would be some response to needs for internal self-determination, using the term 'self' in an existential, not in a legalistic or statist, way. That means some appropriate form of autonomy that allows for the protection and self-control over life in all its dimensions. That obviously involves difficult, maybe intractable, problems of reconciliation with the rights of others, other groups, and with the individual rights mentioned earlier. It also may require some clarification of territorial de-limitation, as well as the in-gathering of dispersed clusters of indigenous peoples.

Second, and perhaps less significantly at this stage, some dimension of external self-determination, some capacity on the part of indigenous peoples to be able to form networks of solidarity with other indigenous groups and with organizations representing indigenous peoples on an in-ternational and transnational level, is a necessary component.

Third, there must be ways to promote human rights in relation to the specific circumstances of individuals and groups properly identified as indigenous, in particular so as to assure protection against exploitation by non-indigenous structures.

Fourth, there needs to be an acceptance of some international personality for indigenous peoples, so that they can present their claims and grievances in arenas outside the national legal system. Achieving international stand-ing seems a very important goal. There has to be a way of appealing to either a special tribunal or by way of special procedures so that the determination of conflicts between indigenous peoples and modern society is not totally subject to the institutions and criteria of modern society.

Fifth, there has to be special attention to the protection of sacred sites, and an understanding that sacred land in some instances must be restored to the extent possible to indigenous peoples, for them to have any kind of cultural or religious integrity. This is not just a matter of assigning equi-valent or sufficient land, or offering monetary compensation. There is a relationship to specific land and to specific aspects of nature that are part of what human dignity means in those civilizational settings associated with indigenous peoples, and no equivalent can be devised.

Sixth, and finally, the notions of restitution, as well as protection, have to be introduced into this regime in the form of land rights and the financial resources and facilities that might be needed to overcome the distress many of these peoples have and are experiencing, especially those who find themselves at the brink of extinction. Tragically, this terminal situation currently exists in many countries.

Such a call for a special regime could be formalized in a Draft Convention on the Rights of Indigenous Peoples. If this call commands a consensus then the movement to adopt a convention could be a focus for a social movement on behalf of indigenous peoples. In my view we have a historic opportunity, and because of the pace of modernization perhaps our last opportunity, to preserve part of the common heritage of the planet that is of enormous value, and to end the crimes against those who reject or are unable to participate in, the dynamics of modernization and development. What is being sought, in other words, is a way to end a criminal process that has persisted for centuries, noticed only when its excesses temporarily shock sensibilities of the dominant society. At this stage it may be the indigenous peoples themselves who will be the main bearers of this emerging right of peoples. They must be the ones, I think, to give it most of its specific content, although subject to interaction with other viewpoints. The role of jurists is to validate and legitimate this enterprise, and to suggest that for vulnerable peoples to survive at the edge of modern civilization requires an enormous mobilization of moral, legal, and political energy. It will not happen on its own. It will not happen merely by waiting for it to happen, and waiting for the existing framework of laws and human rights to be applied in these directions. A special circumstance of emergency must be acknowledged and acted upon. Only on this basis can we begin to do justice to this very fundamental challenge to our moral identity, and perhaps to our survival prospects as a species.

At this stage, the image of comprehensive protection of indigenous peoples by way of legal regime is aspirational in the extreme. At most such a formulation gives substance to the co-ordinated claims being advanced in forums controlled by indigenous peoples. Whether this co-ordination will proceed to become an international movement that is itself a factor in the contest of social forces out of which come new realities remains to be seen.

What can be said is that there is a dramatic upsurge all over the world in awareness of the plight of indigenous peoples. Further, indigenous peoples have become conscious of their need for co-ordinated action on an international level including a variety of efforts to shape the normative climate. Finally, commentators have increasingly come to appreciate the overall human importance, ecologically and as an intrinsic benefit, of keeping indigenous peoples from being either extinguished through encroachment or by way of assimilation.

4. Conclusion

The instance of indigenous peoples is only one dimension of the more general debate about the rights of peoples. It is expressive of the idea that peoples can be bearers of rights, but it is restricted to particular categories of peoples who have chosen to be excluded or whom others have excluded from participation in the 'modern societies' in which they now live. The broader concept of the rights of peoples assesses the overall State–society relationship, including patterns of victimization that are carried on within the framework of modernity. For example, the insistence that the State is not empowered to threaten or use nuclear weapons can be an expression of an emergent right of peoples to security policies in accord with international law. As with the situation of indigenous peoples, the assertion of anti-nuclearist claims may have to proceed mainly outside traditional international law frameworks, frameworks that continue to reflect the statist insistence that governments exert unconditional control over security policy.

3

The Right to Development: A Right of Peoples?

ROLAND RICH[1]

1. Introduction

In 1982 I set out some of the arguments for recognition of the right to development as a human right.[2] That paper stopped short of the claim that the right to development was a part of positive international law. That being the case I did not believe I needed to make explicit what seemed implicit—that major international law texts do not list the right to development as an existing human right. My aim was to cite authorities who had recognized the right to development as a means of gauging the level of acceptance it had achieved.

The right to development remains a putative right not fully accepted into the body of generally accepted international law. It is part of the body of *lex ferenda* and not *lex lata*. Its claim for inclusion in the latter was strengthened, but not finally confirmed, by the passage, on 4 December 1986, of General Assembly Resolution 41/128 adopting the Declaration on the Right to Development. However, there are commentators who hold a different view. Professor Brownlie quotes with approval Alston's plea for a system of quality control in the proclamation of new human rights.[3] One would expect Alston to exercise care in giving his own 'appellation contrôlée' or seal of approval to a new human right. While acknowledging a number of difficulties, Alston has this to say about the right to development:[4]

It is appropriate to acknowledge that, as a general proposition in terms of international human rights law, the existence of the right to development is a *fait accompli*. Whatever reservations different groups may have as to its legitimacy,

© Roland Rich 1988

© Roland Rich 1988

[1] Department of Foreign Affairs, Canberra. The views expressed here are the author's, and do not necessarily represent those of the Department.

[2] R. Rich, 'The Right to Development as an Emerging Human Right' (1983) 23 *Virginia JIL* 287.

[3] P. Alston, 'Conjuring up New Human Rights: A Proposal for Quality Control' (1984) 78 *AJIL* 607, quoted by Brownlie above, p.12 n.10

[4] P Alston, 'Development and the Rule of Law: Prevention versus Cure as a Human Rights Strategy' in *Development, Human Rights and the Rule of Law, Report of a Conference held in The Hague on 27 April–1 May 1981* (1981) 31, 106.

viability or usefulness, such doubts are now better left behind and replaced by efforts to ensure that the formal process of elaborating the content of the right is a productive and constructive exercise.

I propose to be guided by Alston's injunction. I do not believe it is possible to discuss the rights of peoples solely in terms of existing international law. Questions of law and policy can be divorced, but only at the cost of creating a degree of artificiality in discussion of the subject. The right to development is a political issue. To Third World countries it may be the most pressing political issue they face. That is why I was surprised at Professor Brownlie's advice to the practitioner not to stray from the confines of positive international law. My experience as a practitioner is that this advice will only lead to a dialogue of the deaf, a dialogue which will not achieve my purpose. In this context the human rights I am concerned about are the rights of the peoples of the Third World. It is these rights which require promotion and which add an element of urgency to any discussion of the right to development.

In this Chapter I raise four subjects for discussion:

1.   The framework in which the right to development has been elaborated;
2.   A brief overview of relevant State practice, including the question of the linkage between development assistance and human rights;
3.   The articulation of the right to development, especially in the United Nations General Assembly;
4.   Finally, the question whether this putative right has a useful role to play in international law.

2. The Conceptual Framework

In a sense we are at a disadvantage in that discussion of these issues is not taking place in French. Most of the thoughts on this subject have been thought in French. Much of the literature is in French. The method of approaching the subject differs from the method which a lawyer schooled in the Anglo-Saxon tradition would adopt. Questions of practical application, workable definitions and the examination of State practice are often considered by the French as secondary considerations best left for others. True nobility of purpose is to be found in the development of the concept, and in fixing its place in history.

(1) Generations, Phases and Colours: Some Attempts at Conceptualization

In this context a conceptualization that has become popular is that of a 'third generation of human rights'. The Senegalese jurist Keba M'Baye was the first commentator to refer to a right to development,[5] but it was Karel Vasak, formerly UNESCO'S Legal Adviser, who popularized the concept of the third generation of human rights, which is said to include the right to development.[6] It is within this framework that many people, especially from developing countries, tend to view the right to development. Vasak called the third generation rights the solidarity rights, a term which loses something when translated from the French. His thesis is as follows:

● The first generation rights were those rights which emerged from the American and French revolutions. They were aimed at securing the citizen's liberty from arbitrary action by the State. They correspond by and large to the Civil and Political Rights in the International Bill of Rights. They are said to be negative rights in that they call for restraint from the State.
● The second generation rights emerged with the Russian revolution and were echoed in the welfare state concepts which developed in the West. They correspond largely to the Economic, Social and Cultural rights and they require positive action by the State.
● The third generation rights, as Vasak sees them, are a response to the phenomenon of global interdependence. Individual States acting alone can no longer satisfy their human rights obligations. The problems that are now being faced require international cooperation for their resolution. These problems include the maintenance of peace, the protection of the environment and the encouragement of development. The third generation rights necessarily benefit individuals and peoples.

Vasak's thesis is open to criticism especially in the positive/negative dichotomy he postulates in respect of the first two 'generations' of rights. It could be argued that civil and political rights require considerable activity on the part of the State for their full enjoyment, and that economic rights may often be enhanced through the absence of government involvement. None the less this classification of the 'generations' of human rights is attractive, and has considerable persuasive power.[7]

Combined with this idea is a growing acceptance of a 'structural approach' to human rights. Alston has argued that since 1977 there has been a new trend in human rights activity.[8] Led by the Commission on Human Rights, the trend has been to identify and attempt to remove structural obstacles to the enjoyment of human rights. Thus writers have

[5] K. M'Baye, 'Le Droit au Développement comme un Droit de L'Homme' (1972) 5 *Revue des Droits de L'Homme* 503.
[6] K. Vasak, 'A Thirty Year Struggle—the Sustained Efforts to give Force of Law to the Universal Declaration of Human Rights' *UNESCO Courier* (Nov. 1977) 29.
[7] Indeed one commentator argues that the three generations of rights are simply a restatement of the three-worded rallying cry of 1789; liberty, equality, fraternity: S. Marks, 'Emerging Human Rights: A New Generation for the 1980's' (1981) 33 *Rutgers LR* 440.
[8] Alston (1981) 37.

identified four phases of the activities of the Commission on Human Rights. Writing in 1975 Jean-Bernard Marie categorized the first three phases:[9]

- 1945-55 was the standard setting or normative phase. The Universal Declaration on Human Rights was drafted, the bulk of the work on drafting the two Covenants was completed. Other Conventions including those on Genocide and Refugees were drafted. This lofty work however stood in stark contrast to the UN's inability to react to specific human rights violations.
- The 1955-65 phase was an attempt to correct this by the promotion of human rights. It was a period of attempting to influence the situation by working with governments through the procedure of periodic governmental reports and the provision of advisory services. The achievements in this phase were modest.
- Within the next decade, 1965-75, came the phase of protection of human rights and an attempt to do something more directly about violations of human rights. New techniques were developed for appointing special rapporteurs to investigate situations. The problem of what to do with the thousands of communications received by the UN on human rights issues was tackled, and in 1970 ECOSOC adopted the procedures under resolution 1503. The idea of a High Commissioner for Human Rights was launched.

Clearly these distinctions are not watertight, but the trends appear to be clearly enough identified. They provide a backdrop to developments in human rights in the mid-1970s when the concepts behind the New International Economic Order took hold of the imagination of the Third World. Previous methods of looking at human rights, which concentrated essentially on the civil and political rights, began to lose relevance. In 1977 the Commission on Human Rights began considering the right to development and the General Assembly adopted Resolution 32/130. What can be described as the structural phase of human rights work had begun. Indeed, the right to development has been described by Alston as 'the single most important element in the launching of a structural approach to human rights at the international level'.[10]

Historical classifications aside, it is important also to consider how perceptions of the process of development changed. In addition to three generations and four phases, one might mention Johan Galtung's description of the three colours of development:[11]

- Galtung describes 'blue' development as the method of achieving economic growth by fostering the activities of an entrepreneurial class. The nation is seen as a market-place, the role of the government is seen as essentially negative, i.e. to take as few economic initiatives as possible and not to fetter the activities of the entrepreneurial class.
- 'Red' development, as one can guess, is economic growth controlled and initiated by a governmental bureaucracy. The ultimate determinant of economic direction is not the market but the plan.

---

[9] J.-B. Marie, *Le Commission des Droits de L'Homme de l'ONU, Deuxième Partie* (1975).
[10] Alston (1981) 99.
[11] J. Galtung in *Development, Human Rights and the Rule of Law* (1981) 121.

● Thirdly, perhaps as a synthesis, comes 'green' development. It is development based on concepts such as those elaborated by Schumacher.[12] It calls for more autonomy at the local level, for smaller economic cycles, for concentration on village economies and for agriculture based on more traditional models.

There may well be a place for all three types of development, even in the one country. The right to development would require that the choice of development policies not be based solely on macro-economic models, but that it should take fully into account the needs of the primary subject of human rights law, the individual.

(2) Persons and Peoples

The dichotomy between persons and peoples as subjects of international human rights law lies at the heart of the problem of the 'third generation' of rights. I wish to propose three premises which any conclusions on this question should take into account:

(1)   The individual necessarily remains the primary subject of international human rights law.
(2)   International human rights law recognizes the existence of groups.
(3)   The full enjoyment of individual human rights requires certain human rights to devolve, wholly or in part, upon groups.

Something should be said about each of these propositions in turn.

The first proposition would require no elaboration if it avoided the assertion that there is a hierarchy among the subjects of human rights law. I believe it is important to make that assertion, to insist that the individual, as the ultimate beneficiary of all human rights, has primacy. An important corollary is that there can be no human rights which detract from the individual's human rights. I must concede that this assertion sits uncomfortably with one aspect of UNGA Res. 32/130, which tends to speak in the same breath about the rights of the human person and of peoples. However I would not accept another possible criticism, which is that the primacy of the individual gives priority to civil and political rights over economic, social, and cultural rights. Both Covenants place primary emphasis on the individual, and both use the same formulations in describing the beneficiary of the rights; 'all persons' or 'everyone'. (The one exception, the right of self-determination, I discuss below.) When human rights law recognizes groups, the individual is nevertheless usually singled out as the primary beneficiary.

The second proposition asserts that human rights law does recognize certain rights of groups. Human rights law has recognized groups as a matter of necessity, because groups have so often been the victims of abuses

---

[12] E. F. Schumacher, *Small is Beautiful* (1973).

of human rights. The subject deserves study in depth but I simply list a few examples.

- *Protection of minorities.* An extensive system of provisions protecting minorities was built into the network of treaties concluded at the end of World War I. For many newly created States of Europe, a price for nationhood had to be paid in the form of a guarantee to respect the cultural, religious, and even linguistic freedom of minorities within their borders, and a promise that there would be no institutionalized discrimination.[13]
- *Proscribing racial and other forms of discrimination.* Various conventions, including the International Convention on the Elimination of All Forms of Racial Discrimination, the ILO's Discrimination Convention (No 111) and UNESCO's Convention against Discrimination in Education, extend their protection to members of groups defined by reference to race, colour, descent, sex, national or ethnic origin, political or other opinion, economic conditions, or birth.
- *Protection of indigenous populations.* ILO Convention No 107 concerning indigenous and tribal populations sanctions affirmative action in favour of the populations concerned. ECOSOC in its Decision 1982/34 established a Working Group to review developments relating to the promotion and protection of the human rights and fundamental freedoms of indigenous populations, with special attention to the evolution of standards concerning the rights of indigenous populations.

In each of these areas the recognition of groups is essential for the effective protection of the rights of the individual members. The recognition of the group is necessary to allow human rights law to define the individual requiring special protection. The instruments cited are for the most part careful not to grant rights directly to peoples, as distinct from persons belonging to the groups. But there are at least two instances where, in support of my third premiss, it is the group itself which is the direct beneficiary of human rights. The Convention on the Prevention and Punishment of the Crime of Genocide is intended for the protection of groups defined by national, ethnic, racial, or religious criteria. The Convention implies an acceptance that the group is qualitatively different from the sum of its parts. The International Convention on the Suppression and Punishment of the Crime of Apartheid has similar provisions. While extending rights to members of the group, other provisions, like Article II(b), refer to the crime of 'deliberate imposition on a racial group . . . of living conditions calculated to cause its . . . physical destruction . . .'. These two cases appear to be instances where rights devolve directly upon groups.

The two best-known examples of peoples' rights are of course the right of self-determination and 'the rights of peoples and nations to permanent sovereignty over their natural resources' as stated in Art. 1 of UNGA Res. 1803 (1962). Two conclusions from the existence of these rights may be

---

[13] See F. Capotorti, *Study on the Rights of Persons belonging to Ethnic, Religious and Linguistic Minorities*, E/CN 4/Sub 2/384/Rev 1 (1979).

relevant to an examination of the right to development. First, the proposition that the right to development may be a right of peoples in human rights law does not break new ground in principle. The precedent was set decades ago. If there is a third generation of human rights then the first-born of that generation is the right of self-determination. Second, the possibility that a State could itself be one of the beneficiaries of human rights law is foreshadowed in the principle stated in UNGA Res. 1803, which recognizes the right of peoples and nations to permanent sovereignty. If peoples are capable of being subjects of human rights law, then why should these same peoples, organized as nations, lose this capacity?

There are however two important distinctions to be drawn between the right of self-determination and the right to development. Many commentators refer to the former as a precondition for the enjoyment of individual human rights. Given the subjugated condition of colonized peoples, this may be valid. But the same description should not be attached to the right to development, lest this right be used as a justification for violating or delaying the implementation of civil and political rights.

The other distinction is that the right to development is widely said to be a right of peoples and, simultaneously, of individuals. In this way the traditional individual human rights are considered to be the necessary base on which to erect the broader structure. There is no derogation from existing individual human rights. Rather they are reinforced.

(3) The Universal Declaration of the Rights of Peoples (1976)

To complete this comment on the theoretical framework, I wish to refer briefly to the Universal Declaration of the Rights of Peoples adopted in Algiers on 4 July 1976.[14] The Universal Declaration was drafted not by States but by individuals. It was drafted in French and it shows the Gallic tendency to devise abstract principles before full consideration of the substance of a matter is undertaken. I raise this document not as evidence of positive international law but as an example of the importance with which the rights of peoples are held by some commentators.[15]

The Declaration is in seven parts. Section I deals with the right of peoples to exist and to maintain their national and cultural identity. Section II concerns the right of political self-determination, including the right to be represented democratically. Section III on economic rights refers to permanent sovereignty, the common heritage of mankind, equity in international trade and the right of peoples freely to choose their own path to development. Section IV on cultural rights includes a suggestion that peoples have a right to their artistic treasures and an implication that they

[14] See A. Cassese & E. Jouve (eds), *Pour un Droit des Peuples* (1978).
[15] Those involved in the drafting and adoption of the Declaration included G. Abi-Saab, A. Cassese, F. Rigaux, J. Salmon, R. Falk: id., 22.

have a right to have these treasures returned to them. Section V deals with the right to protect the environment and enjoy the common heritage of mankind. It also contains a rather cryptic reference to the need of peoples 'to coordinate the demands of economic development with those of solidarity between all the peoples of the world'. Section VI concerns minority rights, which do not include any right of secession. The final Section on guarantees and sanctions contains some interesting ideas on enforcement of international law. The Declaration makes no attempt to define the term 'peoples'. However it tends to equate peoples with nations.

2. State Practice

We must now confront the difficult issue of what constitutes State practice in the present case. Professor Brownlie has taken me to task for adopting what he considers to be an unacceptable view of State practice. He appears to require a fairly strict positivist interpretation. But the positivist method requires a State to concede that its actions flow from obligations. I do not believe that this test can be the sole qualification for an act to constitute State practice. States often consider themselves obliged to undertake certain actions but nevertheless prefer to couch these actions in the language of discretion. Those working in government will be familiar with this need to portray all official actions as based on decisions freely selected from various options. International law must lift this veil of claimed discretion and examine the actions themselves to determine if they are sufficiently widespread and consistent to constitute State practice. Articulation of a particular practice by governments is an important piece of evidence, but its absence should not automatically be a disqualifying factor.

In contrast to the French approach, the common law tradition tends to put more emphasis on assessing relevant State actions. I intend briefly to state four conclusions which may be derived from State practice and also to examine the emerging links between human rights and development. I do not consider these four conclusions constitute proof of the existence of the right to development, but they are evidence of a distinct trend in that direction, and are thus foundation stones in the construction of the right to development. I propose to state the four conclusions without elaboration but with some illustration.

(1) States behave as if they were under an obligation to provide development assistance. The Brandt Commission[16] and the Development Assistance Committee of the OECD[17] have provided ample documentation

---

[16] Report of the Independent Commission on International Development Issues, *North-South: A Programme for Survival* (1979).

[17] The Development Assistance Committee of the Organization for Economic Co-operation and Development publishes an annual review entitled *Development Co-operation*.

of the development assistance phenomenon. In absolute terms, it has to-talled well over $US30 billion a year in each of the first years of this decade.[18] It may not have reached the targets set, but it is a substantial and consistent flow.

The development assistance phenomenon provides an interesting test case of what may constitute State practice. Donor countries have stopped short of admitting that aid is an obligation owed to developing countries. Yet the practice of giving such aid is so consistent as to require closer examination. All Western donors belong to the Development Assistance Committee of the OECD, where they compare notes on each other's per-formance and experiences. Many have established government agencies dedicated to this function (for example USAID (United States), CIDA (Canada), ADAB (Australia)). Some have made the provision of de-velopment assistance part of their domestic law.[19] Others collect domestic taxes earmarked for development assistance purposes.[20]

There is also a considerable level of articulation of governmental po-sitions concerning development assistance. The OECD's annual pub-lication, *Development Cooperation*, spells out donor motives. The 1981 issue summarized these as 'global solidarity'.[21] The General Assembly has passed numerous resolutions urging donors to undertake to achieve certain aid targets.[22] Among academics, Oscar Schachter argues that the in-ternational law of development incorporates 'a new conception of in-ternational entitlement to aid and preferences based on need'.[23] Maurice Flory argues that 'the international community is moving towards the recognition of the developing countries' right to aid'.[24]

Donor countries through their consistent actions and their statements and votes in international institutions have represented themselves as in-tending to provide development assistance. Recipient countries, who are usually required by donors to match foreign exchange contributions with local support for development assistance projects, have, in accepting to co-operate with donor countries, moved from their original positions. An analogy may be made with national law. Though there may be no con-sideration flowing directly to donor countries, the common law doctrine of equitable estoppel would arguably preclude them from reneging on their

---

[18] According to the OECD, total ODA flows were as follows: 1980 $US 33.35 billion; 1981 $US 33.36 billion; 1982 $US 34.24 billion; 1983 $US 33.65 billion.

[19] Austrian Federal Law of 10 July 1974; Swiss Federal Law of 19 March 1976.

[20] Norway has had such a tax since 1963. Denmark's excise tax on coffee serves the same purpose. See M. Flory, *Droit International du Développement* (1977) 185-6.

[21] OECD, *Development Cooperation* (1981) 86.

[22] All three UNGA resolutions inaugurating Development Decades, Res. 1710 (1961), Res. 2626 (1970) and Res. 35/56 (1980) were adopted with unanimous support.

[23] O. Schachter, 'The Evolving International Law of Development' (1976) 15 *Columbia JTL* 1, 9.

[24] Flory (1977).

original offers and representations. It is difficult to escape the conclusion that the relationship between donor and recipient is one of obligation.

In 1971, the United Nations Secretary-General said of the view that development assistance was a right of developing countries, that 'no such obligation has been accepted in positive law'.[25] In 1979, a study commissioned by the Secretary-General argued that the 1971 conclusion required reconsideration.[26] If the obligation to provide aid is a part of international law, then it would be a cornerstone of the right to development.

(2) International organizations have adopted as one of their major goals the advancement of developing countries. Though international organizations emerged late last century, their number, influence and fields of activity have grown significantly since 1945. Their constitutions recognize the need to assist developing countries, and their programmes are to an increasing extent geared to helping meet that need. The Constitution of UNIDO is particularly significant as the most recent expression of community goals. It describes international development co-operation as the 'shared goal and common obligation of all countries'.[27]

(3) Developing countries appear to have become distinct subjects of international law (that is, they are beneficiaries as such of special rights in international law). The evidence for this proposition is weighty, particularly when one takes into account the numerous references to the term 'developing countries' in a wide range of international instruments adopted over many years. These instruments range from the International Bill of Rights (developing countries are set a slightly less onerous duty than other parties in Art. 2(3) of the International Covenant on Economic, Social and Cultural Rights) to the Law of the Sea Convention (where the concept of the benefit of mankind is qualified by reference to the special interests and needs of developing countries).[28]

(4) There has been a recognition of the substantive inequality of developing as against industrialized States, entitling the former to affirmative action. The conclusion that affirmative action is an applicable principle in the relations between the developed and developing world is of considerable significance. It would form a key element of the right to development. Three of the starkest examples are:

[25] 'Survey of International Law—Working paper prepared by the Secretary-General' Doc A/CN.4/245 (1971) 83.
[26] 'The International Dimensions of the Right to Development' Doc E/CN.4/1334 (1979) 141.
[27] Preamble, Doc A/CONF.90/19.
[28] United Nations Convention on the Law of the Sea, Montego Bay, 10 Dec 1982, Art. 141.

- the granting of trade concessions to developing countries, accompanied by a renunciation on the part of the grantor to reciprocity.[29]
- the practice of international financial institutions to grant the most concessional terms to the poorest countries. Thus the worst risk borrowers attract the most favourable rates.[30]
- the provisions of the Law of the Sea Convention granting developing countries preference in such areas as access to foreign fishing zones (Art. 62), access to seabed mining technology (Annex III, Art. 5(3)(e)) and compensation for adversely affected land-based mining industries (Art. 151).

These four propositions are not presented to show that the problems of the developing countries have been resolved. But they do show that practices have evolved which address these problems. These practices contribute to the emergence of the right to development and would form an important part of that right.

An important factor in the establishment of the right to development would be the adoption by States of links between human rights and development assistance. State practice in forging this link however can be said to be tentative.

Some years ago consideration was given to creating these links in a negative way. The Development Assistance Committee of the OECD spoke of 'a disposition on the part of donors to turn down or even off the aid flow to developing countries guilty of persistent human rights violations'.[31] Two countries, Holland[32] and the United States,[33] the latter through domestic legislation, made this link one element of their aid policies in the late 1970s. But this method of linking the two issues does not appear to have taken hold. The then Government of Holland and the Carter Administration which instituted these links have both lost office. Their successors have adopted a more cautious approach. Among European countries there appears to be a general disinclination to adopt the 'negative link' as a matter of policy.[34]

[29] T. Murray, *Trade Preferences for Developing Countries* (1977). GATT has on its agenda 'the legal framework for differential and more favourable treatment for developing countries in relation to GATT provisions, in particular the most-favoured nation clause': *Yearbook of the International Law Commission* (1978) vol. II, pt. 1, 26.

[30] See W. D. Verway, 'The Recognition of the Developing Countries as Special Subjects of International Law Beyond the Sphere of United Nations Resolutions' in R. J. Dupuy (ed.), *Hague Academy of International Law and United Nations University Workshop* (1980) 30.

[31] OECD, *Development Cooperation* (1980) 61.

[32] *Human Rights and Foreign Policy* (Memorandum presented to the Lower House of the States General of the Kingdom of the Netherlands on 3 May 1979 by the Minister for Foreign Affairs and the Minister for Development Cooperation) Policy Conclusions, 32-42.

[33] United States Department of State, [1975] *Digest of United States Practice in International Law 222.*

[34] According to a survey on the issue undertaken by the Australian Department of Foreign Affairs. The closest approach to such a 'link' was the proposition accepted by a few countries that persistent violators of human rights were so unpopular domestically that it became difficult to justify aid to these countries in the domestic political context.

The increasing unpopularity of the negative link complicates the question of justiciability posed in Professor Crawford's paper. Justiciability is not inappropriate on legal grounds but rather on the basis of aid policy. As the Australian Minister for Foreign Affairs recently put it, linking development assistance to human rights protection 'would probably lead to a repudiation of the aid proposals—and therein rests a moral dilemma... namely that aid denied where it is desperately needed means punitive experiences for the most exposed and dependent groups in a particular community'.[35]

Attempts have also been made to bind the two concepts in a positive way rather than in the form of a sanction. A move in this direction was the development in the late 1970s of the Basic Human Needs approach to development planning. This was an attempt to make the individual and his basic needs the centre of the development process. It seemed that it could provide the bridge between human rights and development. But the approach was soon discredited. The developing countries argued that it distracted attention from issues of the New International Economic Order, played down the importance of economic growth and encouraged foreign interference in their domestic affairs.[36] In short, it smacked of paternalism.

The structural approach to human rights, mentioned above as a possible new phase in human rights activity, by requiring the removal of structural obstacles to the enjoyment of human rights, would certainly create the link in a positive fashion. And the Commission on Human Rights also adopted a positive and constructive approach in the cases of Equatorial Guinea,[37] the Central African Republic[38] and Uganda.[39] The Commission's resolutions, rather than simply condemning human rights violations, required advisory services, action plans and other concrete forms of assistance to be provided to help those countries to establish a system which would safeguard respect for human rights and fundamental freedoms.

More attention needs to be given to this question of reinforcing respect for human rights through a constructive application of aid and affirmative action programmes. Organizations like ADAB and CIDA should in my view consider general human rights questions in their aid project planning. It must be concluded however that this link, so important in founding the right to development, is only in its infancy.

3. The Articulation of the Right to Development

For some, the repetition of the assertion that there is a right to development by such bodies as the General Assembly,[40] the Commission on Human

---

[35] Hon. W. G. Hayden MHR, *Sydney Morning Herald*, 8 March 1985, 2, commenting on the relationship between Australian aid and human rights in Laos.   [36] P. Alston (1981) 70-2.

[37] CHR Res. 31/37 (1981).   [39] CHR Res. 30/37 (1981).

[38] CHR Res. 15/37 (1981).   [40] UNGA Res. 34/46 (1979).

Rights,[41] the Conference of Heads of State of Non-Aligned Countries,[42] and the Assembly of Heads of State and Government of the Organization of African Unity,[43] is sufficient proof of its existence. But such assertions cannot be conclusive. They need to be backed by State practice and by the detailed articulation of the content of the right in an instrument enjoying widespread support.

In 1981 the Commission on Human Rights established a Working Group to draft a Declaration on the Right to Development.[44] The fifteen-member Working Group (including France, the Netherlands, and the United States) was unable to conclude a text and the Commission decided to refer the issue to the General Assembly. Yugoslavia accepted responsibility for securing progress on the issue and at the 40th Session of the General Assembly in 1985 circulated a draft declaration drawn from the drafts prepared by the Working Group. The draft attracted a surprising level of acceptance but consensus proved elusive and the Yugoslav delegation decided not to press the issue at that session.[45]

In 1986 Yugoslavia circulated the draft declaration at the 41st Session of the General Assembly but this time made clear its willingness to press the matter to a vote. On 4 December 1986 the General Assembly, by a vote of 146 in favour to 1 against with 8 abstentions, adopted Resolution 41/128, the 'Declaration on the Right to Development'. The Chairman of the Third Committee of the General Assembly at the 41st Session described the adoption of the Declaration as 'perhaps the Committee's most significant achievement'.[46]

In the course of the negotiations Yugoslavia accepted one amendment and deflected another. An amendment submitted by France and the Netherlands to make clear that references in the Declaration to the right of peoples to full sovereignty over all their natural wealth and resources is governed by Article 1, paragraph 2 of the International Covenant on Civil and Political Rights, was incorporated in the Declaration.[47] With this amendment the support of 15 OECD countries was secured.[48] A Pakistani amendment incorporating references to specific aspects of 'new international economic order' was deflected so as not to risk losing the support of those industrialized countries prepared to vote in favour. It was sub-

[41] CHR Res. 4/33 (1977), Res. 10/34 (1978), Res. 4 & 5/35 (1979), Res. 6 & 7/36 (1980), Res. 36/37 (1981).

[42] UN Doc A/34/542 (1979) Annex, para. 1, 266.

[43] Banjul Charter on Human and Peoples' Rights, OAU Doc CAB/LEG/67/3/Rev 1-5.

[44] CHR Res. 36/37 (1981).

[45] See A/40/970 (1985) 3-9, 17.

[46] UN Doc A/C.3/41/SR61, 36 (1986).

[47] UN Doc A/C.3/41/L34.

[48] Viz. Australia, Austria, Belgium, Canada, France, Greece, Ireland, Italy, Luxembourg, Netherlands, New Zealand, Norway, Portugal, Spain, and Turkey.

sequently adopted as a separate resolution with a significantly reduced majority.[49]

The absence of consensus raises questions about the authority in which the Declaration should be held. The largest international donor in monetary terms, the United States, voted against Res. 41/128. In its explanation of vote,[50] the United States delegation described the Declaration as 'imprecise and confusing', took exception to the connections drawn between disarmament and development, and disagreed with the view that development was to be principally achieved by transfers of resources from the developed to the developing world (a view not elaborated in the Declaration). The eight countries abstaining included four Nordic countries, Japan, the United Kingdom, and the Federal Republic of Germany, all significant aid donors and all countries which have promoted the observance of human rights in recent times. From their explanations of vote,[51] two major preoccupations emerged: first, that priority should be given to individual human rights rather than the concept of a human right of peoples and, secondly, that the provision of development assistance could not be seen as an obligation under international law.

It is interesting that these aspects of the Declaration should be singled out for criticism. The duties imposed on States in the Declaration are not specific, let alone quantified; rather they are couched in quite general language. The claim in Article 3 that 'states have the duty to cooperate with each other in ensuring development and eliminating obstacles to development' sounds more like a description of existing development assistance objectives than an onerous new obligation. Where the Declaration calls for 'more rapid development of developing countries' (Article 4) it does so in the passive voice and juxtaposes this as 'a complement to the efforts of developing countries'.

The Declaration is more strident in its insistence that 'the right to development is an inalienable human right' devolving on both persons and peoples (Article 1) and that all aspects of the right to development are indivisible and interdependent (Article 9). It seems that some countries are still not prepared to accept this arresting new notion.

The reluctance of a few countries should not obscure the force of the innovative concepts elaborated in the Declaration. It contains the unequivocal statements that 'the human person is the central subject of development' (Article 2), that in formulating national development policies States must 'aim at the constant improvement of the well-being of the entire population and of all individuals' on the basis of 'the fair distribution

---

[49] UNGA Res. 41/133, adopted by 133-11:12. Only 2 OECD countries (New Zealand, Turkey) voted in favour.
[50] UN Doc A/C.3/41/SR61, 32 (1986).
[51] UN Doc A/C.3/41/SR61 (1986); A/41/PV.97 (1986).

of the benefits' of development (Article 2), that 'failure to observe civil and political rights' can be 'an obstacle to development' (Article 6), that States shall ensure 'equal opportunity for all in their access to basic resources, education, health services, food, housing, employment and the fair distribution of income' and shall encourage 'popular participation in all spheres' (Article 8).

The objections expressed to the Declaration, some of which were also shared by countries voting in favour of Resolution 41/128, must be given due weight when assessing the degree of acceptance of the Declaration in the international community. The adoption of the Declaration by such a broad majority should be seen as an important and perhaps decisive step in the progress of the right to development to the status of international law. While the dissenting opinions are significant, there is a likelihood that dissent will wane as the years pass and as the Declaration is given practical application.

4. The Necessity for a Right to Development

The final section of this paper is devoted to a presentation of arguments on the usefulness of the concept of a right to development. I noted above the precedent for 'nations' to be beneficiaries of human rights. As a right of peoples, I see no effective means of implementing the right to development other than through States and their governments. There is no other acceptable method of representing peoples in the post-decolonization era than through their national governments which are recipients of development assistance.

Many would consider this aspect an unacceptable concession to Socialist bloc doctrine. In practice however, the principle of affirmative action in favour of developing countries is already largely established. The right to development would place this practice in the framework of international human rights law. Affirmative action would no longer be considered as a discretionary practice, nor as amends for past guilt, nor as a political concession, but as a human rights obligation. The acceptance of aid and affirmative action programmes by recipient countries would also be seen in a human rights context. As things stand, and bilateral agreements aside, the acceptance of such assistance creates no corresponding obligation. The right to development would link the acceptance of the benefit with a corresponding obligation on developing countries to respect and advance the human rights of their people. It would be a further avenue through which individuals could base claims on their own governments.

The right to development would thus disallow any suggestion that economic rights have priority over civil and political rights. It would give substance to the claim that such rights are 'indivisible and interdependent'.

It would reject the notion that civil and political rights are luxuries beyond the means of developing countries.

The right to development would provide a rationale for development beyond the impersonal calculations of economic growth targets. It would insist that the development of the individual is the ultimate objective of all development projects. It would therefore work as a corrective to mal-development. Development projects requiring coercive pressures on individuals, forced removal of indigenous or agrarian populations, or even unacceptable environmental damage, could no longer be supported by foreign aid or concessional loans or assistance from international organizations. Indeed there are now indications that countries are beginning to take these factors into account when assessing aid requests.

The issue of the quality of aid would be squarely faced. Donors would not be entitled to dump unwanted produce that did not meet the needs of foreign recipients. The trend to tie aid grants to trade concessions would be reversed. Project planning would be required to go beyond macro-economics. E. F. Schumacher once described official development assistance as 'a process where you collect money from the poor people in the rich countries, to give it to the rich people in the poor countries'.[52] The right to development would make unfounded at least the second half of that statement.

We are all aware of the criticism of international law from Third World countries.[53] To these countries, international law is tainted. It was developed without their participation and, initially at least, worked against the interests of their peoples. Human rights law is often tarred with the same brush. It also suffers from another criticism. It is believed that the Western emphasis on civil and political rights is a reflection of the Western conception of the individual's role in society. Asian and African societies tend to place more emphasis on the welfare of the group, whether family, clan or tribe, than on the rights of the individual.

The right of self-determination played a role in rehabilitating human rights law in the Third World. However, that right is now less a war-cry than a ceremonial chant of remembrance. The right to development would be a positive force in involving Third World countries in human rights, including the less fashionable civil and political rights. The right to development acknowledges the importance of both the individual and the group. It would associate traditional human rights with the issue of greatest concern to developing countries—development.

[52] Quoted in *The Canberra Times*, 5 December 1981.
[53] e.g. M. Bedjaoui, *Towards a New International Economic Order* (1979) 51.

4

The Rights of Peoples:
'Peoples' or 'Governments'?

JAMES CRAWFORD

1. The Rights of Peoples and the Structure of International Law

From the perspective of international law, the key feature of the phrase 'rights of peoples' is not the term 'rights', but the term 'peoples'. From a philosophical point of view, no doubt, the term 'rights' is itself problematic. But lawyers, including international lawyers, are used to talking about rights, and so long as one accepts Hohfeld's point that one person's right must mean another person's duty, the term seems unremarkable even in the context of peoples' rights. Moreover, international law is familiar with the notion of 'collective' rights. References to the State, the basic unit of international law, involve a reference to the social fact of a territorial community of persons with a certain political organization, in other words, a reference to a collectivity. In this sense, international law rules that confer rights on States confer collective rights. However, when international law attributes rights to States as social and political collectivities, it does so *sub modo*—that is to say, it does so subject to the rule that the actor on behalf of the State, and the agency to which other States are to look for the observation of the obligations of the State and which is entitled to activate its rights, is the government of the State. This basic rule drastically affects the point that the State *qua* community of persons has rights in international law, especially where the view or position taken by the government of a State diverges from the interests or wishes of the people of the State that government represents. And it is, so far at least, axiomatic that international law does not guarantee representative, still less democratic, governments.[1]

[1] Cf. the *Tinoco Arbitration* (1924) 1 RIAA 369. But the 'right to have a democratic government representing all the citizens without distinction as to race, sex, belief or colour' is asserted by Art. 7 of the Algiers Declaration, and F. Rigaux comments that 'le peuple est l'ensemble ou la majorit d'une population d'un Etat dont un des droits fondamentaux est de n'être pas soumis au pouvoir d'une minorité: 'Remarques Générales sur la Déclaration d'Alger' in A. Cassese & E. Jouve (eds), *Pour un Droit des Peuples. Essais sur la Déclaration d'Alger* (1978) 41, 46.

The proposition that the international law rights of States as communities of persons are moderated through a government (not necessarily representative, but legally the representative, of the people of the State) still represents the general rule. And it is that proposition which makes the term 'peoples' in the phrase 'rights of peoples' remarkable. Has international law taken up the task of conferring rights on groups or communities of people against the State which those people constitute, and against the government of the State? If so, it would be no great step for it to confer rights on those groups or communities as against other States and their governments. But the people of a State are—to put it mildly—at least as likely to have their rights violated by their own government as by the governments of other States. If the phrase 'rights of peoples' has any independent meaning, it must confer rights on peoples against their own governments. In other words, if the only rights of peoples are rights against other States, and if there is no change to the established position that the government of the State represents 'the State' (i.e. the people of the State) for all international purposes irrespective of its representativeness, then what is the point of referring to the rights in question as rights of peoples? Why not refer to them as the rights of States, in the familiar, well understood, though somewhat elliptical way?

I think it is more profitable to try to answer this question in the context of specific formulations of the 'rights of peoples'. Which of these rights are really rights of States in disguise? Which of them are really individual human rights—or aspirations to them? Which can properly be treated as rights of peoples, as distinct from individuals or States? And if they can so be treated, what is it that distinguishes them from the other two classes of rights? It should be stressed that these questions are independent of the actual status of any particular right as a matter of general international law, or, if (as I suspect) this is a different category, as one of the recognized body of 'human rights'. But the questions must be answered before we can make sense of the practice in relation to any asserted 'right', so that to this extent at least, the issues are related.

2. A Survey of 'Peoples' Rights'

Sieghart's compilation of general human rights texts[2] identifies six classes of 'collective rights'. For present purposes, these may be described as follows:

- self-determination and equality of rights
- rights relating to international peace and security
- permanent sovereignty over natural resources

[2] P. Sieghart, *The International Law of Human Rights* (1983) 367–78.

- rights in relation to development
- rights in relation to the environment, and
- rights of minorities.

One cardinal omission from this list, from the point of view of the 'rights of peoples', is the right of groups to exist, which may be conceived of, in the first place, as an obligation on the part of States not to engage in, or allow, genocidal acts.

In addition to these seven classes or categories, there are undoubtedly other asserted rights, or provisions in international texts which might be reformulated as 'peoples rights', that could be added. Although the rights set out in Part III of the International Covenant on Economic, Social and Cultural Rights of 1966 are for the most part formulated in terms of individual rights, a number of them could be seen as having collective elements, including the right to form trade unions (art 8), the right to a 'continuous improvement of living conditions' (art 11), and the rights in art 15(1) with respect to 'cultural life' and 'the benefits of scientific progress and its applications'. None the less, the seven categories mentioned above are those which are sufficiently clearly formulated in terms of 'collective' rights, and which have achieved recognition in at least one international human rights instrument in treaty form.[3] For the purposes of assessing the validity of the 'rights of peoples' as a distinct concept or category, these seven seem a sufficient test.

The seven classes of 'rights' under examination fall into two distinct categories. One immediately apparent category is the group of rights which in some respect deal with the existence and cultural or political continuation of groups. This category would include the right to self-determination, the rights of minorities, and the rights of groups to existence (i.e. as a minimum, not to be subjected to genocide).[4] But, it may be significant that the phrase 'rights of peoples' tends to be used, at least by its proponents, primarily to refer to the other and more miscellaneous category of rights, concerned with a variety of issues relating to the economic development and the 'coexistence' of peoples. This second category includes rights in respect of permanent sovereignty over natural resources, rights to development, to the environment and to international peace and security. However, one cannot exclude the first category in asking basic questions

---

[3] This is not to suggest that other instruments, such as General Assembly resolutions, may not be significant. But such resolutions do not create obligations even for States voting for them, however influential they may be as evidence or sources of argument.

[4] Another 'right' sometimes asserted in this context which would also fall into this category (if it is not merely a reformulation of the three 'rights' referred to) is the 'right to be different': cf. Art. 1(2) of the UNESCO Declaration on Race and Racial Prejudice, 27 November 1978: 'All peoples have the right to be different, to consider themselves as different, and to be regarded as such.' Principles of equality and non-discrimination are also relevant, though usually expressed as individual rather than group rights: cf. *Case Concerning Minority Schools in Albania* PCIJ Ser A/B No 64 (1935) 17.

about the 'rights of peoples', in particular because the three group rights referred to (self-determination, minorities, genocide) appear on their face to be 'rights of peoples', and because each has gone through a considerable process of development in this century (and in the case of the rights of minorities, in earlier centuries also). By contrast the asserted rights in the second category are substantially new, and in most cases embryonic.

(1) Self-determination

The principle of self-determination has been one of the most vigorous, and vigorously disputed, collective or group rights in modern international law, and has generated a vast literature.[5] The major focus for arguments about self-determination has of course been the question of decolonization, and it is controverisal whether the principle of self-determination is restricted to cases of decolonization, or whether it can have consequences in terms of 'metropolitan' States, including, for example, minority groups or peoples. As it happens, the term 'self-determination of peoples' in the United Nations Charter occurs twice, in Art. 1 para. 2, and in Art. 55, in each case as part of the phrase 'respect for the principle of equal rights and self-determination of peoples'. In each case the context is quite distinct from questions of decolonization (which are dealt with in the Charter in Arts 73 and 76). In the United Nations Human Rights Covenants, the phrase has a similar tone of universality, although in each case it is described as a 'right' rather than a 'principle', and is dissociated from the term 'equal rights'. Thus Art. 1 para. 1 of both the Economic, Social and Cultural Rights Covenant, and the Civil and Political Rights Covenant, proclaims that:

All peoples have the right of self-determination. By virtue of that right they freely determine their political status and freely pursue their economic, social and cultural development.

The link between self-determination and 'economic, social and cultural development' is already explicit, and it is spelt out further by linking with self-determination in para. 2 the notion that 'all peoples may, for their own ends, freely dispose of their natural wealth and resources ... In no case may a people be deprived of its own means of subsistence'. Decolonization is only expressly referred to in para. 3 of Art. 1, and then in terms which imply that States parties to the Covenants may have obligations by reference to the notion of self-determination which extend beyond 'Non-Self-Governing and Trust Territories'.[6]

[5] See J. Crawford, *The Creation of States in International Law* (1979) 85-102 and works there cited.
[6] Art. I(3) provides that States parties '*including* those having responsibility for the administration of Non-Self-Governing and Trust Territories, shall promote the realisation of the right of self-determination . . . '(emphasis added).

Whatever view is taken about the scope of the principle of self-determination in international law, from the point of view of the present enquiry the situation is clear. Self-determination is plainly a collective rather than an individual right, although obviously enough individuals are to be involved in the exercise of the right, and a majority of them at least will benefit directly from it in the sense of retaining or achieving a measure of self-government in accordance with their wishes or preferences. Secondly, self-determination is plainly to be thought of as a right of 'peoples' rather than governments. To the extent that it applies, it qualifies the right of governments to dispose of the 'peoples' in question in ways which conflict with their rights to self-determination.

(2) Genocide: The Right to Physical Existence

There can be no doubt that international law recognizes the obligation of States not to commit or condone genocide. This idea may be implicit in the notion of self-determination as expressed in Art. 1 para. 1 of the Human Rights Covenants, but it goes well beyond those provisions, because the 'peoples' or 'groups' protected by the rules about genocide include groups which would not be classed as beneficiaries of the right to self-determination. Article II of the Genocide Convention of 1948 describes the beneficiaries of the rule as any 'national, ethnical [*sic*], racial or religious group' and proscribes certain acts committed against members of such groups with intent to destroy them in whole or in part.[7] It is true that the Genocide Convention is directed at offenders rather than victims; that is to say, the problem is treated in that Convention as a matter of the duties of 'persons . . . whether they are constitutionally responsible rulers, public officials or private individuals' (Art. IV), rather than in terms of the rights of 'national, ethnical, racial or religious groups'. But plainly the definition of 'genocide' can be regarded as having as its object the preservation of those groups, and in this sense it is meaningful to talk about their rights. It should be noted, however, that these rights are of a distinctly limited character, notwithstanding (or perhaps because of) the breadth of the notion of a 'group' in the Convention. Thus the Convention only prohibits acts which involve or conduce to direct or indirect physical destruction of the group or a substantial part of it, whether by homicide, terrorism, mass deprivation, eugenics or forcible transfer of children. The Convention is not concerned with 'cultural genocide' or what has been described as

---

[7] 78 UNTS 277. See also L. Le Blanc, 'The Intent to Destroy Groups in the Genocide Convention: The Proposed US Understanding' (1984) 78 *AJIL* 369. The requirement of intent has led to arguments that the disappearance of indigenous groups as a more or less direct effect of government policies is not genocide because unintended: cf. id., 380–1 (Aché Indians in Paraguay).

'ethnocide',[8] in the sense of the destruction or disappearance of the distinctive values, traditions, or culture of a group, as distinct from the survival of the members of the group as individuals, and its continued existence as a group assuming its members so wish.[9]

(3) Rights of Minorities

As mentioned already, the notion that minority groups may have rights guaranteed to them as such is not a new one in international relations. Indeed, to the extent that minority rights are thought of as more than the product of the individual human rights of members of minority groups (including their rights to associate with each other), these rights were better protected under the international law of the pre-World War II period (in those cases where particular minorities were protected by treaties or other arrangements), than they are now under general human rights law.[10] The relevant provision of the International Covenant on Civil and Political Rights, Art. 27, hovers between being a mere extrapolation from the individual rights of members of a minority group, and being a genuinely 'collective' right. Both the formulation of Art. 27 in terms of individual rights ('persons belonging to such minorities shall not be denied the right . . . '), and its association in international jurisprudence with notions of equality and non-discrimination, suggest that minority rights are not necessarily to be thought of as collective rights at all, in modern international law. The crucial issue is that of 'minorities of minorities': if minority rights are genuinely collective, then it presumably follows that dissenting members of minority groups can be compelled to comply with the wishes of the majority of the group, in the same way that dissenting members of 'peoples' with a right to self-determination can be compelled to accept a form of self government which the majority of that 'people' have elected or accepted.[11]

One of the difficulties here is the underlying assumption that the category 'minorities' bears some necessary relation to the category 'peoples'. This need not be so. A minority cannot cease to be a 'people', if it is one, just because, as a result of demographic or territorial change or for some other reason, it becomes a majority of the national population of a State. By definition, a 'minority' implies the existence of a 'majority' (not necessarily a coherent one, since it could be made up by a collection of other minor-

---

[8] Cf. P. Thornberry, 'Is There a Phoenix in the Ashes? International Law and Minority Rights' (1980) 15 *Texas ILJ* 421, 444.

[9] On the other hand, acts of genocide as defined in the Convention may well take place with a view to the forced assimilation or destruction of the culture of a group, so that to this extent the two concepts are linked.

[10] On the pre-World War II minorities treaties and their replacement by general human rights provisions after 1945 see e.g. J. B. Kelly, 'National Minorities in International Law' (1973) 3 *Denver JILP* 253.

[11] As is the case of dissentients in the various UN-supervised plebiscites in trust and non-self-governing territories: see A. Rigo-Sureda, *The Evolution of the Right of Self-Determination* (1973).

ities). By contrast, the notion of a 'people' says nothing about the relationship of that people to other peoples inhabiting the same State or
territory. Thus an individual might have rights as a member of a minority
which coexist with rights that person enjoys as a member of (the same or a
broader) group properly classified as a 'people', for the purpose of the right
to self-determination, or for some other purpose. One of the difficulties
with nineteenth-century practice in the area of minorities was that it was
seeking to protect what are logically and practically distinct values: the
'collective' value of national existence or continuity or autonomy within a
broader 'multi-national' State or empire (a problem now partly at least
subsumed under the category of self-determination), and the rights of
individual members of minority groups to associate with each other, and
to practice their culture, language or religion. The latter right is certainly
capable of being thought of, and is perhaps best thought of, as in principle
an individual one: no one can be forced to practice a religion. On this view
the Human Rights Committee's treatment of Sandra Lovelace as a member
of a 'minority' under Art. 27 of the Civil and Political Rights Covenant[12]
was not necessarily inconsistent with the view that the Indian group to
which she claimed to belong, or other indigenous groups with a sufficiently
distinctive character, might be 'peoples' for the purposes of Art. 1 of the
Covenant, that is to say, for the purposes of the right to self-determination.
But in practice such claims are likely to be met with considerable hostility,
especially from the 'newly independent' States themselves, whose primary
concern is stated to be nation building rather than respect for, or even
tolerance of, the cultures and beliefs of local populations.[13]

(4) Rights to International Peace and Security

In this insecure and not particularly peaceful world, the idea that there
might be individual or collective rights to international peace and security
has a certain paradoxical quality. There have been various attempts since
1945 by legal means to address some of the causes of war, in particular
measures prohibiting incitement to racial, national, or religious hatred, and
a number of the international human rights instruments contain provisions
requiring certain forms of incitement to 'national, racial, or religious
hatred', and 'any propaganda for war' to be prohibited by law.[14] Article 23
(1) of the African Charter goes beyond this, and declares that:

[12] GAOR 36th Sess, Supp. No 40 (A/36/40), Annex XVIII, 166.
[13] Cf. the Human Rights Committee's reluctance to deal with an application brought on
behalf of the Miqmaq Indians under the Optional Protocol to the ICCPR, alleging a violation
of self-determination under Art. 1 of the Covenant: *Miqmaq Tribal Society* v. *Canada*, noted
in (1984) 33 *Int Com Jurists Rev* 45.
[14] See e.g. ICCPR Art. 20 (1) ('any propaganda for war') (2) ('any advocacy of national,

All peoples shall have the right to national and international peace and security. The principles of solidarity and friendly relations implicitly affirmed by the Charter of the United Nations and reaffirmed by that of the Organization of African Unity shall govern relations between States.

Article 23(2)(b) goes on to provide that the territory of States parties 'shall not be used as bases for subversive or territorist activities against the people of any other State party to the present Charter'. Article 23 is of considerable interest in revealing the interplay, or perhaps one should say the confusion, between the notions of 'people' and 'State'. The first sentence of Art. 23(1) declares a right of all peoples. The second sentence refers to principles of solidarity and friendly relations between States. But Art. 23(2), for the purpose of 'strengthening peace, solidarity and friendly relations' imposes an obligation not to allow territory to be used as a base for subversive or terrorist activities against 'the people of any other State party'. Evidently the 'people' referred to is assumed to be synonymous with the whole population of the State, at least for the purpose of Art. 23(2)(b). Moreover Art. 23(2)(b) might appear to allow 'subversive or terrorist activities' against governments which are wholly unrepresentative of the 'people' of the State, a proposition contradicted by the principles of international law expressly affirmed in the Charters of the United Nations and the Organization of African Unity, which principles Art. 23 had apparently earlier endorsed.

Of course, there is a practical relationship between the maintenance of general human rights, individual or collective, and the existence of a state of peace, if not friendly relations, between States. As a reference to this important though underlying reality, provisions such as Art. 23 of the African Charter, or for that matter Art. 28 of the Universal Declaration of Human Rights,[15] cannot be criticized. But to treat rights to international peace and security as distinct and independent, as it were 'foreground' rights, whether individual or collective, raises questions of an altogether different kind. To say that States have the right to international peace and security is to repeat, in obverse, established and well-known duties such as those stated in Art. 2 para. 4 of the United Nations Charter. But to say, as Art. 23 of the African Charter does, that 'peoples' have that right, even if in this context 'peoples' means the populations of States as a whole, might appear to make a wide range of sensitive foreign policy questions justiciable in the African Commission of Human and Peoples Rights, particularly since Art. 23 makes no distinction between actions (e.g. invasion, military intervention) which themselves breach the peace, and actions, policies, or

racial or religious hatred that constitutes incitement to discrimination, hostility or violence ...'). To similar effect Art. 13(5) of the American Convention on Human Rights of 1969. The African Charter contains no equivalent prohibition.

[15] This provides that 'Everyone is entitled to a social and international order in which the rights and freedoms set forth in this Declaration can be fully realised.'

attitudes which have a more diffuse disruptive tendency. As is well known the United Nations Charter, and the international law founded on it, while acknowledging the link between respect for human rights and maintenance of international peace and security, placed a considerable priority upon avoiding outright conflict between States, whatever its origins, requiring underlying disputes to be settled by other means. Provisions such as Art. 23, in avoiding these distinctions and in conflating respect for human or peoples' rights and international peace and security, tend further to blur or confuse the basic premisses upon which the Charter order was to be based. To be sure, there are other aspects of modern international relations and diplomacy having the same tendency, but it is by no means clear that debate on this central question is assisted by reformulating the issue in terms of peoples rights.

(5) Rights to Permanent Sovereignty over Natural Resources

The notion of permanent sovereignty over natural resources has gained considerable currency in the last two decades, and is recognized in the same terms both in the Civil and Political Rights Covenant, and in the Economic Social and Cultural Rights Covenant. Article 1 para. 2 of both instruments provides that:[16]

All peoples may, for their own ends, freely dispose of their natural wealth and resources without prejudice to any obligations arising out of international economic co-operation, based upon the principle of mutual benefit and international law. In no case may a people be deprived of its own means of subsistence.

The precedent for treating questions of permanent sovereignty over natural resources as rights of peoples, rather than as rights of States, is thus an established one. The African Charter is to that extent on firm ground when it elaborates upon the notion of permanent sovereignty in a similar, though more explicit, way. Article 21 provides that:[17]

(1) All peoples shall freely dispose of their wealth and natural resources. This right shall be exercised in the exclusive interest of the people. In no case shall a people be deprived of it.
(2) In case of spoliation the dispossessed people shall have the right to lawful recovery of its property as well as to an adequate compensation.
(3) The free disposal of wealth and natural resources shall be exercised without

[16] Art. 47 of the ICCPR (Art. 25 of the ICESCR) further states: 'Nothing in the present Covenant shall be interpreted as impairing the inherent right of all peoples to enjoy and utilise fully and freely their natural wealth and resources.'

[17] Art 21 (4) refers to the need to exercise this right 'with a view to strengthening African unity and solidarity'; by contrast, Art 21 (5) entails an obligation 'to eliminate all forms of foreign economic exploitation', so as to maximise a people's benefits from their natural resources. Apparently, local economic exploitation has no such deleterious effects.

prejudice to the obligation of promoting international economic co-operation based on mutual respect, equitable exchange and the principles of international law.

Despite the substantial body of support for rule or principle of permanent sovereignty over natural resources, there are difficulties in treating it as a collective right of peoples as distinct from States. In its application to States, the notion of 'permanent sovereignty' (though something of an euphemism—States are not necessarily 'permanently sovereign' but can be extinguished in a variety of ways) none the less makes reasonable sense as an extrapolation from underlying notions of sovereignty and independence. Agreements, whether on the international or municipal level, with respect to the use of natural resources do not extinguish a State's sovereignty over those resources while they remain within its territory. The notion of permanent sovereignty may also be concerned with establishing, or reaffirming, certain hierarchies of international law rules. For example, States may remain 'sovereign' over their natural resources though their conduct in relation to those resources violates other principles of international law (e.g. in the context of expropriation of foreign-owned property).

So far 'permanent sovereignty' fits sufficiently well within existing categories, whatever conclusions one arrives at as to the merits of particular issues. But introducing the notion that the 'permanent sovereignty' is a sovereignty of 'peoples' adds another dimension. If those 'peoples' constitute a part only of the population of the State, then the notion of permanent sovereignty presumably limits the power of the national government freely to dispose of the natural resources of the region without the consent (or against the wishes or contrary to the interests) of the 'people' in question. Alternatively, if the 'people' is the whole population of the State, the principle apparently establishes that transactions entered into by or on behalf of the State and involving the disposal of natural resources are subject to subsequent scrutiny, and to invalidation or avoidance, if these turn out not to have been in the interests of the population. Moreover, such a rule can hardly make sense when it is limited to 'foreign economic exploitation' (which to be effective cannot be wholly foreign: like charity, exploitation usually begins at home). Formulated in this way, the principle of permanent sovereignty over natural resources is certainly capable of operating as a guarantee of peoples against their own governments, limiting the capacity of governments for the time being in the interests of the community.[18] In the case of provisions such as Art. 21 of the African Charter, that would tend to make a State's natural resources policy justiciable in the African Commission on Human and Peoples Rights. No

[18] But, wholly exceptional situations apart, in the existing conditions of international relations the State acts through its government, and if a State's acts are ever to be definitive so too must the government's be.

doubt the real point of provisions such as Art. 21, or Art. 1 para. 2 of the United Nations Human Rights Covenants, is that they provide a forensic basis for disputing existing contractual and other arrangements relating to natural resources. But thought of as a right of 'peoples', the argument seems a dangerously double-edged one.

(6) The Right to Development

So far this is recognized as such in human rights treaties only in the African Charter, Art. 22 of which provides that:

(1) All peoples shall have the right to their economic, social and cultural development with due regard to their freedom and identity and in the equal enjoyment of the common heritage of mankind.
(2) States shall have the duty, individually or collectively, to ensure the exercise of the right to development.

Notwithstanding its scanty recognition in international human rights treaties, the notion of a right to development as a human or peoples' rights is very much at the centre of the debate about peoples' rights.[19] For present purposes the analysis of the possible distinctions between a right to development as a peoples' right, and that right as a right of States, does not differ significantly from the situation with respect to the right of permanent sovereignty over natural resources. The right to development is, outside specific contexts and specific instruments (e.g. relating to development aid, or the distribution of benefits in the law of the sea regime), less well integrated into the body of international practice than the notion of permanent sovereignty.[20] So far as other States are concerned, the notion that

[19] e.g. H. G. Espiell, 'The Right of Development as a Human Right'(1981) 16 *Texas ILJ* 189. For a more objective account see Roland Rich's discussion in this volume.

[20] It is instructive in this context to compare the provisions of General Assembly Resolution 41/128, the Declaration on the Right to Development of 4 December 1986. The preambular paragraphs refer, in relation to development within particular States, to 'the entire population and ... all individuals', recall the rights of peoples to self-determination and to sovereignty over their natural wealth and resources, refer to various obstacles to 'the complete fulfillment of human beings and of peoples', and specify that 'the human person is the central subject of the development process and ... the main participant and beneficiary of development'. Article 1(1) describes the right to development as 'an inalienable human right by virtue of which every human person and all peoples are entitled to participate in, contribute to and enjoy economic, social, cultural and political development, in which all human rights and fundamental freedoms can be fully realized'. Article 1(2) states that 'the human right to development ... implies the full realization of the right of peoples to self-determination, which includes, subject to relevant provisions of both International Covenants on Human Rights, the exercise of their inalienable right to full sovereignty over all their natural wealth and resources'. Clearly these provisions stop short of stating that the right to development is a collective right, or a right of peoples: the contrast between the 'human right' to development in Art. 1(1) and the two rights of peoples referred to in Art. 1(2) is clear, and is continued in Art. 5 by the emphasis on the right of peoples to self-determination. The remaining articles refer to various responsibilities of States with respect to development, again without any implication that development is a collective or peoples' right.

'peoples' have a right to development does not appear to differ from the proposition that States have such a right. But the former proposition might have an independent content if its effect was to countermand deliberate governmental policies *vis-à-vis* the population of the State in question, leading designedly to non-development or to differential development of regions. It is difficult to believe that States would be interested to assert the illegitimacy of such policies on the part of another State against its own peoples (basic questions of racial discrimination or genocide apart), or that the 'defaulting' governments themselves would be prepared to accept such assertions (whether or not accompanying the provision of development aid) as a matter of right. So far, the assessment of one leading African international lawyer seems accurate:[21]

The right to development ... appears not to have attained the definitive status of rule of law despite its powerful advocates. Its inclusion in the African Charter will be as effective as the Charter itself. The negative duty not to impede the development of States may go down well; the positive duty to aid such development, in the absence of specific accords, is a higher level of commitment that still rests on nonlegal considerations.

(7) Rights to the Environment

Much the same can be said of the notion of 'rights to the environment', which are again reflected so far only in the African Charter. Article 24 provides that:

All peoples shall have the right to a general satisfactory environment favourable to their development.

Plainly we are here at the outer limits of the justiciability of rights of this general kind.[22]

3. Some Tentative Conclusions

So far I have only dealt with what might be called the concept of peoples rights, and only by reference to those rights already recognized in international instruments in treaty form. That is a fair test in the longer term,

---

[21] U. O. Umozurike, 'The African Charter on Human and People's Rights' (1983) 77 *AJIL* 902, 907.

[22] See further W. P. Gormley, *Human Rights and Environment: The Need for International Co-operation* (1976), and the works cited in the Bibliography below. This is not to say that treaty provisions about the environment cannot be justiciable. But in the *Tasmanian Dam* case, the Australian High Court was obviously more comfortable with the specific obligation undertaken with respect to the region through its listing under the World Heritage Convention of 1974 than with the notion of an international obligation under Art. 4 and 5 of the Convention with respect to the natural heritage generally: *Commonwealth* v. *Tasmania* (1983) 46 ALR 625.

whatever view one takes about General Assembly (or other international) resolutions. It would be possible to undertake the same analysis of other items in Alston's list, which includes such rights as:[23]

the right not to be exposed to excessively and unnecessarily heavy, degrading, dirty and boring work; the right to identity with one's own work product, individually or collectively (as opposed to anonymity); the right to access to challenging work requiring creativity . . . the right to social transparency; the right to co-existence with nature; the right to be free to seek impressions from others (not only from the media); and the right to be free to experiment with alternative ways of life.

(Parenthetically, they are a remarkably Western, even bourgeois list!) But it is sufficient to draw conclusion from the seven classes of rights surveyed here.

Dealing first with the group rights associated with self-determination, the rights of minorities and related questions, the conventional view is that each of these is, as a collective right, still a rule of exception.[24] On the other hand, for the purposes of this inquiry, and without prejudice to questions of the scope of these rights, there is no difficulty in thinking of them as rights of peoples; some of them are also collective in character, that is to say, the beneficiary of the right is a group rather than its individual members.

So far as the other rights are concerned, as rights of States some are merely affirmative reformulations of existing duties. Others are merely contentious. As rights of peoples, their real content is with respect to the government of the State in question. No doubt this may not be intended by proponents of those rights, but if they do not intend it, perhaps they would do well to revert to more orthodox terminology. Whatever the case, these third generation rights as so interpreted seem consistent with basic concerns about equity between peoples and their governments which are by no means confined to the Third World. Whether such rights can be made internationally justiciable may be another question, although, as modern administrative law, and the experience with Bills of Rights in a number of countries, show, almost anything can be justiciable at a certain level, and given a sufficient political mandate to the adjudicating body. In the case of the African Charter, the mandate is to the African Commission on Human and Peoples Rights, there being no African Court of Human Rights. It will be interesting to see—now that governments (not peoples) have ratified the African Charter and it is in force—to what extent the members of the African Commission turn out to be representatives of peoples, as distinct from representatives of governments.

[23] P. Alston, 'Conjuring up New Human Rights: A Proposal for Quality Control' (1984) 78 *AJIL* 607, 610–11 (where these are listed among 29 candidates).

[24] But see Professor Brownlie's essay in this volume for the suggestion that minority and indigenous rights are to be equated with the general principle of self-determination.

5

Rights of Peoples:
Point of View of a Logician

DAVID MAKINSON[1]

1. Introduction

The purpose of this paper is to review the logical issues involved in the notion of a right held by all peoples. There are two substantive parts. One deals with problems of indeterminacy of various kinds. The other deals with problems of inconsistency and conflict. Throughout, the point of view is that of a logician.

(1) Historical Background

On 4 December 1950, the General Assembly of the United Nations requested the Commission on Human Rights to 'study ways and means that would ensure the right of peoples and nations to self-determination'.[2] On 16 December 1966 the General Assembly adopted, in the opening article of both the International Covenant on Economic, Social and Cultural Rights and the International Covenant on Civil and Political Rights, a declaration that 'all peoples have the right of self-determination'. Since then, declarative texts formulating various rights of peoples have appeared at other levels, including the influential though non-governmental Universal Declaration of the Rights of Peoples issued in Algiers in 1976 by a private foundation, and the intergovernmental African Charter on Human and Peoples' Rights of 1981. Over the same period, debate has continued in international political circles (though with remarkable little repercussion amongst philosophers), with particular vehemence in the early 1950s, around the first resolutions of the General Assembly concerning the right of peoples to self-determination, in the mid-1970s around the inclusion of the right of peoples to compensation in the Declaration on the Establishment of a New International Economic Order of 1974, and again in

[1] Member of the Division of Philosophy and Human Sciences of UNESCO. The contents of this paper are entirely the personal responsibility of the author, and not of UNESCO.
[2] GA Res 421D (V), 4 December 1950 (adopted 30–9:13). By GA Res 545 (VI), 5 February 1952 (adopted 42–7:5) the General Assembly decided to include an article on the right to self-determination in the 'International Covenant or Covenants on Human Rights'.

the late 1970s and early 1980s around the inclusion of references to the right to development and various other rights of peoples in the resolutions and programmes of Unesco.

The question of rights of peoples involves a number of distinct though interrelated aspects. There are evidently serious political issues involved, given the interests and ideologies of States that are affected or see themselves as likely to be affected by the outcome. As in the case of rights of persons there are complex ethical questions. There are economic and social questions concerning the costs and social changes that would be involved in actual implementation of some of the proposals. There are practical and institutional problems of finding ways of observing, reporting on, and arbitrating implementation in a world of sovereign States, and there is of course the even more difficult problem of enforcement.

However, this paper will discuss only one aspect of the question: the logical issues involved. There are a number of issues of considerable importance that are in a broad sense of the term logical in nature, some of which are rather obvious once stated and some more subtle.

(2) Conceptual Background

The notion of a right, whatever the category of bearer, is far from univocal, and normative discourse reveals a variety of different kinds of relationship at play. An attempt at systematic clarification of some of these kinds was made by Jeremy Bentham, in a text thought to have been written in 1782 but not published until 1945 and then in a more complete edition in 1970.[3] Similar work of clarification, although rather less precise and developed than that of Bentham, was published independently by Austin in 1863.[4] The most influential study of different kinds of rights relationships between individuals, still independent of Bentham, was that of Hohfeld's classic, first published in 1913 and reprinted many times since.[5] Its conceptual distinctions have become, at least in broad outline, part of the heritage of Anglo-Saxon jurisprudence and philosophy of law.[6]

In this paper I draw freely on the conceptual capital accumulated in the literature - juridical, logical, philosophical, and even polemical. I assume some familiarity, particularly when discussing the rather delicate problems of inconsistency, with the broad conceptual outlines of the distinctions stemming from Bentham and Hohfeld, which are indispensable for dealing with the subject with clarity. But I use only such concepts and distinctions

---

[3] J. Bentham, *Of Laws in General* (ed. H. L. A. Hart, London, 1970).

[4] J. Austin, *Lectures on Jurisprudence* (London, 1863) vols II, III.

[5] W. N. Hohfeld (ed. W. W. Cook), *Fundamental Legal Conceptions as Applied in Judicial Reasoning and other Legal Essays* (New Haven, Yale University Press, 1964).

[6] As observed e.g. by G. Williams, 'The concept of legal liberty' in R. Summers (ed.), *Essays in Legal Philosophy* (Oxford, Blackwell, 1970) 121; T. Perry, 'A paradigm of philosophy: Hohfeld on legal rights' (1977) 14 *Am Phil Q* 41.

as are directly needed for the logical issues in hand. Moreover, I avoid using symbolic representations in the manner of Kanger[7] and Lindahl.[8] This is not because of any objection in principle to their use, but rather because the arguments need to be in a form which is as accessible as possible, and independent of the fortunes of any one particular mode of formalization.

It is however necessary to be very attentive to details of formulation. The logical properties of norms are extremely sensitive to variations in formulation; apparently insignificant changes of presentation can generate wild fluctuations in logical behaviour. It is thus very difficult, when concerned with logical rather than philosophical issues, to remain at the level of the essential idea or spirit of a norm; fastidious though it may seem, one must also attend to specific formulations.

Examples of such formulations will usually be taken from the texts of international instruments of one kind or another. This choice should not be understood as indicating that whatever has got into such documents is a 'true right', nor the converse, nor the contrary. Nor do we assume that such texts always provide the best or clearest possible formulations of such rights. The point is rather that in order to make logical points both clear and useful it is necessary to work with examples, which should be realistic in the sense of expressing principles that have been widely urged, in the language of that urging.

(3) Some Distinctions

Our concern is with rights of peoples in the sense of rights advanced as common to all peoples everywhere, or under various general conditions, rather than rights of this or that people distinguished in some way. To mark the point, some authors have spoken of 'human rights of peoples' or 'universal rights of peoples', in analogy with human rights of individuals as contrasted with rights of this or that person or 'restricted class' of persons.[9] This terminology is however rather cumbersome, and I will in general follow the usual custom of speaking simply of 'rights of peoples', it being understood that this is meant in the former, general, sense. It may be noted in passing that the difference between a 'general condition' on subjects of a given category, and a 'restricted class' of those subjects is far

---

[7] S. Kanger, 'Law and logic' (1972) 38 *Theoria* 105; S. Kanger & H. Kanger, 'Rights and parliamentarism' in R. E. Olson & A. M. Paul (eds), *Contemporary Philosophy in Scandinavia* (Baltimore, John Hopkins, 1972) 213.

[8] L. Lindahl, *Position and Change, A Study in Law and Logic* (Dordrecht, Reidel, 1977). See further D. Makinson, 'On the formal representation of rights relations. Remarks on the work of Stig Kanger and Lars Lindahl' (1986) 15 *Journal of Philosophical Logic* 403.

[9] e.g. Y. Dinstein, 'Collective human rights of peoples and minorities' (1976) 25 *ICLQ* 102.

from clear at the borders, but that question is outside the scope of this paper.

It should also be borne in mind that the distinction between rights of individuals and rights of peoples is quite different from several other distinctions between kinds of right, and in particular from the distinction between political and civil rights on the one hand and social and cultural rights on the other. Clearly a political right can be borne by individuals (as with the right of vote) or by peoples (as with the right to political self-determination). Similarly an economic, social, or cultural right can belong to individuals (for example the right to equal pay for equal work) or to collectivities such as peoples (for example the right to sovereignty over natural resources, or the right to development).

Further, it should be remembered that, as van Boven and many others have observed,[10] individuals' rights and those of collectivities are not entirely disjoined: a single right, or at least a complex of closely related rights, may have both kinds of bearer. For example, the right to practice one's religion can be seen as involving both a right of each person to his religious beliefs, customs, and observances, and a right of religious collectivities to undertake activities of an essentially communal nature, such as building places of worship and forming clubs, publishing houses, and representative committees. Again, rights to freedom of expression and to trade union activity both have individual and collective bearers. The rights to development and to a cultural identity are also often presented as borne by both persons and peoples, although with the emphasis on the latter.

The focus on rights of peoples should not be understood as suggesting that there are no other collectivities, such as ethnic, linguistic, or cultural groups, lying uncomfortably between entire peoples and single persons, who may be regarded as bearing rights, even universal rights. Attention is focused here on the category of 'peoples' because it is in terms of that category that current international declarations and debate are conducted. However, I will argue that such a restriction gives rise to problems of separability and leads to considerable arbitrariness.

2. Problems of Indeterminacy

(1)   Identification of the General Category of Bearers

The most obvious, pressing, and widely discussed problem specific to the notion of a right of peoples is that of identification of the category of bearers. It is not just a matter of identifying this people or that one; it is a

---

[10] T. Van Boven, 'Distinguishing criteria of human rights' in K. Vasek (ed.), *The International Dimensions of Human Rights* (Westport, Greenwood Press, 1982) I, 43.

question of what peoples in general are and how they are to be distinguished from other collectivities. This kind of question does not arise with anything like the same centrality in the case of individual rights, where such difficulties appear only with respect to marginal cases.

Clearly, as has been remarked by many authors, and in particular Crawford, peoples cannot simply be identified with States.[11] It is not even possible to maintain that, while some peoples are not constituted into States, nevertheless 'States in the international meaning of the word are obviously "peoples".[12] This is a category mistake; the two concepts are different kinds of abstraction. A people is a kind of collectivity, or group of human beings; a State is a kind of governing and administering apparatus. Even when a State serves as representative or spokesman for a people, the two are never identical, just as a municipal council, even in the best and most democratic of circumstances, is something different from its constituency.

It would also be a confusion of thought to see the term 'people' as a simple opposite of 'minority', partitioning the domain of collectivities into two. For the notion of a minority is relational: collectivity x may be a minority within grouping u, whose majority y may in turn be a minority within a larger grouping v, and so on through indefinitely many steps. On the other hand, whether or not a collectivity x constitutes a 'people' is presumably a qualitative question, independent of the choice of any larger group of reference.

(a) Specific Normative Texts: Self-Determination

To fix ideas as clearly as possible, and to retain contact with the world of political affairs, it is helpful to begin by looking at the notion of a people as it manifests itself in declarations of the right of all peoples to self-determination. This right is proclaimed in the first Article of the International Covenants of Civil and Political Rights and of Economic, Social and Cultural Rights, each of 1966. It is moreover of particular interest in that it is still the only right of peoples to be incorporated explicitly and separately into an international instrument under the aegis of the United Nations. The only one, that is, if it is understood as including the right of a people to sovereignty over its natural resources, as seems to be intended by the wording of the two Covenants, and one of the only two if the latter right, also expressed in the same Article of the two Covenants, is conceptually separated.[13]

---

[11] See J. Crawford's essay in this volume.

[12] A. Cristescu, *The Right to Self-Determination: Historical and Current Development on the Basis of United Nations Instruments* (UN Doc E/CN.4/Sub 2/404/Rev 1, 1981) para. 266.

[13] There are a number of other norms that, in one way or another, come close (sometimes very close) to such a special political status. The Declaration on the Establishment of a New International Economic Order 1974 refers to the 'right of all States, territories and peoples'

The two Covenants proclaiming the right of all peoples to self-determination entirely avoid any clarification of what is to count as a people and what is only an ethnic group, cultural community, religious collectivity, or such like. The political needs of the time did not require such clarification. All that was needed was a tacit agreement that inhabitants included within the borders of European colonies in Africa and other regions of the world did constitute peoples—a most dubious assumption given the extraordinary diversity of languages and cultures within some of these borders, and given the well-known historical vagaries of the original delineation of some of the borders by the colonial powers. But the political forces of the time required self-determination within such borders, and the normative ground of this action was expressed in the language or rhetoric of 'peoples'. Thus the first and most important application within the United Nations system of the concept of the right of peoples to self-determination was, ironically, to support the self-determination of former colonies within boundaries that often split single peoples, under almost any conceivable understanding of the notion, between different States and bundled distinct peoples—again, under almost any use of the term—into a single State. A major task facing such States thus became that of forging out of such elements a unit with a sense of being and purpose—a task sometimes undertaken in ways that violated rights of the persons and collectivities involved.

The question arises, however, whether it is possible to give some general characterization of what is to count as a 'people' that will serve to distinguish 'peoples' from other 'lesser' kinds of collectivity for whom it is felt that the right to self-determination cannot reasonably be applied. Of course, it is always possible to do so in a vague manner but that is hardly adequate. It appears, moreover, that there are so many variations and graduations of social bonding as to render extremely arbitrary any attempt

to restitution and compensation for damages incurred under colonial rule. This norm is not formulated as a separate principle in its own right, but in a preambular fashion in support of other more specific matters. Moreover, it includes peoples as merely one among several hardly distinguished categories of collective or corporate bearer. Some logical issues associated with this widely urged right of peoples are considered later in the paper. There is also a second-order principle of equal rights of peoples, proclaimed in both the preamble and the text of the Declaration on Principles of International Law concerning Friendly Relations and Co-operation among States in accordance with the Charter of the United Nations 1970. But this principle occurs only as part of the composite phrase 'principle of equal rights and self determination of peoples', and no attempt is made to unpack its content in the Declaration. Thirdly, the right of peoples to development is proclaimed in several resolutions of the United Nations General Assembly, especially Res 41/128 (1986). Some of the logical issues arising in connection with the right to development are examined later in this paper. In addition, there are some formal international commitments dealing with the protection of collectivities, but not using the language of rights. An important example is the Convention on the Prevention and Punishment of the Crime of Genocide of 1948, which covers all 'national, ethnical, racial or religious groups'. Finally, some quite formal declarations do speak of rights—but of States rather than of peoples. This is for example the case with the United Nations Charter of Economic Rights and Duties of States of 1974.

to draw a neat dividing line marking off a privileged category, of 'peoples' who bear special rights, and others who do not. The only way in which such arbitrariness could be avoided would be by the device of building normative elements into the definition of the concept itself. Under the folds of a more or less complex wording, a 'people' would then essentially be defined as a collectivity whose degree of cohesion and sense of distinctness (based on the elements of descent, language, religion, culture, history, and others) are deemed 'sufficiently strong to merit' attribution of a right of self-determination. Such a logical short cut is a perennial temptation, but inserting a normative component into the very definition of what is to count as a people renders the structure of norms circular, and in particular would render the right to self-determination for all peoples nothing more than an empty tautology.

(b) A 'Semantic Blockage'

The nightmare of States faced with calls for self-determination is of course the spectre of secession, at least from their own territories, and States have sought to make sure that this would not be permitted by the norm proclaimed. For our purposes, it is interesting to see the logical procedure by which this has been done. It is not done by introducing into the two Covenants restrictions on what is to count as a 'people', or exceptive clauses on the right to self-determination. The strategy is much cruder. We simply find other declarations pronouncing the impermissibility of all attempts at secession. In particular, this is done in categorical terms in the Declaration on the Granting of Independence to Colonial Countries and Peoples of 1960, Article 6 of which declares bluntly that:

Any attempt aimed at the partial or total disruption of the national unity and the territorial integrity of a country is incompatible with the purposes and principles of the Charter of the United Nations.

Such a principle—read of course as itself expressing a norm rather than describing an earlier one—is difficult to reconcile with the right of all peoples to self-determination. Under any ordinary understanding of the latter notion, the acquisition of self-determination by a proper subgroup within a country necessarily divides or at least impairs the unity and ter-ritorial integrity of that country; and yet under any use of the term 'people' that still has some connection with ordinary usage, peoples may sometimes find themselves in the position of being such subgroups. What the Cov-enant apparently grants such a people as a right, the Declaration apparently outlaws. Thus, under any ordinary understanding of the terms involved, the two are logically incompatible.

The point can be put in another way. The accumulation of the two texts has led to a 'semantic blockage'—a situation where it is logically impossible to give any meanings to the operative terms involved that at one and the

same time leave the texts mutually consistent and still have some resemblance to ordinary usage. Given this semantic blockage, the natural
reaction of States has been to avoid trying to define or clarify the concept
of a people or that of self-determination, but rather to insist that however
the terms are understood their own citizens form a paradigm example of
one and only one people, thus remaining on the safe side of the norm.

Legal commentators have, however, explored other possibilities for resolution of the inconsistency. One possibility, suggested by certain writers
particularly concerned with the situation of indigenous populations, is to
work with a very much diluted notion of self-determination, admitting an
enormous range of degrees, so that even the least element of decen-
tralization, devolution, or federalization is counted as constituting some
measure of self-determination.[14] Now the acquisition of a certain modest
degree of self-determination need not jeopardize the unity or territorial
integrity of an englobing State, so the Declaration outlawing such impairment can be rendered logically compatible with the Covenants—provided the text of the Covenants is reread as meaning 'all peoples have the
right to at least some measure of self-determination', and provided the
'partial disruption' of the Declaration is not taken to have too low a
threshold.

Such a radical reinterpretation of the operative term of 'self-
determination' is a far cry from what was evidently intended by those who
voted the 1966 Covenants, with their presentation of self-determination as
involving or accompanied by at least sovereignty over natural resources.
But it does have a lot to be said for it. As well as saving the logical
consistency of an existing edifice of norms, it also opens the way to an
equally radical reunderstanding of the notion of a 'people', to cover any
collectivity that feels itself united by some degree of cultural or other
affinity, thereby extending the privilege of (at least some measure of) self-
determination not only to a restricted and arbitrarily selected club of collectivities, but to all collectivities that manifest felt distinctness.

The denunciation of secession is carried out in more conditional terms
in the later Declaration on Principles of International Law concerning
Friendly Relations and Co-operation among States in Accordance with the
Charter of the United Nations of 1970. After repeating in its preamble the
prohibition in bald terms almost identical to those of its 1960 predecessor,
it goes on in its text to pronounce more guardedly on the matter:

Nothing in the foregoing paragraphs shall be construed as authorizing or encouraging any action which would dismember or impair, totally or in part, the
territorial integrity or political unity of sovereign and independent States conducting themselves in compliance with the principle of equal rights and self-
determination of peoples as described above and thus possessed of a government

14 See e.g. G. Nettheim's essay in this volume.

representing the whole people belonging to the territory without distinction as to race, creed or colour.

This circumspect formulation does not give rise to a problem of inconsistency; its logical problems are different. The antecedent of the conditional (expressed in the clause 'conducting themselves... colour') is a mix of descriptive and normative elements. The descriptive constituents are so vague, and the normative elements so self-referential, as to make unambiguous application extremely difficult in contested cases. In particular, in order to determine whether a given collectivity escapes the interdiction on impairing political unity, one would first have to determine whether the government of the encompassing State, which is denying the dismemberment, is really 'conducting itself in compliance with the principle of equal rights and self-determination'—which in turn requires prior determination of whether the collectivity does indeed hold a right to the action it seeks, in circular fashion.[15]

(2) Determination of Representatives of the Bearers

Even in a case where it is agreed that a certain collectivity does constitute a 'people', the logical problems are not over. There remains an issue that always arises for collectivities, although only in exceptional cases for individuals. If a person has, say, a right to express opinions in public, there is in general no difficulty in assigning an authoritative source for what opinions that person wishes to express: the person in question. But if a people has, say, a right to nurture its cultural identity, the question remains who or what organism defines the various strands of this culture, distinguishes it from others, and determines what is to be cultivated and what discouraged.

The problem is familiar to every political scientist. My purpose is not to provide an answer to how it should be handled, but simply to recognize its existence: it is impossible to speak seriously about rights of peoples without recognizing the need for some mechanism (always fallible, but sometimes far less so than others) for expressing in policy and action the multiple strands of a people's aspirations and ideals.

In some conditions, when the governing bodies are elected in a democratic and non-discriminatory manner at regular intervals, the State may credibly serve as spokesman. But even when these conditions are satisfied, tensions arise from the fact that in general, a right of a people will involve claims upon the State itself, so that the State will have a triple role: party upon whom obligations fall, direct spokesman of the party to whom these

---

[15] For further discussion of these texts see J. Charpentier, 'Autodétermination et décolonisation' in *Mélanges offerts à Charles Chaumont* (Paris, A. Pedone, 1984) 117; A. N'Kolombua, 'L'ambivalence des relations entre le droit des peuples à disposer d'eux-mêmes et l'intégrité territoriale des états en droit international contemporain' id, 433.

obligations are directed, and organism containing the judicial apparatus to adjudicate between the two. The task of fulfilling all three roles is not impossible, but it is not an easy one, and requires a sophisticated apparatus with very clear separations of functions and powers. It is already difficult enough in connection with human rights of individuals, where only the first and third roles are in play.

Finally, in those cases where a people exists only as minority in a larger State, or is divided between several States, or lives in a diaspora, the question of representation can arise even more acutely.

(3) Unspecified Correspondents

We turn now to a phenomenon that can arise even when the general category of bearers is clear, and problems of representation are resolved. It can happen that an agent has an obligation to assist a certain category of parties in a general way, without specification of beneficiaries among them.[16] For example, in some kinds of community, where mendicant priests are an accepted part of society, the wandering priest is permitted to seek food and shelter, others are forbidden to interfere with this activity, and moreover the citizen is under a general or diffuse obligation to assist mendicant priests as a category, without having an obligation to assist any specific one among them. It could be argued, again, that according to the mores of western society, the citizen has a similar relationship to charitable organizations. This kind of relationship also manifests itself to a certain extent in connection with some rights of peoples. For example, Article 2 of the International Covenant on Economic, Social and Cultural Rights imposes on each State party an obligation to provide economic assistance, without specifying who, in any case, the beneficiaries should be within the general category of peoples.

This lack of specification of beneficiaries from within an overall category is a logical phenomenon, but not a logical defect in a norm as such. It does however have certain consequences. Since those bearing the obligation do not have a duty to assist any particular party, there is no particular party that has a claim on the bearers of the obligation. The relationship is a far weaker one, and for lack of generally recognized terms we might call it one of a 'diffuse obligation' of one party and a 'preclaim' of the other. Because of the absence of a party with a claim to be assisted, and thus of a party that can consider itself as aggrieved by another under the norm, such preclaims and diffuse obligations are difficult to verify and enforce. For this reason they are often regarded by jurists as quite unsuitable for incorporation into a legal system, and better treated as expressing moral guides, or at most some kind of second-order juridical 'principles' along

---

[16] As observed e.g. by J. Feinberg, 'Duties, rights and claims' in J. Feinberg, *Rights, Justice, and the Bounds of Liberty* (Princeton, Princeton University Press, 1980) 130.

the lines suggested by Dworkin.[17] The logical phenomenon of lack of specification of beneficiaries is thus not a logical flaw in a norm as such, but it generates serious practical difficulties for incorporation of the norm into a legal system.[18]

A similar, and in practice more serious, phenomenon can also arise with a dual lack of specification of the bearers of an obligation. It can happen that a party bears a claim, or something very much like a claim, without specification of which parties from within a given domain are responsible for meeting that claim. This phenomenon has been noted by several moral philosophers, including Becker,[19] Raphael,[20] McCloskey (who calls such claims 'entitlements'),[21] and Feinberg who refers to them as 'claims-to' as contrasted with 'claims-against', and also describes them as 'inchoate' or 'manifesto' claims.[22]

Clearly in such a case, or at least in the extreme instance of it where not even a single bearer of the obligation is specified, there is no party that carries an obligation. Again, we have a weaker relationship, which we might call one of a 'diffuse claim' of one party and a 'preobligation' of the other. Because of the absence of a party upon whom responsibility falls, there is no way of determining who has done as he should, and so no basis for reprobation or punishment. There is only a way of determining who has been rightly done by. There is thus little leverage for enforcement, and jurists are even more loath to accept such diffuse claims or 'claims-to' without specification of addressees as suitable for a legal system. However, these diffuse claims and corresponding preobligations do arise in practice, in connection with both human rights of individuals and rights of peoples.

A salient example is the rule that 'everyone has the right to nationality', expressed in Article 15 of the Universal Declaration. The general category of bearers of the corresponding obligation to confer nationality is clear enough, consisting of States, but the formulation gives no indication of which State or States bear this obligation to any given person. Knowledge of the ways in which borders shift, regimes radically change, States pass in and out of existence, and colonial possessions are disbanded reveals that the disputable cases are far from marginal. There is a partial indeterminacy too in the 'right to food', or 'right of everyone to an adequate standard of

---

[17] R. Dworkin, 'Is law a system of rules?' in R. M. Dworkin (ed.), *The Philosophy of Law* (Oxford, OUP, 1971) 38.

[18] For simplicity, the discussion here has been phrased in terms of the usual case, where the counterparties of an obligation—that is, the parties towards whom the obligation holds— are the intended beneficiaries of the obligation. However, the same basic points may be made for those cases, that sometimes arise in law, where the counterparties may be distinct from the beneficiaries.

[19] L. C. Becker, *Property Rights, Philosophic Foundations* (London, Routledge and Kegan Paul, 1977).

[20] D. D. Raphael (ed.), *Political Theory and the Rights of Man* (London, Macmillan, 1967).

[21] H. J. McCloskey, 'Rights' (1965) 15 *Philosophical Quarterly* 115.

[22] Feinberg (1980) 130-42.

living for himself and his family', expressed in Article 25 of the Universal Declaration and again in the Covenant on Economic, Social and Cultural Rights. In this case, the State of which the individual is a citizen is implicitly indicated as bearing at least some responsibility in the matter, but it is left quite open how far this responsibility extends to other States and parties.[23]

The same phenomenon appears in some widely mooted rights of peoples, sometimes referred to as 'solidarity rights'.[24] For example, the right of each people to ownership of the common heritage of mankind, its right to assistance in times of crisis, and the less radical formulations of its right to development all seem to involve diffuse claims with at least partial indeterminacy of the bearers of obligations to meet those claims.

Once again, this logical phenomenon does not appear to be, strictly speaking, a logical defect for norms in general. Indeed, some philosophers would argue that 'recognized needs' are morally fundamental, giving rise successively to diffuse claims and then directed claims with corresponding obligations, in opposition to a Kantian position that would see obligations as morally fundamental.

But even if we follow the former of these philosophical viewpoints—as I tend to do—the point remains that the impossibility of enforcing relationships in which no one is assigned responsibility for seeing to it that a diffuse claim is satisfied, renders such diffuse claims and their corresponding preobligations far more suitable for moral than for legal codes.

(4)   Open-Ended Commitments

A final problem of indeterminacy arising with acuteness for some canvassed rights of peoples is the open-ended nature of the degree of commitment involved. This is perhaps most clearly evident with the right to development.

The right to development can be regarded as an elaboration and strengthening into more far-reaching principles of the diffuse obligations to assistance of Article 2 of the International Covenant on Social, Economic and Cultural Rights. It is the subject of a declaration of the United Nations General Assembly,[25] and of several other resolutions, and is included in the African Charter on Human and Peoples' Rights of 1981. None the less we are not dealing with a single formulation, definitively accepted at the international level, but rather with a range of varying formulations, of differing degrees of explicitness and clarity.

[23] There is a review of indeterminacies associated with the right to food in P. Alston, 'International law and the right to food' in A. Eide and others (eds), *Food as a Human Right* (Tokyo, United Nations University Press, 1984) 162.

[24] UNESCO, 'Symposium on the study of new human rights, 162, the "rights of solidarity" ' SS-80/CONF 806, SS/HR (1980) (mimeographed).

[25] GA Res 41/128 (4 December 1986), analysed in Rich's essay in this volume.

The right to development is generally regarded as involving a permission to each people to pursue its development, a prohibition on other parties to interfere in this process, and a more or less directed claim for continual assistance and other arrangements to facilitate the task. This claim falls first and foremost upon the State which (it is assumed) represents the people in question. But the literature makes it clear that the responsibility is often also understood as going much further than that, falling upon the entire 'international community' and including what Shue terms 'everyone's minimal reasonable demands on the rest of humanity'.[26] In particular, the prime external bearers of the obligations are conceived as the wealthier and more developed States; in some of the formulations all of the more developed countries are understood as bearing an obligation distributively to all of the poorer ones, and particularly the poorest. The assistance is seen as involving not only advice but also aid, and in addition, as expressed in the demand for a 'new international economic order', a restructuring of the entire system of international economic relationships and the international division of labour.

It is not my purpose in this paper to go into the moral force of these claims, nor into a host of other questions that arise around them—how far assistance should go beyond what have been called 'basic needs', how far development itself should be seen in merely economic terms or as involving other dimensions, to what extent it can be given a more convincing content than the now little-used concept of 'progress', whether it deserves single-minded pursuit in all circumstances, how far various kinds of assistance are of practical efficacy in enhancing development, and so on. My purpose is simply to draw attention to the open-ended nature of the commitments as usually formulated, without much indication of upper bounds. From a strictly logical point of view, this is no more than an element of vagueness in the content of the obligations. But on a practical level, such an element of vagueness is of considerable consequence It is only to be expected that the developed countries, even when accepting some responsibility in the matter, will tend to circumscribe it within limits compatible with enlightened self-interest. And it is even more to be expected that when a right of peoples, such as that to development, is formulated in such vague terms as to leave the upper limits of the obligation open, there will be unease and reticence among those who fear an uncontrolled cascade of commitments. The logical gap of open-ended commitment thus breeds apprehension and distrust towards some rights of peoples, which then by association tend to become attached to peoples' rights in general.

---

[26] H. Shue, *Basic Rights: Subsistence, Affluence and US Foreign Policy* (Princeton, Princeton University Press, 1980), 19.

(5)   Summary of Conclusions in this Section

There are thus several important problems of indeterminacy arising in connection with the concept of a right of all peoples. One of them can be seen as, quite directly, a logical problem. Four others are perhaps better regarded as logical phenomena that generate severe practical problems for inclusion in a legal system. The directly logical problem is the lack of a reasonably clear identification of the general category of bearers, that is, of peoples. It is exacerbated by the complete lack of any attempt to give an even approximate characterization in the principal normative texts themselves. Moreover, it would appear difficult to introduce a dividing line between 'peoples', to whom special rights are then to be attributed, and other 'lesser' collectivities that are not accorded those rights, without being arbitrary, unless one reduces the right of self-determination for all peoples to a mere tautology by introducing a normative component into the characterization of a 'people' itself. The problem is compounded by the existence alongside assertions of the right of all peoples to self-determination, of equally solemn declarations of the impermissibility of any form of secession. Taken together, the two norms create a 'semantic blockage', that is, a situation where it is impossible to give any meanings to the operative terms involved that retain some resemblance to ordinary usage and at the same time leave the norms mutually consistent. The only apparent way to resolve this blockage, whilst leaving the norms intact, would be by radically weakening the force of the notion of self-determination so that it covers any form of devolution or partial autonomy, no matter how limited; which in turn would render feasible a corresponding widening of the notion of a people to cover a very broad range of collectivities.

Logical phenomena that lead to difficulties for the inclusion of peoples' rights in a legal system include the vagueness of criteria for identifying representatives of the peoples concerned, the open-endedness of common formulations of some of the rights in question, and indeterminacy as to counterparties. This takes the form of the attribution of obligations to assist without clear specification of the distribution of beneficiaries (diffuse obligations, without corresponding bearers of claims), and of claims for assistance without clear specification of parties to meet them (diffuse claims, without corresponding bearers of obligations). Diffuse obligations are usually regarded as unsuitable for inclusion in a legal code, because of the difficulties of verifying observance. Diffuse claims are even more unsuitable, for without allocation of responsibility there is no basis for arraignment and little leverage for enforcement.

All of these problems of indeterminacy, to be sure, have counterparts that can already arise, to some degree and in some cases, in connection with human rights of individuals. For example even the question of identifying what is to count as a human being can remain disputed at the edges, as discussions on abortion reveal; and questions of how to represent the mentally deficient, the insane, and the comatose are very real. But in practice such problems have tended to arise in a much more central manner, with greater force and frequency, in the case of rights attributed to peoples.

3. Problems of Inconsistency

This section examines the possibilities of conflict between rights, in particular when one or more of them is formulated as a right of peoples.

(1) Self-Consistency of the Concept

It should be clear that there is no self-contradiction in the very idea of rights or obligations attaching to an abstract or collective bearer, such as a people. For example, Western moral theory and law have for some centuries recognized and worked with rights and obligations of such entities as business firms including limited liability companies, voluntary and community associations, minorities, and the State itself. Neither the step to the collective, nor the step to the abstract character of the bearer is in itself incoherent.

This does not mean, however, that any given canvassed right of all peoples is internally consistent. Indeed, the consistency of a norm, as of an ordinary proposition of any degree of complexity, depends to a considerable degree on the particular manner of formulation. For this reason, almost any right, whether of peoples or of persons, can be formulated in stronger ways that generate self-contradiction, and in weaker ways that avoid it. An example is the right to self-determination. If the right is formulated so as to entitle each people not only to self-determination, but to exercise that right on the territory with which it has been most continuously and deeply associated, then two distinct peoples may find themselves with the right to self-determination on the same territory. In effect, the parties are each given a protected permission (that is, a permission to act with a prohibition on interference) to perform generic actions whose executions not only tend to interfere with each other, but (unless the notion of self-determination is itself radically weakened, in the manner earlier described) necessarily preclude each other.

This said, it is rather exceptional to find considered formulations of rights that are internally inconsistent. Much more common is mutual inconsistency, on which attention will therefore be focused.

(2) Formal Possibilities of Mutual Inconsistency

I pointed out in the Introduction that the concept of a right is far from univocal, and different rights may involve components of quite different logical structures. This section assumes some familiarity with the work of Bentham and Hohfeld in clarifying such components. Some familiarity with the formal work of Kanger or Lindahl is useful although not essential. When a right involves at least a protected permission, as most do, there is a quite straightforward avenue for contradiction to occur. Suppose that r is a protected permission for a certain category of bearers, that is, suppose that every x in the category is permitted to do A, and no agent is allowed to interfere with his doing so. Suppose moreover that r' is a protected permission that allows an agent y to do B and prohibits others from interfering with this. Then if A and B happen to be kinds of activity such that doing one necessarily interferes with or hampers the other, we have a conflict: r has forbidden y to B but r' has permitted him to do so. When rights involve claims as well as permissions, the possibilities of contradiction are multiplied and indeed become systematic. For suppose that a right r includes a claim by one party y to carry out a certain kind of action. Then quite trivially, this is in conflict with the equally conceivable right that provides y with a permission not to perform that kind of action. Dually, any claim by x on y to refrain from doing something is in conflict with a right of y—the right to do that thing.

But this is not really what we are looking for. We are interested in the potentialities for conflict, not merely over the domain of all conceivable rights, but also between more or less recognized or widely mooted rights, without however getting involved in questions of which among these might be 'really correct' or most appropriate. The problem thus arises within the above abstract logical framework, but also involves attention to the logical properties of specific, real-life examples.

(3)   Rights to Choose: General Considerations

Such conflicts already arise between widely accepted human rights of individuals. We shall not consider these extensively, but shall look briefly at two examples that are instructive for later developments.

The norm (implicit from Articles 17 and 18 of the Universal Declaration, taken together) that parents have the right to bring up their children in accordance with the religious customs and traditions of the family, permits actions that sometimes, indeed quite frequently, clash with other rights of individuals, notably 'the right of everyone to the enjoyment of the highest attainable standard of physical and mental health' (International Covenant on Economic, Social and Cultural Rights, Article 12). For it does sometimes happen that deeply felt religious and quasi-religious customs of the family and wider community either impose prohibitions on actions that can be necessary for health (such as blood transfusions or vaccinations) or even involve positive actions devastatingly injurious to the well-being of the children concerned (a notorious example being female excision).

Again, the norm that 'parents have a prior right to choose the kind of education that shall be given to their children' (Universal Declaration, Article 26) clashes in innumerably many individual cases with the principle that girls have equal rights with their male siblings in education at all levels (Convention against Discrimination in Education, 1960, Preamble and Article 1). There are many cases where parents do choose the education of their children in a discriminatory fashion. It is perhaps because of the visibility of this contradiction that in subsequent decades more sensitive to discrimination between the sexes, reformulations of the former right in other international instruments have tended to be more circumspect and conditional.

Not all of the actions countenanced by the one norm are in conflict with the interdiction imposed by the other, but some are. This reveals a rather subtle logical configuration that is very important for this review. On the one hand, as is well known in work in formal deontic logic, permission to carry out a generic action is not generally in logical contradiction with a prohibition on some particular modes of executing it. A doctor may permit his patient to eat eggs, but forbid him to eat them fried. Likewise, permission to carry out a generic activity is not generally in logical contradiction with a prohibition on another generic activity, even given the existence of actions that are simultaneously of both kinds. For example, permission to run a restaurant is not in contradiction with a prohibition on operating with extended opening hours, even though there are ways of doing both at the same time.

On the other hand, the permissions involved in the above two examples have rather special logical structures that generate special logical powers. In the former example, it is implicit in the formulation that parents have the right to bring up their children in accordance with any religious customs and traditions that the family happens to have; it is this element of universal quantification that opens the path to contradiction. The latter example is expressed as a 'right to choose'. Now permission to choose one's manner of doing something, even when hedged around with exceptive clauses, is radically more powerful than simple permission to do it. For it not only permits that it be done in some manner or other, but also permits whatever manner is in fact chosen, within the limits of whatever exceptive clauses are given or understood. For this reason, a conflict between the result of any such choice and the requirements of another norm constitutes an inconsistency between the norms themselves.

(4) Self-Determination and Choice of Political Status

At first sight the right to self-determination and sovereignty over natural resources does not appear to offer much scope for conflict with any generally recognized rights of individuals. Indeed, if the formulation of the right is limited to so many words, it is probably safe to say that there is no conflict. But the formulation as it is given in the two Covenants says considerably more. It states not only that 'all peoples have the right to self-determination' but also that 'by virtue of that right they freely determine their political status'. The former norm is thus presented as including the latter. The latter is, however, a tricky affair. If interpreted quite literally it could be understood as pronouncing the freedom of peoples to choose whatever political systems they see fit, and thus their freedom to choose political systems that do not countenance various human rights of persons, and rights of minorities.

The matter is rather unclear, partly because of the vagueness of a term like 'political status'. But if that term is understood in a broad sense, as indicating any political system, and given that no exclusive clauses are attached to the text, then a literal and natural interpretation creates a straightforward logical contradiction between this norm and a whole range of human rights of persons and rights of minorities.

It might be remarked, of this situation and conflict between norms in general, that almost any system of norms of considerable size is bound to have some inconsistencies within it, that this is just a fact of life, and that the art of the jurists consists in part of finding ways of coping with the problem; the discovery that there are contradictions involving widely mooted rights of peoples is not, therefore, a cause for alarm. It must be admitted that there is some truth in such a response. However, it ignores certain vital points, and abdicates intellectual responsibility to far too great a degree. Whilst inconsistencies do commonly arise when legislation becomes so massive that it is difficult to be familiar with it all at any one time, it is far less common, and much more serious, for inconsistencies to appear already among the very first principles set down in an area. Further, although the jurist, having to apply the norms available to him, sometimes has to work with inconsistencies, it is generally recognized that this causes difficulties in practice, and that when the inconsistencies become too pervasive or fundamental, rendering application too often problematic and contestable, the practical difficulties can become intolerable. The art of the jurist in reaching some kind of reasonable, coherent, and predictable judgement even in the face of conflicting norms is no doubt to be admired, but it is essentially an art of 'damage limitation', and far from univocal. For the same reason as a legal system needs written norms in the first place, it needs consistent ones. Inconsistency is not entirely eliminable, but it needs to be minimized. There is no room for complacency in this regard, particularly when we are dealing with the very first steps in formulating norms in an area of far-reaching consequence.[27]

(5) Development and its Roads

A second example of the ways in which clashes may occur arises in connection with the right to development. It may happen that in a certain situation a government believes that implementation of the economic plans that it has drawn up for development cannot be carried out in the presence of ordinary civil and political liberties or freedom of association into trade unions, consumer organizations, or interest groups. In general, a government is not a very dispassionate judge of the matter, being one of the parties involved, and in many cases the use of imagination, patience, and flexibility in the application of the development of policies can avoid the difficulty. But let us assume, for the sake of the example, that certain highly valued development plans are indeed hindered by such freedoms. How far do we then have an inconsistency between the right to development held by the people as an entity (which for the sake of the example we suppose to be adequately represented by the State) and the rights to association and so forth of the citizens?

The logical situation is again rather complex. On the one hand, there is no contradiction between the protected permission of the collectivity to undertake development, when formulated in so many words, and that of its members to, say, trade union association. As already noted, a permission to build a house does not imply permission to erect any specific style of dwelling, or to construct it in any given manner.

On the other hand, the situation is complicated by the existence of another principle, also enshrined in an international text, which whilst at

---

[27] From the formal point of view, the simplest manoeuvre for restoring consistency to conflicting norms is by assigning them relative priorities, the norm with the higher priority being the one whose application is taken to prevail when conflict arises. In the case of legal norms, such a procedure is sometimes followed quite explicitly. The logical questions involved in this kind of procedure can be quite subtle: see e.g. the formal studies by C. E. Alchourron & D. Makinson, 'Hierarchies of regulations and their logic' in R. Hilpinen (ed.), *New Deontic Logic* (Dordrecht, Reidel, 1981) 125; D. Makinson, 'How to give it up, a survey of some formal aspects of the logic of theory change' (1985) 62 *Synthése* 347. In so far as the manoeuvre requires the determination of a priority relation to be used, it goes beyond the bare norms themselves, and sometimes beyond the contents of the legal system. Moreover, the reasonable resolution of inconsistencies often seems to require more complex kinds of operation. For example, it may be felt that priority between two norms should hold in one direction in one kind of situation, but in the other direction in another kind of situation; resolution would then require priority relations indexed by situations, or another sort of procedure such as introduction of exceptive clauses into the norms themselves. In general, there is a multiplicity of ways of proceeding, each way admitting a multiplicity of results; and in so far as the orderings, exceptive clauses or other devices are not already explicit in the code, the elimination of inconsistency is obtained by transcending the code.

first glance adding little that is not already implicit in the right to development, can be interpreted as transforming that right into a norm sufficiently powerful to enter into direct conflict with other human rights. This
is the right of all peoples 'to determine the road of their development',
proclaimed in the General Assembly's Declaration on the Preparation of
Societies for Life in Peace of 1978.[28] Innocently nebulous as it might
appear, the principle not only presupposes a protected permission to undertake development as such, but also asserts, if read literally, a permission
to do so in whatever fashion is chosen. In this case, we do have an explicit
conflict between the norm itself and various human rights of individuals.
for there are plenty of examples, not only imaginable but occurring in real
life, where certain policies and methods of economic development do curtail
rights of association, movement, expression, and even security. As the one
norm countenances all such policy choices, it is inconsistent with the others
that rule out some of them.

Faced with this situation, some commentators on the right to development have tried to make the inconsistency disappear by means of a
semantic shift in the concept of development. The idea is to incorporate
respect for human rights into the meaning or definition of development.
'True' or 'real development—'development as properly understood' as
contrasted with 'development narrowly conceived'—is thus taken as containing within its very meaning not only an economic component, but also
a range of other elements including in particular observance of human
rights. This semantic shift is particularly common in commentaries from
international organizations which, by their constitutions, are committed to
promoting all rights that have accumulated in the relevant texts, and so
need to search assiduously for ways to minimize or transform conflict
between them.

In one respect, the manoeuvre is a total success. Whenever one is really
developing a country, in the new and 'full' sense of the term, then one is
(definitionally and trivially) not violating any human rights at all. This
remains so no matter how one is conducting the development—so long as
it is still development in the revised sense. In another respect, the shift
achieves nothing. The very same policies, plans and actions for economic
growth that violate human rights of persons or of collectivities before the
terminological shift, continue to do so after. Moreover, in so far as planning
authorities do not adapt their thought habits to the new portmanteau sense
of the term 'development', they will continue to conduct their working
activities as before, in terms of economic and technological development.

However, it is hoped by some that over a period of time the manoeuvre
may achieve something, by inducing a gradual widening of attitudes on the
part of planners. The argument is that by incorporating respect for human

---

[28] GA Res 33/73, 15 December 1978 (adopted 138-0:2).

rights into the very concept of development, it may be possible to transmit to the former some of the enthusiasm shown by even rather ruthless regimes for the latter, and thus to incorporate some care for human rights into the administrative routines that have already been built up for purposes of development. This may be so, but there are also the risks that by over-burdening the content of the term with disparate elements in this way, it might become a vague 'cover all' akin to the older 'progress', and that the loss of clarity resulting from confusion of meanings from the context of apologetics and the context of action may provide endless opportunities for rhetorical sleights of hand.

(6) Cultural Identity of a Collectivity

A third area in which the question of clash of norms arises is in connection with the right to cultural identity. It is often suggested that each people has a right to its cultural traditions and identity, and this is conceived as at least a permission to express and nurture those traditions, with an ac-companying prohibition on others to interfere. here again, we are not dealing with a single, more or less canonical formulation, but with a range of loosely presented ideas. Some presentations go further than we have indicated. For example, Article 17(3) of the African Charter declares that 'The promotion and protection of morals and traditional values recognized by the community shall be the duty of the State'. Article 29(7) pronounces as a duty of each individual 'to contribute to the best of his abilities, at all times and at all levels, to the promotion and achievement of African unity'.

Two general points need to be made. One is the unpleasant but hard fact that there are significant elements deeply embedded in many cultures—indeed, it is probably safe to say, some elements of every culture—that directly clash with widely recognized human rights. An unrestricted right to encourage all such elements would, therefore, give rise to conflict with those human rights. The other point is that the principle, in its generality and vagueness, can give rise to conflicts in its application to communities that are even slightly heterogeneous. A number of questions arise. What kinds of action could be covered by 'encouragement' of a given cultural tradition, and how far could this include discouragement of another? What would constitute 'interference' with such encouragement, particularly on the part of subcultures and minorities that may have been denied the honorific title of a 'people'? In so far as their behaviour is strikingly different from that of the dominant or approved segment—in dress, diet, religious observances, personal relations, sexual behaviour, artistic tastes, leisure enjoyments, that is, in ways of life—it tends to be perceived as a threat to the central or 'official' cultural pattern, tantamount to undermining and interference and therefore proscribed. At some stage in the continuum of restrictions, demands and duties that may be placed on minority groups and individuals in the name of the preservation of mainstream cultural values and traditions, there comes a point of rupture with rights of those groups and of individuals, to follow their own perhaps flagrantly different traditions and beliefs.

(7)   Collective Compensation

Questions of possible conflict also arise in connection with the notion of collective responsibility of an entire people for recent or even distant relations with other peoples. This notion has manifested itself in two principal ways: on the international level, in the right of peoples formerly subject to colonial powers to compensation for spoliation and damages caused, and on the national level, in the right to compensatory action for collectivities formerly held in slavery or oppression or dispossessed of their land. The former can be found, for example, in the non-governmental Universal Declaration of the Rights Of Peoples, issued by a private foundation in Algiers in 1976 Article 24, the African Charter on Human and People's Rights, of 1981 Article 21(2), and the United Nations Declaration on the Establishment of a New International Economic Order, 1974 paragraph 4. The latter is very much a subject of debate in the United States, Canada, Australia, and New Zealand in connection with land rights of indigenous peoples. There are many other countries in which such debates would be equally relevant.

All parties to this discussion appear to be agreed that collective punishment is not acceptable, in view of the widely recognized human right not to be punished for crimes committed by others. Curiously, this principle of personal responsibility does not appear in either the Universal Declaration or the two International Covenants. It does occur, however, in the African Charter on Human and Peoples' Rights Article 7(2), which states that 'punishment is personal and can be imposed only on the offender'. However, the line between compensation without punishment and punishment accompanied by compensation is not always easy to draw, as compensation tends to require other parties giving up things acquired. In practice, therefore, it can be difficult to separate the generally accepted right not to be punished for the actions of others from the contested right not to be responsible for effecting reparations for the actions of others. The latter involves genuine problems of moral and political philosophy. On the one hand, under many moral and legal conceptions, it would be difficult to retain it in its full generality. Many systems already recognize such responsibility in at least some instances—for example, of parents or guardians for actions of minors, and of shareholders (financially, to some limited degree) for actions of their company. On the other hand, there is a considerable difference between a claim borne by x that y take actions of a compensatory nature, and a right on the part of x, or of y, or some third party, to determine the nature and scale of those actions. The difference is particularly important given that in most cases there is no sense in speaking of 'full compensation': no amount of compensation to people today alleviates the sufferings of their ancestors, even if it can alter the condition of their descendants.

Consequently, although the notion of rights may be suitable for setting in motion debate on such an issue, general formulations are not suitable for reaching specific results in negotiations. These will also need to take into account such further elements as interests, consequences, feasibility, and co operation. Until the declared rights are posed in a less sweeping fashion, they lead directly to contradiction, and may serve as an obstacle. This seems to be one reason why many commentators feel that there comes a point in the discussion of land rights and compensation where formulation of specific measures in terms of a right becomes unhelpful, if progress is to be made in reaching an agreed solution, in action, to a debate which that very concept helped initiate.[29]

(8) Summary of Main Conclusions in this Section

The potentialities for conflict observed in this section may be tallied as follows. When the domain of norms under consideration is the purely formal one of all conceivable protected permissions and claims with various categories of bearer, the conflictual relations are systematic and legion, as a formal analysis quickly reveals. However, when the domain is the much more restricted one of widely accepted or canvassed rights, the inconsistencies become occasional rather than systematic, and are very sensitive to variations in formulation. Nevertheless, they do arise in significant fashion, as between human rights of persons, between these and rights of peoples, and between those and rights of minority collectivities—in addition, of course, to the direct conflicts between each and the rights of States under traditional international law to untrammelled sovereignty over their territories.

On the one hand, it must be emphasized that there is no inconsistency between a norm which simply permits a certain kind of activity, and a prohibition of certain modes of carrying out that activity. On the other hand, in so far as the former norm is enlarged to include a permission to choose the mode of performance, without accompanying limitations, there is a straightforward logical inconsistency between the two. This situation arises for some important formulations of the rights to self-determination and development. Indeed, it already arises for some rights which the Universal Declaration recognized as pertaining to individuals. When the element of choice in a norm is left obscure, the possibility of such conflict

---

[29] See e.g. the essays by Brownlie, Prott, and Kamenka in this volume.

remains. Conflict can also appear in connection with some ways of expressing rights of peoples to the preservation of their cultural identity. Ironically, it is the very cultural identity of minority collectivities—which may also regard themselves as 'peoples'—as well as the personal liberty of individuals, that are most exposed by rash or careless formulations. It must be said that most formulations of the right of peoples to cultural identity are so vague as to leave such clashes as latent under elaboration and interpretation, rather than explicit. It would, however, be hazardous to commit oneself formally to principles expressed in terms that so easily admit conflictual elaboration. In the case of compensation of peoples for past spoliation, there are difficulties in drawing a dividing line between compensation and punishment, and in reconciling the more sweeping formulations of a right to compensation with equally sweeping formulations of a right not to be held responsible for the actions of others.

In general, then, inconsistencies can and do arise between widely canvassed rights of peoples, individuals and minority groups. These conflicts are not, however, inherent in the genre. They could be avoided by careful and restrained formulation—more so than has so far been the case.

6

Cultural Rights as Peoples' Rights in International Law

LYNDEL V. PROTT

1. Introduction

It is essential, in this field, to make it absolutely clear exactly what is being discussed. When one talks about peoples' rights, one can mean one of several very different things. One might mean peoples' moral claims. One might mean peoples' rights as established and recognized in law, and this would involve the weighing up of evidence as to whether they are so established or not. Or one might mean, how far can such moral claims be established in law: what is their content? are they clear? do they meet the prerequisites for efficient enforcement by the legal system? In this sort of discussion lawyers have a great deal to contribute, since it is their constant effort to clarify and define. Moreover, this task is essential, if the rights asserted are to be given legal form and enforced. It is to this discussion this paper is directed.

It is important therefore to assert that in analysing and critically dissecting the claims being made lawyers are not being obstructive, or saying that these claims should not be legally enforced. Whether the claims should be recognized by the legal system is a question on which every concerned individual in a society should form a view. Rather the lawyer is emphasizing that the effort to frame rules to meet these claims must meet the same criteria as any other claim for attention in the legal system: they must be formulated in a way that is clear and understandable, that gives adequate notice to those subject to an obligation of the ambit of that obligation, and to those who must administer the rules, of their content. Moral claims may be phrased in ways that are inspirational, promotional and emotive, but to be enforced as legal rights they need restatement in a way which enables the enforcement mechanisms of the State or of the international community to be effective. The contribution of lawyers to this debate is therefore crucial, and they should not be criticized for performing it.

Yet there is clearly some impatience on the part of some Third World statesman and scholars, and indeed on the part of political activists and idealists generally, at the lawyer's approach. For the reasons already described, I think some of this impatience is misplaced. However, for other important reasons which I will discuss in the conclusion to this Chapter, I think their impatience is justified and requires serious attention.

2. Cultural Rights

Before discussing cultural rights it is essential to discuss the idea of 'culture'. The word 'culture' has many meanings: at least two are central to this discussion. The term is probably usually understood to mean the highest intellectual achievements of human beings: the musical, philosophical, literary, artistic, and architectural works, techniques and rituals which have most inspired humanity and are seen by communities as their best achievements. This is the traditional view of the meaning of culture— what we might, for the sake of convenience, call Culture with a capital c. The second view of 'culture' is that developed by anthropologists and means:[1]

the totality of the knowledge and practices, both intellectual and material, of each of the particular groups of a society, and—at a certain level—of a society itself as a whole. From food to dress, from household techniques to industrial techniques, from forms of politeness to mass media, from work rhythm to the learning of family rules, all human practices, all invented and manufactured materials are concerned and constitute, in their relationships and their totality, 'culture'.

In discussions of cultural rights it is not always clear which of these senses of the word is being invoked. Clearly Culture in the first sense is most significant to humankind, and legal measures to ensure its protection are justified, but culture in the wider sense is also to be valued. The preservation of diversity, the understanding of cultural development, may well require the care of everyday objects and practices which do not constitute peaks of cultural achievement. Moreover, the line between 'Culture' and 'culture' is a difficult one to draw: while one era may regard, for example, certain objects as everyday items, another may regard them as 'Art'. An example in recent practice is the reclassification of certain crafts practised by women from 'everyday object' to 'decorative art' to 'Art'— this is true of quilting and other textile work. However, some types of culture (in the anthropologist's sense) which do not seem (at any rate, by standards currently being used) to represent peaks of human achievement, may well be worth preserving simply because they represent an interesting and different response of humanity to its environment.

Clearly assertions of rights to preserve a culture are not all embracing: certain features of ghetto culture may be impossible to sustain without

[1] C. Guillaumin, 'Women and Cultural Values: Classes According to Sex and Their Relationship to Culture in Industrial Society' (1979) 6 *Cultures No 1—Cultural Values: the Cultural Dimension of Development* 41.

abject poverty and deprivation, and may not be desirable in terms of hygiene and health. Yet other aspects of that same ghetto culture may be enriching to the human condition; and one may want to take some pains to preserve them, while eliminating the degrading and restricting conditions in which they first developed.

These different shades of meaning are often ignored in discussions of cultural rights, but their existence shows that any attempt to talk about cultural issues in terms of rights may be slippery and difficult. Culture is not a static concept: cultures change all the time, and even the most enthusiastic supporter of cultural preservation would no doubt find elements in the culture under consideration which no special effort should be made to preserve. Likewise the proponents of cultural development are not urging total change: the degree of development and change of a culture which is desirable may be a subject of the keenest debate between members of that cultural group. Assertions of the right to develop and preserve a culture therefore conceal some of the most difficult areas of cultural policy-making.

3. Peoples' Rights and Human Rights

Even in the context of a discussion of the 'rights of peoples', it is impossible to do justice to the topic without making reference to individual human rights and to the general human rights context out of which the so-called 'third generation' rights have emerged. Cultural rights, in my view, have been present implicitly, if not explicitly, in human rights thought from the start. Freedom to express one's view, to adhere to one's religion, to associate with others for peaceful purposes, are all essential to the maintenance and development of any culture. Though these rights were certainly not designed for this purpose, their existence is a necessary prerequisite for the protection of culture, especially for the culture of minorities. But I agree that certain claims by groups which are not on their face unreasonable have involved matters not adequately covered by the classical formulations: Professor Brownlie lists, among these, 'claims to positive action to maintain the cultural and linguistic identity of communities'.[2] In this context he cites the *Belgian Linguistics Case*[3] to demonstrate that a court will not require a State to provide subsidies or other material underpinning to these rights. I am not so sure that it is possible to decide what is 'refraining from' and what is 'providing' in this context, particularly in the case of education, where the provision of buildings, teacher training, and other material resources may be the inevitable implication of the child's right to education, and the parent's right to choose its form.[4]

[2] Above p.3.
[3] (1968) 11 *Yearbook of Human Rights* 832.
[4] See the discussion of these issues by the Permanent Court of International Justice in *Rights of Minorities in Upper Silesia (Minority Schools)* (1928) PCIJ Series A No 15, 41-6.

There has certainly been a change of emphasis with the effort to extend cultural rights from the individual, or specified minorities protected by detailed and concrete treaty provisions, to broad general formulations as 'rights of people'. The most thorough attempt to do so has been in the Universal Declaration of the Rights of Peoples adopted at a conference at Algiers in 1976. (This was not a diplomatic or inter-State conference, i.e. not a conference intended to create new law by the consent of States in the traditional method of international law). Some of its ideas have been adopted by the OAU in the Banjul Charter on Human and Peoples' Rights of 1981. These two documents have been at the centre of the discussion of the 'third generation' of human rights, the collective rights which are current important political assertions of Third World states, and subject to scepticism and to allegations of vagueness by many Western scholars.

Among the collective or group rights which have been asserted are some new cultural rights. 'Peoples' rights' have been said to include the right to self-determination, to protection against genocide, the rights of minorities, the right to peace and security, to permanent sovereignty over natural resources and the right to development. Cultural rights have also been included, but relatively little work has been done on them. 'Cultural rights' remains a rather hazy category, for reasons which I think have to do with some of the fundamental difficulties relating to 'peoples' rights'.

4. Identifying 'Cultural Rights'

First it is necessary to identify the rights in question. There seem to be a number of rights which can loosely be described as 'cultural rights'. These are:

(1)   The right to freedom of expression, together with the important concomitant rights of freedom of religion and freedom of association. Though generally classified among civil and political rights, these rights seem to be an essential basis for the existence of any cultural rights. They are guaranteed by all the major human rights instruments.

(2) The right to education (Universal Declaration 1948, Art. 26; International Covenant on Economic, Social and Cultural Rights, Art. 13(1); Protocol I to the European Convention on Human Rights 1950, Art. 2; American Declaration of the Rights and Duties of Man 1948, Art. 12; Banjul Charter 1981, Art. 17(1)).

(3) The right of parents to choose the kind of education given to their children (Universal Declaration, Art. 26(3), International Covenant on Economic, Social and Cultural Rights, Art. 13(3); Protocol I to the European Convention on Human Rights 1950, Art. 2).

(4) The right of every person to participate in the cultural life of the community (Universal Declaration Art. 27(1); International Covenant on Economic, Social and Cultural Rights 1966, Art. 15(1)(a); American Declaration of the Rights and Duties of Man 1948, Art. 13; Banjul Charter, Art. 17(2)).

(5) The right to protection of artistic, literary and scientific works (Universal Declaration, Art. 27(2); International Covenant on Economic, Social and Cultural Rights, Art. 15(1)(c); American Declaration of the Rights and Duties of Man 1948, Art. 13).

(6) The right to develop a culture (UNESCO Declaration of the Principles of International Cultural Co-operation 1966 Art. 1(2); Banjul Charter 1981, Art. 22(1); Algiers Declaration 1976 (Art. 13) (in terms of a 'right to preserve and develop its own culture')

(7) The right to respect of cultural identity (Algiers Declaration Art. 2).

(8) The right of minority peoples to respect for identity, traditions, language, and cultural heritage (Algiers Declaration Art. 19).

(9) The right of a people to its own artistic, historical, and cultural wealth (Algiers Declaration, Art. 14).

(10) The right of a people not to have an alien culture imposed on it (Algiers Declaration, Art. 15).

(11) The right to the equal enjoyment of the common heritage of mankind (Banjul Charter, Art. 22(2)).

Of these eleven 'cultural' rights, the first five seem to be cast as rights of individuals. Rights (6) to (11) are, however, cast as peoples' rights, and it is on these that I shall concentrate..

Peoples' cultural rights, as currently formulated in the instruments listed above, seem to fall into two distinct groups. The right to preserve and develop a culture, the right to respect for cultural identity, and the right not to have an alien culture imposed on it, all relate to the cultural identity and uniqueness of a people. A second group consists of the right of a people to its own cultural heritage and to participation in the world cultural heritage. These seem to relate to issues of property, and are, I think, of a different order.

5. Rights Relating to 'Cultural Identity'

The concept of 'cultural identity' is difficult for precisely the same reason as the concept of 'a people' is difficult: it is hard to think of any satisfactory definition of 'people' which would not use some form of cultural criteria. Similarly it is difficult to think of any concept of a culture (other than a universal culture) which would not need to use the concept 'people' (or 'group' or 'community' or other synonym) in its definition. The world abounds in disagreements between groups as to how a culture or 'sub-culture' is to be classified; whether it needs special protection, whether it should be discouraged as a local (and perhaps less valuable) aberration of the pervasive culture, whether it should be given special assistance to develop further. An indication of this confusion is the inclusion in the Algiers Declaration of a people's right to cultural identity (Art. 2) and a minority's right to cultural identity (Art. 19). Niec's suggestion that the benefit of this right should be restricted to a 'nation', whether or not organized as a national state, does not appear to provide a solution.[5] Certain of the older generation of human rights, the right to freedom of expression, the right of parents to choose the education of their children, clearly enhanced the situation of minorities and assisted the survival of threatened minority cultures. Yet the assertion of cultural identity across national frontiers has been a most potent and disturbing political argument (witness pan-Germanism in the nineteenth and twentieth centuries). Small wonder that these so-called 'cultural rights' have the most part been left unexplained and undeveloped.

An illustration of some of the discomfort which can be aroused by assertions of collective rights to cultural identity by minorities might be taken from Ghana. Within the modern State of Ghana are the Ashanti people, formerly an extremely powerful and wealthy tribe against whom the British conducted two expeditions in 1874 and 1900. They took from the Ashanti capital gold artifacts of deep symbolic significance. The objects are currently held in English collections, but the psychological and spiritual significance of the regalia makes any question of its return very awkward. The Ashanti are an unusual and culturally distinct tribe from the other peoples of Ghana; their culture is little understood, and they might justifiably feel a grievance if these materials were to be returned to the Ghanaian Government. On the other hand, the return of the regalia, with its enormously powerful associations, to one tribal unit could very well cause a dangerous imbalance within the country.[6] The close connection between cultural symbols and practical politics is patent.

Identification of one particular group with important cultural resources may not always be so direct. Whose cultural heritage does an object belong to, when it is important to more than one group? The Elgin marbles' dispute is the most obvious but by no means the only example. Under the Canadian Cultural Property Export and Import Act 1975, an item can become part of the cultural heritage of Canada after it has been in the country thirty-five years; or if it has a close connection with Canadian history or national life (thus an early seventeenth century Dutch atlas and papers of Rudyard Kipling, part of a well-known Canadian collection, have both been held to be of outstanding significance to Canada and are preserved there under the provisions of this Act).[7]

6. Rights Connected with the Cultural Heritage

The right of a people to its own cultural, artistic and historical wealth was first mentioned in the Algiers Declaration of 1976. The date, and the use

[5] H. Niec, 'Human Right to Culture' (1979) 44 *Annuaire des Anciens Auditeurs de l'Académie de la Haye* 109, 112.

[6] R. Chamberlin, *Loot—the Heritage of Plunder* (1983) 69-97.

[7] Secretary of State, *Annual Report, Cultural Property Export and Import Act, 1979-80* (Ottawa, Government Printer, 1981) 18-19; *Annual Report, Cultural Property Export and Import Act, 1982-83* (Ottawa, Government Printer, 1984) 20-2.

of the word 'wealth' rather than heritage, suggests that the drafters were not particularly concerned with intangibles such as language, traditions or rituals but had in mind cultural property, in respect of which a campaign has been mounting, through the United Nations and through UNESCO, for the 'restitution' of cultural objects taken from their places of origin, especially in colonial times, and now located in Europe or America. The right to the equal enjoyment of the 'common heritage of mankind' first appeared in the Banjul Charter in 1981, and it seems from the context that the cultural heritage is at least included, though it is not specifically referred to.

It is difficult to be precise about the meaning of either of these two provisions. The right of a people to its 'artistic, historical and cultural wealth' may mean no more than that a State, or a minority in a State, has the right to prevent despoliation of sites of importance on its territory and to prohibit traffic in movables. There is no suggestion that a people should have 'permanent sovereignty' over its cultural wealth in the way that it would have over its natural resources under the UN Declaration on Permanent Sovereignty over Natural Resources of 1962. This would certainly cause bitter problems over immovables: there are many sites which are primarily associated with the culture found in one State but are now within the borders of another. A prime example was seen in the *Case of the Temple of Preah Vihear*,[8] which concerned a religious site built by the Khmer people whose descendants now live in Kampuchea, but which later came under Thai control. The problem of ensuring the care of such sites, especially where the States concerned may be hostile to one another, would hardly be improved by the vigorous assertion of rights such as that here described. (Interestingly, this right was not adopted by the Banjul Charter.)

Although cultural rights relating to education, religious tradition, and language have been studied in relation to minority groups,[9] little attention has so far been paid to the protection of the archaeological heritage in this context. It seems more likely that the formulation of a people's right to its artistic and historical wealth was intended, not to relate primarily to sites, but to shore up the demand for restitution of movable cultural property, especially in respect of those newly independent States which can clearly show that all the most significant items of their cultural heritage were taken from their territory when they had no control over it and that they have not even a nucleus from which to build a national collection. Countries such as Nauru and Vanuatu, which found themselves at their independence

---

[8] ICJ Reports 1962 p.6.
[9] F. Capotorti, *Study on the Rights of Persons Belonging to Ethnic, Religious and Linguistic Minorities* (UN Doc. E/CN 4/Sub 2/384/Rev, 1979) 57–94.

stripped of almost all examples of their traditional cultural material would be States which might want to assert such a right.

The assertion of this right could be intended by its proposers to cover yet another situation: where cultural objects have been exported illegally from their country of origin and the State of their present location refuses to enforce the export prohibition of the State of origin. For example, the Maori carvings concerned in the case of *Attorney-General for New Zealand* v. *Ortiz*[10] had been illegally exported from New Zealand, but the House of Lords held that the New Zealand government was not their owner and could not succeed in a suit for possession in the United Kingdom. Perhaps the assertion of a people's rights to its artistic and historical wealth is intended to improve the prospects of success in such a venture.

Cases such as this may be quite spectacular. Consider the case of the collection of Central Aboriginal artifacts, recordings of songs, rituals, and folklore made by the archaeologist Strehlow from the 1930s on. According to his records, he was entrusted with much of this information, some of it secret, by the elders of the Aranda tribe at a time when they saw their culture under great threat from encroaching Westernization and were fearful of a lack of serious interest of their own younger tribal members. The collection passed with Strehlow's death into the hands of his widow, and in 1984 was reported to have been taken out of the country in defiance of an Australian export prohibition. The collection (popularly called 'the crown jewels of Australian archaeology') had extraordinarily high commercial value (as had been seen by the few commercial uses Strehlow had made of parts of it in his lifetime) and an incalculable spiritual and cultural value to the Aranda community in its resurgence of tribal and Aboriginal identity.[11] An assertion of a 'people's right' to its own artistic and cultural heritage in this kind of context might be more in the manner of an assertion of some permanent right to decide on its location, or even an assertion of the primacy of a spiritual/cultural claim over a commercial one.

There may also be cases where a minority group within a State seeks restitution of movable cultural property or control over its movement within the State. For example, a significant claim being made within Australia is the claim to prevent the movement of Aboriginal material away from its traditional owners, or the community which has the closest association with it. Such claims were originally considered at the time of the passing of the Aboriginal and Torres Strait Islander Heritage (Interim Protection) Act 1984 (Cth) but no agreement was reached. The 1984 Act has since been made permanent,[12] but without any substantive amendment

[10] [1983] 2 All ER 93 (HL), affirming [1982] 3 All ER 432 (CA).

[11] The collection was subsequently reported to have been returned to Australia, after negotiations between the Australian government and those responsible for its exportation. See *The Bulletin* (13 November 1984) 62.

[12] Aboriginal and Torres Strait Islander Heritage Protection Act 1984, as amended by Act No 83 of 1986. See G. Ward, 'The federal Aboriginal Heritage Act and archaeology' (1985) 2 *Aust Aboriginal Studies* 47.

to extend the very limited recognition of these claims in the Act as originally passed. Such claims have been given greater recognition in the New Zealand Antiquities Act 1975, which places certain restrictions on the transfer of ownership of Maori antiquities within that country, as well as on their export.

The right to equal enjoyment of the common cultural heritage is an even hazier notion. Does it mean the right to cultural exchanges? Could it be intended to be the basis of an argument about the right to literacy and to scientific and technological advances made by other peoples? Or is it perhaps an assertion on behalf of the smaller and less affluent cultures to assistance from such international bodies as may have any to give? Is it a reference to the world cultural and natural heritage defined in terms of sites of supreme importance in the development of man in the 1972 UNESCO Convention on the Protection of the World Cultural and Natural Heritage? That interpretation does not seem to make any sense: either such sites are, or are not, on the territory of a 'people'. If they are, then they are part of its own cultural heritage, and if they are not, then the only content this provision would have would be as an assertion that sites of importance to all mankind are also of importance to the world's individual peoples.[13]

7. 'Universal' Culture and 'Specific' Cultures

An important distinction has to be made between general cultural rights (e.g. to education, participation in cultural life), rights related to a specific culture, and rights related to cultural resources of universal significance. A number of UNESCO instruments emphasize the importance of all cultures to the human experience: thus the UNESCO Convention for the Protection of the World Cultural and Natural Heritage 1972 is based on the assumption that everybody has an interest in the greatest cultural achievements, and international campaigns to protect threatened sites (such as Abu Simbel and Borobodur) are supported by the commitment to their preservation of persons outside the local culture. At the same time it is clear that some of the rights discussed above, such as the right to develop a culture, or the right of parents to choose the kind of education they desire for their children, are more in the nature of 'special status' rights which can be claimed by minorities whose cultural survival or creative activity is threatened. The protection accorded by these minority rights could include the protection of sites of special significance to that particular group, even if no other persons outside that group were interested in them. However,

[13] See the World Heritage List annexed to *Report of the Intergovernmental Committee for Protection of the World Cultural and Natural Heritage* (UNESCO General Conference Document 23 C/86 (23rd Session, Sofia, 1985)).

just as distinguishing a 'nation' from a 'people' from a 'minority' is one of the perennial problems of international law, so deciding when a 'culture' is distinct and important enough to need special legal protections and guarantees is a very difficult task.

Consider as an example the case of Kakadu National Park, a site nominated by Australia and accepted for the UNESCO World Heritage List under the 1972 Convention. It is of universal cultural significance because of its unique sites of rock art, still actively being worked within living memory and stretching back in an unbroken tradition many thousands of years. It shows the continuing evolution of the Aboriginal community in its environment, the development of new styles and achievements and new ways of man looking at himself. Some of the features of these rock galleries have important parallels, and equally important contrasts, with other important rock art sites, such as Altamira in Spain and Lascaux in France. The galleries have been little explored, and clearly are an enormous storehouse of artistic and intellectual experience requiring special protection for their significance to all mankind. At the same time they have a special significance for all Australians, including the recently arrived European settlers, confronted with an unfamiliar and at first hostile environment. Indisputably they have special significance for the Aboriginal population of Australia, a group whose interests were systematically ignored or overborne by the immigrant population until very recently, and to whom they permit an assertion of cultural uniqueness, value, and superiority very important in their recent and growing assertions of equality. Above and beyond all those claims are the special claims of those descendants of the original artists, those tribes located in that part of Australia who still have special close connections with the land and are its guardians and 'traditional owners' (using that term in a non-technical sense).

8. Cultural Rights and the Right to Development.

The problems of delineating, understanding, and applying cultural rights are compounded when the areas of conflict and overlap with other collective rights are examined. This can be well illustrated by the conflict with the right to development. The right to development is seen by many Third World partisans of collective rights as central to the scheme of collective rights, since without it the economic basis for the realization of many of the basic human rights, civil, political and, especially, economic rights, may not exist. Yet the assertion of the right to development may run directly counter to the right to preserve or develop a culture. Economic development may obliterate or mutilate important cultural sites and destroy social structures which are essential for the survival of traditional arts and other cultural activities. Pressures to exploit tourism as a source of foreign revenue often lead to degradation of traditional crafts to cater with the increased demand, to the provision of services for tourists inimical to the local environment, and to damage to static life-styles from the constant stamp of tourist feet. Economic development may mean cultural stagnation: cultural development may mean economic stagnation. An awareness of this paradox has led to the suggestion that 'development' must be redefined to include socio-cultural as well as economic factors.[14]

While it is true that these conflicts can be lessened by sensitive planning, they cannot be eliminated. It may be argued by some groups which have a culture which is threatened by a surrounding majority culture, inimical to many of its values (such as an indigenous culture under threat of Westernization) that the group seeks the right not to develop, in order to preserve or redevelop its traditional culture.

The point is that very serious decisions with most far-reaching implications are going to have to be made on matters of cultural policy and social and economic development. None of these decisions is made any easier by framing the issues in terms of 'right' rather than of compromise. For example, the desire to obtain technological knowledge, to participate more fully in international trade or to encourage tourism might lead a government to phrase its claims for aid for the teaching of English as part of the right to development. At the same time the desire to consolidate national identity, to improve literacy, develop local cultural traditions and preserve important kinds of cultural activity might lead the same government to encourage the use, development, and teaching of an indigenous language. The debate concerning the status of Creole in Mauritius is an interesting example.[15] The right to development might also be called on in a situation such as Egypt's when it was decided to build the Aswan High Dam. Against it could be urged the right to participate in the world's cultural heritage: since this was a clear case where sites of extreme and universal significance to all would have been completely removed from access and in due course irretrievably lost.

9. Cultural Policy and Cultural Rights

It will be clear from this discussion that a great deal of further analysis has to be done before these important complexes of cultural policy can effectively be transformed into enforceable law by way of declarations of rights in international legal instruments. This may yet be done, but only through the use of relatively vague formulations and many ambiguities; instruments

[14] M. Makagiansar, 'Preservation and Further Development of Cultural Value' in (1979) 6 *Cultures No 1—Cultural Values: the Cultural Dimension of Development* 11.
[15] P. Lenoir, 'An Extreme Example of Pluralism: Mauritius' in (1979) 6 *Cultures No 1— Cultural Values: the Cultural Dimension of Development* 63, 70-2.

of this type need careful study before they can be regarded as establishing new law.

This does not mean that formulations of cultural rights are not important. Indeed, it seems to me that questions of culture underlie a good many of the political demands from which the classical human rights developed. Many of the issues mentioned in the course of this paper are regarded as of very great significance, particularly by the newer States. A publication by the Association of Conservation of Cultural Treasures of the Republic of Korea insists that the conquest of a nation is only complete, not by military subjection, however thorough, but by destruction of the indigenous culture.[16] Such an attitude illustrates the drive to give threatened cultures additional protection by formulating certain demands about culture into human rights protected by international instrument which cannot be derogated from..

It is this factor which accounts for the drive to phrase cultural issues as human rights issues. If there is any content to be given to *'jus cogens'* in international law, there seems to be reasonable agreement that certain basic 'human rights' are included in it. The vigorous assertion that these critical cultural issues involve 'rights' is understandable in this context. 'Human rights' has been an emotive and potent force in the process of improving the human condition. It is one to which Western States have shown commitment, and, in the achievement of the traditional civil and political rights particularly, great pride. Issues raised as human rights issues will be given serious attention. Critical attention is better than no attention..

But there is another side to this. There seems in many Third World States to be resentment and criticism of the caution of Western legal scholars in the acceptance of newly formulated rights, and a belief that their attitudes may be obstructive. For reasons set out already, I think that this is to confuse different issues. None the less I do think that many Western scholars are not altogether realistic in their approach to these issues. Professor Brownlie comments that:[17]

As policy goals, as standards of morality, the so-called new generation of human rights would be acceptable and one could sit round a table with non-lawyers and agree on practical programmes for attaining these good ends. What concerns me as a lawyer is the casual introduction of serious confusions of thought and this in the course of seeking to give the new rights an actual legal context.

This statement seems unexceptional. But Third World States would be justified in arguing that there has been no sitting round a table and no agreement on practical programmes on issues of cultural policy, indeed no

---

[16] Association for Conservation of Cultural Properties of Korea Inc, *Conservation of Cultural Properties* (in Korean, Seoul, n.d. (?1978)) 13. See L. V. Prott & P. J. O'Keefe, *Law and the Cultural Heritage*, Vol 1: *Discovery and Excavation* (Professional Books, Abingdon, 1984).

[17] Above p.14.

willingness shown to pay attention to issues of cultural policy of very serious concern to them. To take an example: archaeologically rich countries have been concerned for generations with the despoliation of their sites for the benefit of Western markets. Discussions on the international control of illicit exploitation of antiquities took place in the League of Nations between 1919 and 1922 but resulted in no international instrument (though they did become the basis of the first antiquities legislation in Iraq). A draft Convention on the Repatriation of Objects of Artistic, Historical or Scientific Interest, Which Have Been Lost, Stolen or Unlawfully Alienated or Exported was submitted to the Member States of the League of Nations in 1933, but was not adopted. A draft Convention for the Protection of National Historic Artistic Treasures was submitted to the Member States of the League in 1936 and referred back for further study. A draft Convention for the Protection of National Collections of Art. and History drawn up in 1939, which would have applied only to objects individually catalogued as belonging to a State but which were stolen and unlawfully expatriated, was never adopted because of the outbreak of war. The final Act of the Cairo Conference of 1937, which adopted certain international principles applicable to archaeological excavations, failed to receive the implementation it needed because of the worsening international situation, though it later formed the basis of the 1956 UNESCO Recommendation on that topic.

Thus it took fifty years and the failure of several major instruments to get a viable international instrument to deal with the problem (the 1970 UNESCO Convention on the Means of Prohibiting and Preventing the Illicit Import, Export and Transfer of Ownership of Cultural Property). That Convention is a very much weakened version of the instrument originally proposed,[18] and even that draft had differed from its unsuccessful predecessors. Of the 58 States which are currently parties, of European States only Italy is a party; the United Kingdom, Switzerland, and the Federal Republic of Germany, all major art markets, are not. Although the United States is a party (since 1983), its acceptance is extremely limited. Despite evidence of persistent and serious concern for the protection of cultural resources, Western statesmen and international lawyers have shown that their interests are not engaged by the serious and complex problems in this area. Examining current periodicals of international law, for example, one is struck by the hundreds of articles being written on exploitation of the seabed, changes in laws relating to maritime transit, and the sharing of economic resources of the sea. On international issues of cultural policy there are probably no more than 10 international lawyers showing any interest in the subject, and probably not more than 5 working

[18] Cf. *Kingdom of Spain* v. *Christie, Manson & Woods Ltd* [1986] 1 WLR 1120, 1124 (Browne-Wilkinson VC), and the discussion in L. V. Prott & P. J. O'Keefe, *Law and the Cultural Heritage*, Vol 3: *Movement* (Professional Books, Abingdon, 1987).

on the problems as a whole with any degree of serious effort, rather than dabbling with one or more specific issues as an 'instant expert'.

In this context I understand and sympathize with the efforts of lawyers from newer States to formulate cultural issues as human rights issues. If States will not utilize the existing techniques of formulating new, conceptually satisfactory, and practically effective rules to control a serious source of international friction, one can hardly blame those who seek to use techniques which may be conceptually unsatisfactory but do make use of an existing strong ideological commitment, to achieve their ends. There is an international political momentum behind the 'peoples' rights' movement which may be unstoppable. I suspect that much of the distaste of Western international lawyers for the intellectual disarray of current international formulations of international rights conceals a complacent commitment to the interests of Western States. It is easy to say, 'Let us sit around a table and discuss these issues', but that statement ignores the long record of failure of Western States and Western scholars to do any such thing, and the present apparent lack of serious effort to address the policy issues in the area of cultural protection.

In concluding this critical analysis of cultural rights as they are presently formulated, it is very important to recognize the very strong pressures existing to refine and expand rights which are now embryonic or emerging. It is likely that more will be formulated, proclaimed and promoted, despite all we can say or do, despite all our hand-wringing and nay-saying. If we really care for the texture of international law and its intellectual integrity, we should do something solid about the practical problems that are encouraging its distortion, and not simply spend our time lamenting it.

7

'Peoples' and 'Populations'—Indigenous Peoples and the Rights of Peoples

GARTH NETTHEIM

1. Introduction

Since the early 1970s there have been attempts by a number of individual nation states, including Australia and Canada, to come to terms in their different ways with the claims of indigenous peoples. The international legal system, too, has begun to acknowledge that indigenous populations may have claims worthy of response in terms of international law.

An early landmark in the international development was the 1957 ILO Convention No 107 concerning the Protection and Integration of Indigenous and Other Tribal and Semi-Tribal Populations in Independent Countries.[1] A later landmark was the 1971 decision of the Sub-Commission on the Prevention of Discrimination and Protection of Minorities to commission a study of the problems of the world's indigenous populations. The Martinez Cobo study was finally published in 1984.[2] In the meantime the Sub-Commission had received authorization to have five of its members constitute a pre-sessional Working Group on Indigenous Populations. That Working Group met annually from 1982 to 1985, for one week in August.[3] It opened its deliberations not only to those non-governmental organizations (NGOs) which have formal UN accreditation but also to organizations of indigenous peoples, and to knowledgeable individuals. In 1984 it approved a scheme for a Trust Fund to assist attendance of representatives of indigenous peoples who would otherwise be unable to participate. The Working Group has been one of the most accessible entities in the United Nations system.[4]

[1] G. Bennett, 'The Developing Law of Aboriginal Rights' (1979) 22 *ICJ Review;* G. Bennett, *Aboriginal Rights in International Law* (Occasional Paper No 37, Royal Anthropological Institute of Great Britain and Ireland (in association with Survival International), 1978).

[2] *Study of the Problem of Discrimination against Indigenous Populations* (E/CN 4/Sub 2/476 & Add 1-6; E/CN 4/Sub 2/1982/2 & Add 1-7l E/CN 4/Sub 2/1983/21 & Add 1-8).

[3] Its 1986 meeting was cancelled as a result of the UN financial crisis.

[4] D. E. Sanders, 'The Re-Emergence of Indigenous Questions in International Law' (1983) 1 *Canadian Human Rights Yearbook* 3; D. Weissbrodt, 'The Third Session of the UN Working Group on Indigenous Populations 29 July-3 August, 1984' (1985) 13 *ALB* 12; G. Alfredsson, 'Fourth Session of the Working Group on Indigenous Populations' (1986) 55 *Nordic J Int L* 22.

Indigenous peoples moved rapidly to take up the opportunity. Several organizations gained formal NGO status in order to facilitate participation in this and other agencies such as the Sub-Commission and the parent Commission on Human Rights. Some of those organizations represent particular groupings of indigenous peoples, e.g. the International Indian Treaty Council, the Inuit Circumpolar Conference, the National Aboriginal and Islander Legal Services Secretariat (NAILSS). One body which attempts a global coverage is the World Council of Indigenous Peoples (WCIP).[5] The contrast between the WCIP's title, which speaks of indigenous 'peoples', and the Working Group's, which refers to indigenous 'populations', is significant.

The point of this account is that there have, for several years, been moves at the international level to formulate the claims of indigenous 'peoples' or 'populations', just as there have been similar moves at the level of national legal systems. In so far as bodies such as the Working Group on Indigenous Populations are supposed to move towards the evolution of standards, we can usefully attempt to formulate the claims of indigenous peoples as actual or potential rights. And we can attempt to discover to what extent the claims or rights of indigenous populations coincide with the claims or rights of peoples generally.

2. Claims of Indigenous Peoples at National and International Level

The following account attempts therefore to identify the claims being advanced on behalf of indigenous peoples in two national systems (Australia and Canada), and to relate these to each other and to claims being advanced on behalf of indigenous peoples in the international system.

(1) Australian Claims

The campaign for recognition of Aboriginal rights has been continuous since the time of European invasion and settlement. The modern history of the campaign can be related to a series of events which serve to indicate the nature of Aboriginal claims on Australian society.

● In 1966 Gurindji stockmen went on strike in protest against conditions of employment with the Vestey beef-cattle interests. The entire community walked off the settlement and established camp on a portion of their traditional country at Wattie Creek.

[5] D. E. Sanders, *The Formation of the World Council of Indigenous Peoples* (IWGIA Document 29, Copenhagen: International Work Group for Indigenous Affairs, 1977).

- In 1967 a long campaign by Aboriginals and their supporters culminated in a successful referendum to amend the Commonwealth Constitution by deleting a provision confining legislative power over Aboriginals to State Parliaments. Aboriginals looked to the Commonwealth Parliament to use its new, concurrent power to override repressive State laws.

- Clans at Yirrkala on the Gove peninsula in the Northern Territory went to court in 1969 to assert their continuing ownership of their traditional lands in an (unseccessful) challenge to the validity of mining leases granted over their land by the Commonwealth Government.[6]

- In 1972, in protest at the McMahon government's refusal to contemplate any substantial recognition of land rights in the Northern Territory, Aboriginals established an 'Aboriginal Embassy' tent encampment on the lawns in front of Parliament House in Canberra. Its presence there over several months highlighted the land rights campaign, nationally and internationally, and embarrassed the Commonwealth Government. Heavy-handed measures to remove the campersonly served to attract additional publicity and support for the cause.

- In 1973 the newly elected Whitlam government redeemed its electoral pledge to move towards recognition of Aboriginal land rights in the Northern Territory by commissioning Justice Woodward as Aboriginal Land Rights Commissioner to explore how this goal might best be achieved. The principal recommendations of the Woodward Report[7] were eventually enacted by the Fraser government in the Aboriginal Land Rights (Northern Territory) Act 1976 (Cth). The Act transferred Aboriginal reserves to local Aboriginal ownership, set up a system for adjudicating traditional claims to unalienated Crown land, and established powerful regional land councils to represent Aboriginal interests. (In the meantime critical issues of mining, Aboriginal land and environment protection in the 'uranium province' of the Northern Territory had also been addressed in the course of the Ranger Inquiry.[8]) Over the years the Northern Territory government has sought to limit the scope of the land rights legislation but most of the court decisions have favoured the Aboriginal interest.

- In 1975 the Whitlam Government ratified the International Convention on the Elimination of All Forms of Racial Discrimination and, by way of implementation, enacted the Racial Discrimination Act 1975 (Cth). In the same year, in order to override repressive features of Queensland legislation, it enacted theAboriginal and Torres Strait Islanders (Queensland Discriminatory Laws) Act 1975 (Cth). The latter Act appears to have had some influence in subsequent changes to Queensland legislation.[9] The Racial Discrimination Act was not confined in its application to Aboriginal people but, consistently, 30-40 per cent of the complaints under the Act are brought by Aboriginals althought they number less than 2 per cent of the population. The High Court of Australia

[6] *Milirrpum* v. *Nabalco Pty Ltd and Commonwealth* (1971) 17 FLR 141. The correctness of the *Milirrpum* decision is to be questioned in pending litigation before the High Court: *Mabo* v. *Queensland*.

[7] Aboriginal Land Rights Commission, *First Report* (Parl Pap 1973/138); *Second Report* (Parl Pap 1974/69).

[8] Ranger Uranium Environmental Inquiry (Chairman: Justice RW Fox), *Second Report* (AGPS, Canberra, 1977).

[9] G. Nettheim, *Victims of the Law. Black Queenslanders Today* (Allen & Unwin, Sydney, 1981)

upheld the validity of key provisions of the Racial Discrimination Act against a challenge by Queensland in *Koowarta* v. *Bjelke-Petersen*.[10]

- In Queensland the Aboriginal people of Aurukun opposed the State government's grant of mining leases over their lands, without consultation, and without any clear provision for them to participate in profits.[11] Subsequent moves in 1978 by the Queensland government to take over management of the reserve from the Uniting Church led to a bitter Commonwealth–State confrontation, enactment of the Aboriginal and Torres Strait Islanders (Queensland Reserves and Communities Self-Management) Act 1978 (Cth) (neatly sidestepped by the Queensland government), and a 'local government' compromise solution for the future governance of Aurukun and another Uniting Church mission community on Mornington Island.

- In 1980 the integrity of land held in leasehold by Aboriginal people at Noonkanbah in Western Australia was threatened by the insistence of the Western Australian government that exploratory oil drilling should proceed in close proximity to a sacred site. The Commonwealth Government spoke against the move but did nothing, and its failure was made the subject of complaint by a three-man delegation from the National Aboriginal Conference to the UN Sub-Commission on Prevention of Discriminaion and Protection of Minorities at Geneva. Aboriginal delegations have continued to go to Geneva to contribute to the development of international standards for indigenous rights.

- In 1966 South Australia legislated to transfer ownership of reserves from the government to a state-wide Aboriginal land trust. Some other states followed suit. In 1981 South Australia enacted the Pitjantjatjara Land Rights Act 1981 (SA) transferring the vast Pitjantjatjara reserve lands to Pitjantjatjara ownership. The Maralinga Tjarutja Land Rights Act 1984 (SA) was similar. The validity of exclusion provisions in the Pitjantjatjara Land Rights Act was challenged in *Gerhardy* v. *Brown*[12] as inconsistent with the Racial Discrimination Act 1975 (Cth), but the High Court rejected the challenge.

- New South Wales enacted the Aboriginal Land Rights Act 1983 (NSW) to transfer existing reserves to local Aboriginal ownership, to allocate a portion of land tax revenues to a three-tier system of aboriginal land councils, and to provide for a system of land claims.[13] Victoria has been moving towards lands rights legislation. Queensland has been progressively refining a scheme of deeds of grant in trust for Aboriginal and Islander communities. For Western Australia, the scheme proposed by the Seaman Report[14] in 1983 was effectively blocked by a political campaign waged by mining interests opposed to any measure of Aboriginal control over mining. The same campaign also led to the Hawke government abandoning in 1986 its promise to enact national land rights legislation based on a set of principles including Aboriginal control over mining.[15]

[10] (1982) 39 ALR 417.
[11] *Director of Aboriginal and Islanders Advancement* v. *Peinkinna* (1978) 24 ALR 118.
[12] (1985) 57 ALR 472.
[13] M. Wilkie, *Aboriginal Land Rights in NSW* (APCOL, Sydney, 1985).
[14] Aboriginal Land Inquiry, *Report* (Perth, Government Printer, 1984).
[15] G. Nettheim, 'Justice or Handouts? Aborigines, Law and Policy' (1986) 58 *Australian Quarterly* 60.

● The question of Aboriginal land rights—and of Aboriginal control over mining and other resource development—has received differing responses in the several Australian jurisdictions. So has the issue of protection of sacred sites and other elements of Aboriginal cultural heritage, though the Commonwealth Parliament has enacted national 'back stop' legislation in this area.[16] The Commonwealth Government has also assumed primary responsibility for funding programmes of Aboriginal social and economic development.

● In 1979 the National Aboriginal Conference (an elected assembly of Aboriginal and Islander Representatives, funded by the Commonwealth Government) proposed the negotiation of a treaty between Aboriginal Australia and Australia. The Fraser government resisted use of the language of 'treaty' but expressed some acceptance of the concept of a 'compact' or Makarrata (an Aboriginal word) as a basis for resolving outstanding issues. The concept also won significant non-Aboriginal support, notably from the Aboriginal Treaty Committee.[17] The NAC developed a series of negotiating points, and the Senate Standing Committee on Constitutional and Legal Affairs affirmed the feasibility of such a compact.[18] But the momentum towards a Makarrata seemed to have died with (or even before) the demise of the NAC itself when the Commonwealth Government terminated funding in mid-1985. There is no prospect of such a negotiated settlement in time for the 1988 Bicentennial of British occupation.

Against this background, five major categories of claim which have at some stage been pressed on Australian governments by Aboriginal and Torres Strait Islander peoples may be identified.

(a)   Land rights (on several possible bases—for instance, traditional association, long occupancy, economic need, or compensation for dispossession).

(b)   Rights associated with land rights (for example, control of access to Aboriginal lands, self-management on Aboriginal lands, an effective voice on issues of resources development, protection of sacred and significant sites, hunting and fishing rights).

(c)   Self-management (especially in regard to lands occupied by Aboriginal people, but also in regard to Aboriginal affairs generally and particularly in the delivery of services for Aboriginals).

(d)   Special assistance (in matters of health, housing, education, employment, justice, and so on, not only on the basis of evident present need but also on the basis of compensation for past dispossession).

(e)   Cultural identity (recognition as a people, and recognition of specific cultural needs in regard to land, sacred and significant sites, law, languages, and other aspects of culture).[19]

---

[16] Aboriginal and Torres Strait Islander Heritage Protection Act 1984 (Cth).

[17] Judith Wright, *We Call For A Treaty* (Fontana, Sydney, 1985).

[18] Senate Standing Committee on Constitutional and Legal Affairs, *Two Hundred Years Later* (AGPS, Canberra, 1983).

[19] G. Nettheim, 'Justice and Indigenous Minorities: A New Province for International and National Law' in A. R. Blackshield (ed), *Legal Change. Essays in Honour of Julius Stone* (Butterworths, Sydney, 1983) 257-8.

(2) Canadian Claims

Compared with Australia, the situation of indigenous peoples in Canada presents contrasts as well as similarities.[20] One major contrast arises from the fact that in Canada the Crown did sign treaties with some (though not all) of the native peoples. Another contrast is that, independently of treaties, aboriginal land rights in Canada are judicially recognized. Moreover, since confederation in 1867, the Canadian government has had exclusive legislative power over 'Indians and lands reserved for the Indians'. The Constitution Act 1982 defined the aboriginal peoples of Canada as comprising Indians, Metis, and Inuit and recognized and affirmed 'existing aboriginal and treaty rights'. The Constitution also established a process (the First Ministers' Conferences (FMC)) whereby the leaders of the federal, provincial, and territory governments and of four national native peoples' organizations would attempt to identify those rights. Thus Canada's aboriginal peoples have constitutional recognition not just as the objects of legislative power but as the possessors of rights worthy of recognition at the constitutional level.

Much of the current Canadian debate focuses on the right to self-government. The report of a parliamentary committee in 1983 proposed recognition of Canada's native peoples as constituting a separate level of government.[21] The Trudeau government drafted a bill which offered much less than the report recommended—indeed, not much more than local government powers on Indian reserve lands. That Bill lapsed with the change of government.[22] Aboriginal self-government remains as the major item on the agenda for the last of the currently mandated FMC meetings for April 1987.

Land rights have been recognized in the courts, though there has been no authoritative judicial analysis of the nature and extent of those rights. Where land is claimed on the basis of treaty, the terms of the treaty can be referred to. The process of negotiating native rights continues, though in terms not of treaties but of comprehensive settlements. The Indians and Inuit have gained considerable negotiating strength from judicial recognition that their rights survived in common law despite the acquisition of British sovereignty.

[20] B. Keon-Cohen & B. Morse, 'Indigenous Land Rights in Australia and Canada' in P. Hanks & B. Keon-Cohen (eds), *Aborigines and the Law* (George Allen and Unwin, Sydney, 1984) 74. For a more detailed Canadian compendium, see B. Morse (ed), *Aboriginal Peoples and the Law. Indian, Metis and Inuit Rights in Canada* (Carleton UP, Ottawa, 1985).

[21] House of Commons, Report of the Special Committee on Indian Self-Government, *Indian Self-Government in Canada* (Ottawa, 1983).

[22] Hon John C. Munro, Minister of Indian Affairs and Northern Development, *Response of the Government to the Report of the Special Committee on Indian Self-Government* (5 March, 1984); Bill C–52 for 'An Act relating to Self-government for Indian Nations', first reading 27 June, 1984.

Much of the impetus for the recent and continuing negotiation of settlements derives from proposals for resource development in some of the more remote lands inhabited by native peoples. Such proposals in Canada led to the Mackenzie Valley Pipeline Inquiry conducted by Justice Thomas Berger,[23] the litigation that sparked the James Bay agreement and much else.

In Canada as in Australia, land rights seem to lie at the heart of indigenous claims on the wider society. Not all indigenous communities retain sufficient connection with traditional lands to themselves be direct beneficiaries of settlements. But the claim to land rights also has a symbolic significance—to acknowledge the rights in land of some indigenous people is to acknowledge the prior indigenous ownership of the entire country.

Recent Canadian federal practice has been to require extinguishment of common law rights as a term of negotiated settlements, but the practice is now being reconsidered. In 1984 the Council of Yukon Indians declined to sign an Agreement partly for this reason.[24]

Even a term that extinguishes prior rights recognizes the existence of those rights. The most recent negotiating position of Australia's National Aboriginal Conference was to require a momentary recognition of Aboriginal title in a Makarrata compact which would relinquish such title in return for the other terms of the settlement.[25] In Canada the comprehensive settlements are being negotiated in various parts of the country with various Indian and Inuit groups.[26] Examples include the James Bay and Northern Quebec Agreement of 1975 and the 1984 Inuvialuit (Western Arctic) Agreement. The claims negotiated in those settlements include recognition of the rights of specific native groups in defined areas of land; rights in relation to that land; compensation; environment protection; hunting, fishing, trapping, and gathering rights; culture and language rights; social and economic development.[27] The nature of the claims is very similar to the claims being advanced by Australia's Aboriginal peoples. But they are being advanced in Canada from a stronger base of judicial recognition and some treaty recognition, and to a large extent in the context of the national Constitution.

(3) International Claims

What then are the claims of indigenous peoples on international law? ILO Convention No 107 of 1957 gives some indication. Its concerns were land

[23] *Northern Frontier, Northern Homeland: Report of the Mackenzie Valley Pipeline Inquiry* (Ottawa, 1977)
[24] B. Morse, 'Canadian Developments' (1985) 12 *ALB* 8.
[25] Senate Standing Committee on Constitutional and Legal Affairs, *Two Hundred Years Later ... Report on the Feasibility of a Compact or 'Makarrata' between the Commonwealth and Aboriginal People* (AGPS, Canberra, 1983).
[26] Hon John C. Munro, Minister for Indian Affairs and Northern Development, *In All Fairness. A Native Claims Policy. Comprehensive Claims* (Ottawa, 1981).
[27] Keon-Cohen & Morse, 76.

rights, cultural identity, and socio-economic disadvantage. But the Convention addressed those concerns in terms of protection and integration, goals which most indigenous peoples' organizations would now regard as inadequate, and which are now conceded to be inadequate by the ILO itself which, in 1986, commenced the process of revising the Convention.[28]

The sessions of the Working Group on Indigenous Populations in Geneva also provide evidence of indigenous peoples' claims, particularly as the Working Group was asked 'to give special attention to the evolution of standards concerning the rights of indigenous populations . . . '. At its 1983 meeting, the Working Group organized the following structure for its agenda item 'Review of Developments . . . ' which gives some indication of the way in which those attending the meeting perceived the claims/rights of indigenous populations:

- The right to life, to physical integrity, and to security of the indigenous populations.
- The right to land and to natural resources.
- The right to autonomy or self-determination, and political institutions and representation of indigenous populations.
- The right to develop their own cultural traditions, language, religious practices, and way of life.
- The economic and social rights of the indigenous populations.[29]

The 1983 meeting also devised a more detailed 'Plan of Action from 1984 onwards' in which it proposed to concentrate on particular topics in successive years for the purpose of its other main agenda item on 'Evolution of Standards'.[30]

At its 1984 meeting the Working Group proposed to consider two topics—the definition of indigenous populations, and land and natural resources. Not much headway has been made in establishing an agreed definition of indigenous peoples. But in international as in national fora, land is clearly at the heart of indigenous claims:[31]

From the very first session of the Working Group it was obvious that land constituted the most significant issue facing indigenous peoples around the world. For some indigenous communities the problem was preserving their present territories from further encroachment by the culture which possessed control of the government. Other indigenous peoples want to obtain the return of land taken from them in the past. In some countries the indigenous communities are not permitted to hold title to land and to control their land on the same terms as other individuals and groups.

[28] S. Leckie, 'Indigenous Peoples: Recent Developments in the International Labour Organization' (1986) 16 *SIM Newsletter* (Netherlands Institute of Human Rights) 22.
[29] UN Doc E/CN.4/Sub 2/1983/22.
[30] UN Doc E/CN.4/Sub 2/1983/22, Annex 1.
[31] Weissbrodt, 13.

At its first meeting in 1982 the Working Group accepted a document presented by the Indian Law Resource Center entitled 'Principles for Guiding the Deliberations of the Working Group on Indigenous Populations'.[32] The claims embodied in the document include protection of the physical, cultural, and political integrity of indigenous peoples and groups; land rights, including control of natural resources and protection of the environment; self-determination; and international status for treaties and other agreements.

There have been other attempts to define the claims of indigenous populations. The World Council of Indigenous Peoples, at its second General Assembly at Kiruna, Sweden, in 1977, listed claims to land rights; self-determination; self-government; culture, language and, traditions; control of natural resources; social and economic development. In 1981, the Legal Commission of the International NGO Conference on Indigenous Peoples and the Land, held at Geneva, stressed the 'inseparable connection between land rights of Indigenous Peoples and the right of self-determination'. In particular, they endorsed the following proposals from the 1977 Conference:[33]

that the right should be recognized of all indigenous nations or peoples to the return and control, as a minimum, of sufficient and suitable land to enable them to live an economically viable existence in accordance with their own customs and traditions, and to make possible their full development at their own pace... that the ownership of land by indigenous peoples should be unrestricted, and should include the ownership and control of all natural resources. The lands, land rights and natural resources of indigenous peoples should not be taken, and their land rights should not be terminated or extinguished without their full and informed consent.

Another restatement of indigenous claims appears in the Declaration of Principles of Indigenous Rights adopted at the Fourth Assembly of the World Council of Indigenous Peoples in Panama, September, 1984. That document was presented to the fourth session of the Working Group on Indigenous Populations in 1985, together with a Draft Declaration of Principles adopted by six other NGOs. Both were published as annexes to the report of the Working Group, together with the Working Group's own initial set of draft principles.[34]

So, bit by bit, we can discover the range of claims being advanced by indigenous peoples on international law. Most are listed below. We can then take each one and consider whether it is a claim that is particular to indigenous peoples or one which may be shared by peoples generally, and the extent to which it already has recognition in international law.

[32] UN Doc E/CN.4/Sub 2/AC4/1982/R1.
[33] Reproduced in (1982) *Canadian Legal Aid Bulletin* 193.
[34] E/CN 4/Sub 2/1985/22, Annexes II-IV.

3. Indigenous Claims and International Law

On this basis, ten classes of claims can be identified—physical survival; cultural survival and cultural identity; sovereignty; self-determination; self-government; land rights; control of land and its resources; compensation; non-discrimination, and affirmative action. Though overlapping to some extent, these claims are to a certain extent distinct, and they will be considered in turn.

(a) Physical Survival

This, the ultimate claim, is not confined to indigenous peoples. As a right of peoples generally (as distinct from individuals) it is recognized in the Convention on the Prevention and Punishment of the Crime of Genocide. Indigenous peoples in many parts of the world have experienced genocide in the past. Some still do so.

The Genocide Convention was carefully drafted. The offence goes beyond direct killing, although it probably does not extend to 'cultural genocide'. Article II provides:

In the present Convention, genocide means any of the following acts committed with intent to destroy, in whole or in part, a national, ethnical, racial or religious group, such as:

(a) Killing members of the group;
(b) Causing serious bodily or mental harm to members of the group;
(c) Deliberately inflicting on the group conditions of life calculated to bring about its physical destruction in whole or in part;
(d) Imposing measures intended to prevent births within the group;
(e) Forcibly transferring children of the group to another group.

(b) Cultural Survival and Cultural Identity

If the concept of genocide as defined in the 1951 Convention does not cover the destruction of a people's 'peoplehood', the concept of ethnocide may be appropriate. Again, the claim may be a claim for peoples generally, not just indigenous peoples. The same may be said of such international law recognition as the claim receives under Article 27 of the International Covenant on Civil and Political Rights, which provides that:

In those States in which ethnic, religious or linguistic minorities exist, persons belonging to such minorities shall not be denied the right, in community with the other members of their group, to enjoy their own culture, to profess and practice their own religion, or to use their own language.

In terms, this is a limited right. Like most of the human rights recognized in international law it is focused on individuals, though it is predicated on the group. Does it forbid activity which is not directed against individuals or the group as such but which destroys or damages the essential bases for the continuance of culture, religion, and language? It may well do so for those indigenous peoples whose culture, religion and, possibly, language, are intimately bound up with a continuing relationship with land.

This is certainly the case with regard to traditional Aboriginal communities. It was the basis on which a delegation of the National Aboriginal Conference went to Geneva in 1980 to address the Sub-Commission on Prevention of Discrimination and Protection of Minorities when the Western Australian Government insisted on oil drilling at a sacred site on Aboriginal land at Noonkanbah.[35] It appears to be the case with at least some other indigenous peoples. Weissbrodt, writing about discussions at the Working Group on Indigenous Populations, generalizes:[36]

Indigenous peoples have a unique, spiritual relationship to their land... In general, indigenous peoples have organized their communities so that they hold their land in common, not as individuals. They do not view their land as a commodity, but as an intimate part of their life, culture, personality, religion, self-determination, and governmental structure.

To the extent that this is true, Article 27 would provide some guarantee of indigenous land rights. But it would not avail those communities whose culture and religion are not so intimately involved with the land or whose claims in regard to land proceed on other bases.

Article 27 may thus have a particular utility for some indigenous groups. But it applies in terms to all 'ethnic, religious or linguistic minorities'. Independently of the land-nexus Article 27 has been applied against Canada in a complaint brought by an Indian in the Human Rights Committee.[37]

The mandate of the United Nations Educational, Scientific and Cultural Organization (UNESCO) includes culture. Its procedures permit complaints of violations of human rights in matters of culture. In addition, it has held a series of regional conferences (in Latin America, Europe, in Africa) to consider concepts of 'ethnocide' and 'ethnodevelopment'. These conferences may become steps in the evolution of a more detailed set of international standards for cultural survival and cultural identity. Indicative of these developments is the Declaration of San José of 1981.

(c) Sovereignty

By sovereignty I refer to the claim to recognition as an independent nation state in international law. Some indigenous peoples have regained sov-

---

[35] J. Hagan in G. Nettheim (ed.), *Human Rights for Aboriginal People in the 80s* (Legal Books, Sydney, 1983) 26-9.

[36] Weissbrodt, 13.

[37] *Lovelace* v. *Canada*, UN Doc CCPR/C/DR(XII)/R6/24 (31 July 1983); (1981) 2 *Human Rights LJ* 158. See also Australian Law Reform Commission Report 31, *The Recognition of Aboriginal Customary Laws* (AGPS, Canberra, 1986) ch. 10.

ereignty, after a period of colonial rule or UN Trusteeship. Other indigenous peoples have not achieved this but have simply experienced a
transfer from what they perceive as one colonial master to another. In this
context one might mention the peoples of East Timor and West Papua.
So, even where indigenous people are a majority in a particular territory,
they may not always win through to sovereign independence but may,
instead, be aggregated with a larger neighbour in relation to whose people
they become a minority. It pays to be well away from large neighbours, as
in the South Pacific.

Even in the South Pacific colonialism continues in American and French
territories. The metropolitan powers for these places are thousands of
miles away, across 'blue water', and the international community is able to
discuss the future of the indigenous peoples in terms of a range of options
which include decolonization and self-determination to sovereign independence. Problems may remain, of course, especially if the indigenous
population becomes outnumbered, as in New Caledonia.

It is very different for an indigenous minority where the colonizing
majority in the territory have achieved their own sovereign independence
over a long period of settlement, as in Australia and Canada. In Australia,
at least, some Aboriginal people seek to derive advantage from the lack of
any treaties to argue that they have never conceded sovereignty. The assertion of a continuing Aboriginal sovereignty was treated as unarguable
in the High Court of Australia in *Coe* v. *Commonwealth of Australia*.[38]
There seems to be no way it can be argued in the International Court of
Justice. A slightly stronger claim for decolonization might be advanced by
Torres Strait Islanders, because of the Islands' territorial separation from
the mainland and the absence of substantial European settlement. But for
the majority, if not all, of Australia's indigenous people, the best advice
might be to stop talking in terms of sovereignty and to argue instead for
self-determination.

(d) Self-Determination

It is significant that both the International Covenant on Economic, Social
and Cultural Rights and the International Covenant on Civil and Political
Rights give pride of place to the right of self-determination in an identically
worded Article 1. Self-determination is normally thought to permit a
people a range of options from absorption within another nation, at one end
of the range, to full sovereign independence, at the other. If the sovereignty
option is not, realistically, open to those indigenous populations in 'internal
colonial situations', can one apply the concept of self-determination to such
'peoples' at all? If self-determination necessarily connotes a choice between
independence on the one hand and association with other peoples (in a

[38] (1978) 13 ALR 592; (1979) 24 ALR 118.

variety of possible models) on the other, self-determination cannot be offered to internally colonized peoples without jeopardizing another value of international law, the integrity of existing national boundaries. The representatives of existing nations at the UN undoubtedly place greater weight on the latter value.

Yet 'all peoples' are entitled to self-determination. Are not indigenous peoples 'peoples'? Presumably the Working Group on Indigenous Populations was so called to avoid the use of the term 'peoples'. Similarly the Martinez Cobo study was published under the title Study of the *Problems of Discrimination against Indigenous Populations*.[39] On the other hand, the study was treated as coming under the 'discrimination' wing of the Sub-Commission's mandate, not the 'minorities' wing. So the indigenous 'populations' have not been identified as 'minorities'. These symbols are important, if sometimes ambivalent.

In 1974, the Sub-Commission initiated another study, by Hector Gros Espiell, published in 1980 under the title *The Right to Self-Determination. Implementation of United Nations Resolutions*.[40] Gros Espiell cited not only the formal instruments but a body of General Assembly resolutions, juristic writings and so on, which suggested that the right of self-determination was confined to 'peoples under colonial and alien domination' from an 'external' source. A concern for the preservation of 'territorial integrity' is the countervailing, and prevailing consideration. In the classical colonial context the colonized peoples' right to self-determination permits (if not mandates) the option of secession to sovereign independence. But what nations will run the risk of dismemberment of their own territory?

Gros Espiell's analysis—and the materials on which it is based—have been questioned. Pomerance is critical of the distortion which General Assembly resolutions have imposed on the legal foundations of the right to self-determination in the UN Charter and in the International Covenants. Self-determination, he argues, is a process, not one particular outcome of that process. In so far as the UN has displayed a bias in favour of the independence outcome as the only proper outcome of the process for the classical colonial situation, it has adopted a corollary bias against the process itself in other situations where the independence outcome would be unacceptable.[41]

Yet the UN Charter itself and a number of the General Assembly resolutions clearly contemplate that a people exercising their right to self-determination may choose from—and may even be confined to—a range of possible outcomes other than independence: these include federal arrangements, regional autonomy, and full integration. It would seem to

---

[39] See n. 2.
[40] E/CN.4/Sub 2/405/Rev 1.
[41] M. Pomerance, *Self-Determination in Law and Practice. The New Doctrine in the United Nations* (Martinus Nijhoff, The Hague, 1982).

follow that indigenous 'enclave' peoples may be allowed to claim a right to self-determination only if they renounce independence as one possible outcome. One of the formulas being considered in the current Canadian discussions on Aboriginal self-government is one that speaks of self-government 'within the Canadian federal system'.

Some indigenous peoples will not wish to discard the option of independence. The Iroquois Six Nation Confederacy, for example, still asserts the right of its people to travel on their own passports. Is it possible to locate objective criteria to distinguish which peoples would have the full range of self-determination options and which would not?

Clinebell and Thompson find guidance in Article 1 of the 1933 Montevideo Convention on the Rights and Duties of States, which formulated the following criteria as defining a state for the purposes of international law: a permanent population, a defined territory, an effective government, and the capacity to enter into relations with other States.[42] Accordingly, a people that potentially met these criteria so as to be capable of constituting a State in international law would have a right of self-determination which would include the choice of independence; a people that did not so qualify would still have a right to self-determination but one which would not extend beyond a degree of self-government and autonomy within the nation.

My point is that international law ought to be sufficient in principle to meet the autonomy claims of indigenous peoples. It is the implementation of the law which blocks them. With careful thought it may therefore be possible to devise a concept of self-determination which, while not embracing the possibility of complete independence against the wish of the encompassing national State, does permit as wide a range of other forms of association as the self-determining people might select. After all, the right of self-determination is promised to 'all peoples'. Why should one particular set of peoples—a particular sub-category of indigenous peoples—be denied any of the options that international law permits merely because one of those options may not be available?

It is clear that much work needs to be done on this issue. But here, again, the right of self-determination is not peculiar to indigenous populations. It belongs to 'all peoples'. It is most likely to be asserted by colonized peoples, including indigenous populations.

(e) Self-government

If self-determination options other than sovereign independence were available to indigenous peoples, the options would include the possibility of various forms of self-government. These could, in theory, range over a variety of possibilities—a separate state or province within a federation; a

---

[42] J. H. Clinebell & J. Thomson, 'Sovereignty and Self-Determination: The Rights of Native Americans under International Law' (1978) 27 *Buffalo LR* 669.

self-governing territory; local government in a broad sense; local government in a narrow sense like that of a village council. Canadians are currently giving serious consideration to self-government as the primary current focus for the process of constitutional reform as it relates to aboriginal peoples. But Canada's aboriginal peoples have no single agreed model in mind in discussing 'self-government': proposals have ranged from 'nationhood' down to local school boards, so that any approach would have to be flexible enough to accommodate diverse structures and allocations of policy responsibility.[43]

In Australia these issues are not usually thought of in terms of or discussed in the language of self-government. The Fraser government (1975–83) preferred the phrase 'self-management' though, on the one occasion when it used the term in legislation, it contemplated at least powers of a local government type.[44] And yet governmental authorization has been given, by both Federal and State governments, to a range of forms of Aboriginal self-government. Morse has singled out the following examples of what he perceived as forms of Aboriginal self-government in Australia: land councils in the Northern Territory, South Australia and New South Wales, Queensland's Aboriginal Councils, Island Councils, Aboriginal Industries Board and Island Industries Board; and Western Australia's community councils. He also referred to the Aboriginal Development Commission and the several Aboriginal-controlled organizations for the delivery of legal, medical, and other services.[45]

One question that arises is whether there can be self-government without a land base. Among Morse's Australian examples, the Northern Territory Land Councils do not themselves have a land base, but land—formally held by Aboriginal land trusts—is clearly the basis of their power. The Anangku Pitjantjatjaraku and the NSW Land Councils have land bases. The Aboriginal Development Commission and the Aboriginal-run service delivery organizations—the legal services, medical services, and so on—do not have land bases, though they do have a base on another 'resource', federal funding.

If self-determination is, whether or not avowedly, on the agenda, so is self-government for Aboriginal peoples. For the most part, however, self-government is seen as depending on some degree of control over land.

(f) Land Rights
As noted, a claim for land rights appears to be at the heart of the claims of indigenous peoples on national and international law. In so far as the

---

[43] D. C. Hawkes, *Aboriginal Self-Government: What Does It Mean?* (Discussion Paper, Institute of Intergovernmental Relations, Queen's University, Kingston, l985).

[44] Aboriginal and Torres Strait Islanders (Queensland Reserves and Communities Self-management) Act 1983 (Cth).

[45] B. W. Morse, *Aboriginal Self-Government in Australia and Canada* (Background Paper No 4, Institute of Intergovernmental Relations, Queen's University, Kingston, 1984).

cultural and religious life of such peoples is tied to land, that fact explains and supports the claim as a key to their 'peoplehood'. The claim to land rights also seeks acknowledgement of the priority of the claimant peoples, as prior occupiers and owners. Either way, the claim is particular to indigenous populations. Other groups within a society will not be able to make the same claim. Measures, for example, to make land available to landless peasants or returned soldiers proceed on quite different bases.

The claim of indigenous people to land receives limited international law recognition, as noted, in Article 27 of the International Covenant on Civil and Political Rights. It is directly and expressly endorsed in Article 11 of the 1957 ILO Convention No 107 in these terms:

The right of ownership, collective or individual, of the members of the populations concerned over the lands which these populations traditionally occupy shall be recognized.

If it is not yet a complete 'right' in international law, it is arguable that it is on the way to becoming one.[46]

(g) Control of Land and its Resources

To be permitted merely to reside on land would not meet the aspirations of traditional indigenous peoples. They claim also a number of control powers—over access and over disturbance to the physical or social environment which includes control over the development of the land's natural resources for purposes of mining, tourism, or whatever. As Justice Woodward said in his Second Report:[47]

To deny to Aboriginals the right to prevent mining on their land is to deny the reality of their land rights.

In so far as these claims derive from the basic claim to land they, too, are particular to indigenous peoples. Other peoples within a society can reasonably be expected to abide by whatever general regime that the society's laws attach to land ownership.

However, there is a danger of exaggerating the impact of the claim of indigenous people to control access to their land. The danger arises from the individualistic pattern of land holding accepted in many societies as against the communal nature of indigenous land rights. There is a tendency to treat the power of an indigenous community to control access to their land as different in kind from the power of individuals or corporations to control access to their land. With respect, judges of the High Court of Australia fell into this error in *Gerhardy* v. *Brown*.[48]

[46] E. Lucas, 'Towards an International Declaration on Land Rights' (1984) 33 *ICJ Review* 61.
[47] Aboriginal Land Rights Commission, *Second Report* (Parl Paper No 69, 1974).
[48] (1985) 57 ALR 472.

(h) Compensation

In essence, the land rights claim is a claim for restitution. It presupposes either that indigenous people remain on their traditional lands or that they can be returned to it. For many indigenous people this is not possible, either because the links with the land have been irrevocably lost or because the land has passed to others. For those who cannot require return of traditional lands other forms must be found by way of restitution, reparation, compensation, or (to use Colin Tatz's potent analogy) atonement. The basis for such claim is the same as the basis for the primary land rights claim, and is particular to indigenous people. So, too, is a claim for compensation for the effects of dispossession in the past, even for those people who can regain traditional lands.

Claims to compensation can seek alternative land or money or services. Where indigenous peoples seek government funding they frequently insist that there is a fundamental distinction between their case and that of other groups in a nation that may need assistance: they will argue that their claim is not one of welfare or charity but one of compensation and justice. The claim to compensation, then, appears to be particular to indigenous peoples and to derive directly from the same basis as the claim to land rights.

(i) Non-Discrimination

By contrast, claims to non-discrimination, equality under the law and equal protection of the law are not particular to indigenous peoples but extend to members of all groups who, as such, may encounter negative discrimination in a society. The claim has recognition in international law as, perhaps, the primary human right. It is the one matter, apart from self-determination, on which references to human rights in the United Nations Charter are specific—Articles 1(3), 13(b), and 55(c) all speak against 'distinction as to race, sex, language or religion' in regard to human rights and fundamental freedoms.

The principle is developed further in Article 2 of the Universal Declaration of Human Rights, Article 2(2) of the International Covenant on Economic, Social and Cultural Rights, Article 2(1) of the International Covenant on Civil and Political Rights, and in a number of other international human rights instruments. Perhaps the most notable of these other instruments dealing specifically with discrimination is the International Convention on the Elimination of All Forms of Racial Discrimination.

So strong has the principle of non-discrimination become that some have suggested that it is now a principle of customary international law. Stephen J was favourably disposed to this view in *Koowarta* v. *Bjelke-Petersen*.[49] In this case the High Court of Australia affirmed the validity of the relevant

---

[49] (1982) 39 ALR 417, 455-6. See also Mason J, id., 467-8.

sections (ss 9 and 12) of the Racial Discrimination Act 1975 (Cth), enacted to implement Australia's obligations under the International Convention on the Elimination of All Forms of Racial Discrimination. It is significant that validity was upheld (by majority) on the basis of Constitution s 51(29), the 'external affairs' power, rather than s 51(26), the power to pass laws with respect to 'the people of any race for whom it is deemed necessary to make special laws'. Section 51(26) was treated by most of the judges as inapplicable because the Racial Discrimination Act was a law with respect to the people of *all* races, not for any race or races for whom special laws were deemed necessary.

So the non-discrimination principle in national and international law is not particular to indigenous peoples. None the less, indigenous peoples may well be major beneficiaries of the principle. Experience during the first years of the operation of the Racial Discrimination Act 1975 (Cth) indicated that a disproportionate share of complaints—about 36 per cent—came from Aboriginals, even though Aboriginals constitute little more than 1 per cent of the population.[50]

(j) Affirmative Action

This is the obverse of negative discrimination—a claim that circumstances require positive discrimination in favour of a people in order to bring them into a position of approximate equality with other peoples in a society.

ILO Convention 107 requires governments to take measure for enabling indigenous and tribal populations to benefit on an equal footing from the rights and opportunities which other elements of the population enjoy, and for promoting their development and raising their standard of living. Article 3 goes on to provide that:

(1) So long as the social, economic, and cultural conditions of the populations concerned prevent them from enjoying the benefits of the general laws of the country to which they belong, special measures shall be adopted for the protection of the institutions, property, and labour of these populations.
(2) Care shall be taken to ensure that such special measures of protection -
  (a) are not used as a means of creating or prolonging a state of segregation; and
  (b) will be continued only so long as there is need for special protection and only to the extent that such protection is necessary.
(3) Enjoyment of the general rights of citizenship, without discrimination, shall not be prejudiced in any way by such special measures of protection.

The International Convention on the Elimination of All Forms of Racial Discrimination, Article 1(4), also permits affirmative action for groups, indigenous or other, whose socio-economic situation may warrant it. Article 2(2) of the Convention goes on, in effect, to require governments to take such measures when circumstances so warrant.

[50] Commissioner of Community Relations, *Fifth Annual Report, 1970-80* (AGPS, Canberra, 1980) 1.

The Racial Discrimination Act 1975 (Cth) s 8(1) excludes the operation of the Act in respect of measures that fall within the terms of Article 1(4). It was on this basis that the High Court of Australia decided in *Gerhardy v. Brown*[51] that s 19 of the Pitjantjatjara Land Rights Act 1981 (SA), which makes it an offence for non-Pitjantjatjaras to be on Pitjantjatjara land without a permit, was not invalid for inconsistency with the Racial Discrimination Act—it was held to be a 'special measure' within Article 1(4).

Like the right of non-discrimination, the right to affirmative action is not particular to indigenous peoples.

4. Conclusion

The conclusion that seems to emerge from this analysis is that many of the claims being pressed on national and international legal systems by indigenous peoples are claims that are also pressed on behalf of peoples generally, or particular classes of peoples, and are not specific to indigenous peoples. Nearly all those claims have recognition in international instruments, in whole or in part.

Of course, the needs of indigenous peoples may be more urgent than the needs of other groups. In many nations, the indigenous people tend to be the most disadvantaged in terms of the major social and economic indicators. This is certainly the case in Australia and Canada. In Australia it is often stated that the reason for this lies in the denial of those claims that are particular to indigenous peoples, namely, those claims that derive from dispossession of their lands and consequent destruction of their culture and way of life.

It is this set of claims that distinguishes indigenous peoples from other peoples. For the indigenous peoples of Australia, Canada, Latin America, and elsewhere it is the issue. Acknowledgement of the claim, recognition, or restoration of ownership, where possible, or compensation (in land, services, or money) where it is not, substantial control over access to the land and uses made of it, combined with other forms of self-government as the people 'self-determine', may provide a basis for physical survival and a revival of cultural pride that will, in time, diminish the need for affirmative action and reduce the bases for negative discrimination.

But is the acknowledgment and recognition of the land rights of indigenous people merely one particular means of bringing them to a position of social and economic equality within a broader society so as to achieve their assimilation within that society? The one international instrument that directly endorses land rights, ILO Convention 107, does so in precisely that context of the 'progressive integration' of indigenous populations into

---

[51] (1985) 57 ALR 472.

the life of the nation. It is precisely for that reason that indigenous peoples no longer support the 1957 Convention. Indigenous peoples' organizations today are claiming not just short-term special measures to allow them to integrate; they are claiming long-term differential status as a distinct peoples, with their own base on land or other resources, and the ultimate right of self-determination of their political destiny. The substantial degree of acceptance of such claims within the national legal systems of Canada and (although to a lesser extent) Australia has been a revolutionary development of very recent origin. The international legal system is only now beginning to come to terms with it.

Land rights legislation like the Pitjantjatjara Land Rights Act 1981 (SA) recognizes the claims of Pitjantjatjara people to be a distinct people and to continue to be a distinct people within Australia for as long as they see fit. By contrast, existing human rights instruments such as the International Convention on the Elimination of All Forms of Racial Discrimination seem to perceive human rights primarily in terms of individuals enjoying equal status within a nation. Differentiation of groups is permissible only in the case of 'special measures' of limited duration designed solely to assist the integration of individual members of those groups within the national society. In *Gerhardy* v. *Brown* the Pitjantjatjara Land Rights Act was in contest with the Racial Discrimination Act 1975 (Cth), based on the Racial Discrimination Convention. The result in the High Court was the right one, but there are problems in the basis for the decision. The Pitjantjatjara Land Rights Act was saved from invalidation only as a 'special measure' within Article 1(4) of the Convention via s 8(1) of the Racial Discrimination Act. But there is much to be said for the view of Millhouse J in the South Australian Supreme Court in rejecting that argument, namely, that the Land Rights Act was not designed as a short-term measure for the purposes of assimilation but as acknowledgment of the claims of the Pitjantjatjaras to long-term differential status as a distinct people within the nation.

Some national legal systems such as those of Australia and Canada have begun to come to terms with the notion that a 'people' may have rights as distinct from the rights of individuals and the rights of the total community. International instruments listed give some recognition to the rights of peoples but it has yet to come to grips with the special claims of indigenous populations. It is, perhaps, now in the process of doing so.

8

Human Rights, Peoples' Rights

EUGENE KAMENKA

RIGHTS are claims that have achieved a special kind of endorsement or success: legal rights by a legal system; human rights by widespread sentiment or an international order. All rights arise in specific historical circumstances. They are claims made, conceded or granted by people who are themselves historically and socially shaped. They are asserted by people on their own behalf or as perceived and endorsed implications of specific historical traditions, institutions and arrangements or of a historically conditioned theory of human needs and human aspirations, or of a human conception of a Divine plan and purpose. In objective fact as opposed to (some) subjective feeling, they are neither eternal nor inalienable, neither prior to society or societies nor independent of them. Some such rights can be singled out, and they often are singled out, as social ideals, as goals to strive toward. But even as such, they cannot be divorced from social content and context.

Claims presented as rights are claims that are often, perhaps usually, presented as having a special kind of importance, urgency, universality, or endorsement that makes them more than disparate or simply subjective demands. Their success is dependent on such endorsement—by a government or a legal system that has power to grant and protect such rights, by a tradition or institution whose authority is accepted in those circles that recognize these claims as rights, by widespread social sentiment, regionally, nationally, or internationally.

Claims, whether presented as rights or not, conflict. So do the traditions, institutions and authorities that endorse the claim as a right. They conflict both with each other and, often, in their internal structure, implications and working out. It is a feature of rights propaganda, for this very reason, to emphasize and elevate one right at a time or seriatim, but not to examine their relationship to each other too closely. Bringing rights claims in relation with each other at the practical level is the distinctive and central task of law, a task the importance of which is matched only by its complexity. It is a task that requires attention to the plurality of interests and of endorsed rights found in any society and in any situation of conflict. It requires care in gauging the practical effect and social and moral impact of decisions, not only on the parties directly involved. It requires dedication to the rational and impartial examination of problems and the learning and awareness that come only from considering systematized experience over time and over a wide range of social situations and demands. Justice consists not in the strident proclamation of rights, but in considering carefully how to give every man, woman, and child his or her due. Whatever the professional deformations of the lawyer, those of the moral philosopher, the politician and the demagogue are in this respect infinitely greater. When the lawyer, or anyone else, out of shallow moral and political engagement, political careerism or a simple desire to be loved, consistently abandons his or her expertise for the crudity and the demagoguery of less intellectual life, the social consequences can be disastrous.

The concept of human rights is no longer tied to belief in God or natural law in its classical sense. But it still seeks or claims a form of endorsement that transcends or pretends to transcend specific historical institutions and traditions, legal systems, governments, or national and even regional communities. Like moral claims more generally, it asserts in its own behalf moral and sometimes even logical priority—connection with the very concept (treated as morally loaded) of what it means to be a human being or a person, or of what it means to behave morally. These are questions on which moral philosophers do have a certain expertise, at least in seeing where the difficulties lie, and on which they, like ordinary people throughout the world, have long disagreed and continue to disagree.

For the international lawyer, however, and increasingly for the lawyer in general, human rights are no longer simply moral or political claims, statements of the law that ought to be which have no base as such in the law that is. From a prehistory in certain (famous) national constitutions and bills of rights, they have entered by way of international declarations, covenants and agreements into the growing body of formal international law associated with the formation of an international community through the League of Nations and the United Nations. From such international law, they have returned, in expanded and revised form, into some municipal laws, entered others they have not entered before, and informed the law and judicial practice of some regional associations, most notably that of the European Communities. The impact, at least in democratic countries, of the United Nations' proclamations, campaigns, and procedures for the promotion of human rights has been remarkable and is coming to be well-known. That impact has converted in some countries, but not in others, claims for human rights into legally recognized or at least justiciable claims as opposed to moral exhortations.

The eighteenth century, in Europe and America, drew to its close as the century that had clearly and unequivocally proclaimed the inalienable and imprescriptible rights of man. The proclamations were not, in any years except 1792–3, the creatures of Gallic enthusiasm, of a revolutionary category of reason run riot in human affairs. They were the product of sober

English philosophies, English puritanism, and nonconformity, 'respectable' English resistance to absolutism and concern for freedom and toleration. They drew above all on the philosophy of John Locke and the traditions of the Glorious Revolution of 1688, with its Act of Settlement and its compromise, non-individual, Bill of Rights, but with its muted undertones of the great trial of Charles I in 1649. That trial may have had the most dubious standing legally; the king for once may have confronted his accusers with dignity and much logic on his side. But the trial, as the regicides said later, was not 'a thing done in a corner', not an assassination or a summary execution. It was a bungled, illegal, but breathtakingly daring trial of a king as king, for failing in his duties to his subjects, for committing treason against a new implicit but not yet fully recognized sovereign, the people. Its implications were world-shaking. They came to fruition a hundred and thirty years later, in the declaration dated 12 June 1776, made by the good people of Virginia assembled in full and free Convention. The unanimous declaration of the thirteen United States of America made on 4 July 1776, elevated the same sentiments—that all men are created equal and endowed with 'unalienable Rights', including life, liberty, and the pursuit of happiness.

Fifteen years later, after the great revolution in France, the French National Assembly promulgated, as a document prefixed to the constitution, its Declaration of the Rights of Man and of Citizens a declaration firmly rooted, in language and in sentiment, in the American declarations and the political and philosophical tradition that shaped them, except for its (Rousseauist but half-hearted) elevation of the nation beside the individual. By 24 June 1793, in a new declaration, the French had proclaimed that the goal of society is the common happiness and that government is established to guarantee to man the enjoyment of his natural and imprescriptible rights, which are those of equality, liberty, security, and property.

In these declarations lies the whole philosophy of liberal democracy, in whose name most of the political struggles of the nineteenth century and many of the twentieth were to be fought. It had, and has, its critics. The guarantee of political rights and political equality contained in this constitution, the young Marx commented scathingly, was accompanied by and promoted the guarantee of the economic rights of property and the social inequality which they necessarily produced. Behind the republic of the market lay the despotism of the factory; behind political equality lay social inequality.

The eighteenth century invented the idea of happiness, in which the concept of natural rights as political rights was deeply grounded. It also invented the idea of revolution, an idea that was to dominate much of Europe in the nineteenth century and all of the world in the twentieth. The slogan 'Liberty, Equality, Fraternity' could be read politically, but it could

also be read socially, as calling for an economic, social, and cultural re-
construction of society that went far beyond the political claims of the
American revolutionists. The history of the doctrine of natural rights from
the eighteenth century onwards, with the shift to a doctrine of human
rights and of economic, social, and cultural rights, can be seen as the
story of the increasing concretization of rights, of an overcoming of their
abstractness, or as a movement from concentration on the problem of
liberty to that of equality. It is at least partly the story of new and different
concerns, of battles with different enemies, of demands that have quite new
implications. The demand for rights in the seventeenth and eighteenth
centuries was a demand against the existing State and authorities, against
despotism, arbitrariness and the political disfranchisement of those who
held different opinions. The demand for rights in the nineteenth and twentieth centuries becomes increasingly a claim upon the State, a demand that
it provide and guarantee the means for achieving the individual's happiness
and well-being, his welfare. These two different conceptions of rights, like
the opposed conceptions of 'freedom from' and 'freedom to', stand in
constant danger of fundamental conflict with each other—a conflict that
dominates the modern world.

Let us focus first on the positive aspects of human rights, not on the
stridency and abstraction with which they are often proclaimed and supported or the frequent lack of care with which they are drafted or discussed.
Behind these rights lies a proper concern for human autonomy and development. Perhaps the central and fundamental concept elevated by the
Enlightenment and the French Revolution was that of self-determination,
both for individuals and for a people or nation. The working out of that
principle gave birth to all the important modern ideologies—liberalism,
democracy, socialism, nationalism and, as an offshoot, anti-colonialism.
From Europe and North and South America, it spread to the Middle East,
Asia, Africa, and even the Pacific. It brought the whole world into relation
with European developments and ideologies, creating for the first time a
world history that can no longer sensibly be split into separate components.
It made possible an international law that aims to be more than the custom
and practices of what used to be known as 'civilized' nations. The most
positive feature of those developments, largely facilitated by technological
achievements and a rising standard of living in certain fortunate countries
that still lead the world in moral sensitivity, is the breaking down of social
and geographical distance, the extension of what the philosopher David
Hume called 'sympathy', the spontaneous feeling and recognition that
other people are ourselves once more. That feeling, Hume rightly emphasized, grew weaker in proportion to distance in time or space and
dissimilarity in appearance, behaviour, and custom. We find it easier to
feel 'sympathy' for people, or even non-human creatures, more like ourselves, than for the totally alien. Dogs engage our sympathies in a way ants

do not. This capacity for 'sympathy' has perhaps been strengthened more by those developments that are often characterized as the creation of a universal Coca-Cola culture than by League of Nations or United Nations proclamations. It has always been dramatically advanced by publicity for glaring and often uncharacteristic abuses of people—whether as slaves, prisoners, blacks, or servants. The human capacity for sympathy, fragile as it may be, is real. It has been historically active and in the end it is all that stands between us and barbarism.

Be that as it may, there is no doubt that we have learnt, in little more than a century, to count—for the first time—the lower classes, servants, Asians and Africans, convicts and indigenous peoples as fully human, as ourselves once more. We do so more easily when we are not deprived or frightened ourselves.

The sympathy that European societies began in the nineteenth century to extend to slaves, workers, servants, and people of other races, they also extended to another claim for self-determination, that of peoples or nations, even if they did so, especially in the case of other races, fitfully, more at some times and in certain social groups or political parties than in others. Nevertheless, the Russian philosopher Vladimir Solovyev, who rejected sharply the fanatical concern with one's own nation at the expense of others, captured a widespread and growing nineteenth-century liberal European sentiment when he wrote in his book *The Justification of the Good. An Essay in Moral Philosophy* (in Russian, St Petersburg, 1897):

Let it be granted that the immediate object of the moral relation is the individual person. But one of the essential peculiarities of that person—the direct continuation and expansion of his individual character—is his nationality (in the positive sense of character, type and creative power). This is not merely a physical, but also a psychological and moral fact. At the stage of development that humanity has now reached, the fact of belonging to a given nationality is to a certain extent confirmed by the individual's self-conscious will. Thus nationality is an inner, inseparable property of the person—something very dear and close to him. It is impossible to stand in a moral relation to this person without recognizing the existence of what is so important to him. The moral principle does not allow us to transform a concrete person, a living man with his inseparable and essential national char-acteristics, into an empty abstract subject with all his determining peculiarities left out. If we are to recognize the inner dignity of the particular man, this obligation extends to all positive characteristics with which he connects his dignity; if we love a man we must love his nation, which he loves and from which he does not separate himself.

I have written extensively about nationalism elsewhere. Its rise as po-litical nationalism and much of its career as cultural nationalism is con-nected with the changeover from subject to citizen and the consequent need for defining and unifying the new sovereign, the people. It is also connected, as the late John Plamenatz stressed,[1] with feelings of cultural insecurity and even inferiority—when these connections are strong, as they were in Eastern Europe, Germany, much of Asia and Africa, nationalism tends to become especially illiberal. Nationalism has also a close early connection with Romanticism, with the elevation of the past, of the primitive, the spontaneous, of feeling over reason, of blood, soil, and language over administrative arrangements and political ties. This, too, carries more danger than promise, as the world learnt in a horrifying way only fifty years ago. Generally speaking, we may say that much nationalism in Europe in the half century before the revolutions of 1848, and as represented by such figures as Jules Michelet and Guiseppe Mazzini, stood for human liberty, democracy, and progress, for elevating ordinary people, attaching the nationalist message to such universal and universalizable principles as liberty, democracy, self-determination, and also social or economic justice. It welcomed, as morally and socially valuable, the plurality of nations, customs, and languages in the world; it did not seek to elevate any particular nation as a master race or as the repository of all that is right and just. Of course, even then nationalists in the heat of struggle developed less pleasant characteristics—hatred or contempt not only for foreign rulers but for nations and peoples seen as threatening, a gradual conviction in the special mission and general superiority of their own nation, etc. But it was only in the second half of the nineteenth century, especially among nations that had achieved their independence, that this dark side of nationalism became primarily the cult of blood and soil, race and place, that it became anti-democratic, chauvinist and self-glorifying. Is what happened in Europe in the nineteenth century happening in many non-European countries today?

Socialists of a sincere and democratic kind have long been aware of this problem and have always had ambivalent feelings about nationalism or tribalism as an ideology, distinguishing progressive nationalism from reactionary nationalism, the nationalism of emergent nations or peoples seeking only the right to self-determination from the nationalism of secure and established peoples whose nationalism can only be directed against other countries and against the stranger in their midst. Perhaps we can make and accept this distinction by drawing a sharp line, at least in principle, between nationalism as an end and nationalism as a means. The former militates directly and viciously against the principal moral values that I hold dear above all lists and proclamations of abstract rights—the recognition of all people as individuals, as equally human, as ourselves once more. There may be different experiences and customs; I do not believe that there are different national or racial minds, fundamental needs or potentialities. The differences between members of any one nation in values, attitudes, and

---

1 J. Plamenatz, 'Two Types of Nationalism' in E. Kamenka (ed.), *Nationalism: The Nature and Evolution of an Idea* (London, 1976) 22.

capacities are as great as those between one nation or race and another. In short, what we know to be true biologically is also true culturally. Nations and peoples, like genetic populations, are recent, contingent and have been formed and reformed constantly throughout history. They do not form a natural kind.

Peoples, in other words, are above all people, members of the human race. As such, they are entitled to dignity, respect, and the recognition that they are fully members of the human race. They are not entitled to immunity from outside or internal criticism of their dominant customs, practices and traditions in so far as these are themselves destructive of respect for persons, of moral compassion and of the recognition of the moral equality of all people and the destructive character of pain, suffering, and deprivation as regular features of social life. They do not have a moral right, in the name of collective self-determination, to deal as they wish with their own people, any more than we now believe that governments and nation States have such a moral right. The rights of peoples can become rights against one's own people. They regularly do. They should not. The fact that a people has no right to immunity from moral criticism made from outside is not a general licence for the moral officiousness we have so frequently practised in relation to alien peoples and to social inferiors in the past. There is a difference between making moral judgements and moralising. Part of the difference is that the moralizer fails to consider the possibility that he or she may be wrong, may know too little, lack sensitivity to another person's position or situation, or fail to grasp the point of different customs and arrangements and the consequences of simply setting them aside. In other words, our attitudes to peoples need to be the same as our attitudes to people and to human rights—principled in moral outlook but recognizing complexity and conflicts between values, avoiding strident and abstract moralism. In that respect, human rights and peoples' rights, like the concept of self-determination that underlies them, pose the same problems, problems that call for discussion and sensitivity rather than propaganda and moralism, not to speak of demagoguery.

Individuals are defined for us, physically at least, by the independent singularity of their bodies in a way that foetuses are not, which is why the concept of the rights of a foetus raises immediate initial problems that do not arise over the rights of a person. Peoples are more like foetuses than like persons. *Sub specie aeternitatis*, and even over a span of centuries, they are formed, dissolved, reformed with remarkable rapidity. In the struggle against Holland at the beginning of the nineteenth century, Flemings and Walloons saw themselves as one nation, the Belgians. Today, many Flemings and some Walloons are convinced they are two peoples. The Berbers and Arabs of Algeria, in their struggle against the French, suddenly became one nation, the Muslims of Algeria. There are no nation states that I know of that have not been put together by political force and cultural pressure from what were initially distinct cultural and national groups. Transitional periods must have been painful and conflict-ridden; the final outcome, more often than not, was not only immediately non-reversible but in important respects represented, for the individuals involved, a gain in material welfare, intellectual capacities, social, and political opportunities, and the development of wider cultural horizons. It is not obvious to me that the Channel Islands, or the Hebrides, would be better off if they had become independent in the course of their history, nor, I think, is it obvious to them. Here again, there are no abstract princples to fall back on. We have to consider the total situation of a people or region, and the character of the wider society that seeks to incorporate them. On two points, however, we can have general principles, not always, or even often, observed in the past. One is the importance to human beings of a sense of identity, given them not so much by material improvement, but by customs and traditions, by historical identifications, by religion. That sense of identity can be and constantly is altered, given new content and attachments. But it is not something to be ridden over roughshod or to be dismissed as immaterial. It is, for most people, essential to their dignity and self-confidence, values that underlie, in part, the concept of human rights itself. The second point is that pluralism, variety, is itself a good, and especially so at both the cultural and the political level. Language and skills may atrophy, so may literatures and traditions. To destroy them deliberately for no reason but the desire for uniformity and political control is exactly like smashing works of art. It is a habit common to religions and to the more fanatical of political creeds and it is easily done through economic pressure and rationalization, even more so in socialist countries than in non-socialist ones. But to define abstractly, as part of moral philosophy or of the protection of human rights, what constitutes a people, without reference to nation states or to complex social and historical particularities that cannot be turned into general abstract criteria, seems to me to be preposterous.

In all the preceding, I will not have been telling any competent lawyer anything he or she does not know—though much of the United Nations' norm-creating activity and much writing on and in international law depend upon deliberately obscuring such difficulties and pretending there is consensus and coherence where there is conflict, unspoken but crucial reservation, mere lip-service and internal contradiction and ambiguity. One professional but nevertheless questionable tendency for the international lawyer is to by-pass questions about the foundation of rights altogether—to insist that covenants and conventions of the United Nations, and perhaps even its Charter, and General Assembly resolutions and declarations that attract overwhelming support, constitute rules and norms of international law. For the international lawyer—the argument runs—they are given; his task is to interpret them, not challenge them. The reservation I have here is not the product of a crude demand that lawyers criticize positive law instead of seeking only to apply it, or to understand its ramifications, as coherently as possible. I have little time for the more trendy law schools that elevate such a 'critical' approach to municipal or international law into a principle that saves students the trouble of working or thinking about existing law and its traditions. My disquiet, rather, is about the insecurity of some international lawyers, about their desperate desire and need to make international law respectable and to show that in such crucial areas as human rights it is more than a set of pious platitudes or cynical compromises whole-heartedly supported by no one. The United Nations is no doubt all we have, but the vast majority of its member nations are neither honest nor respectable. That point must not be glossed over in the interests of elevating and promoting international agreement and the respectability of international law at any cost.

Lawyers, I am delighted to say, nevertheless remain lawyers, displaying attitudes, virtues, and skills that can and do make up for many a deficiency of character, that enable them to transcend themselves. The propaganda based on the United Nations' Universal Declaration and Covenants, and concern with human rights and with the rights of peoples, especially when carried out by politicians, human rights commissions, and United Nations and human rights support groups, is infinitely cruder, more dishonest, and less conducive to moral and intellectual responsibility than the actual legal documents or the pronouncements and interpretations of lawyers who work with them. One of the greatest dangers of our municipal concern for human rights and rights of peoples is and will continue to be the by-passing of proper judicial procedures and techniques, the giving of power to the shallowly committed, to those who make a career out of human rights, and to those considered suitable because they have an overwhelming concern with particular grievances or claims not balanced by the habit of considering other rights and claims.

There are certain developments in international law that distinguish the attitudes and documents of the United Nations from those of the League of Nations. The notion that rights under international law can be vested in groups of individuals or in individuals as such and not only in States is a major one—though it is insufficiently emphasized to a wider public in Western democracies that all Communist-governed countries accept this innovation only to the most limited extent, even in theory, and that most United Nations members do not and will not accept it in respect of any individuals or groups within their own territories. Something like agreement on the rights of (some) peoples and on the rights of self-determination (for some) has been reached in the United Nations only by interpreting self-determination not to mean democratic government, but merely the rejection of formal colonial rule and (Western) economic imperialism or neo-colonialism. In the rhetoric of the General Assembly, all this has become identified with racism and Western European domination; economic, military, and political hegemony on the part of socialist, African, or Asian states is passed over in silence. An eminent international lawyer, Antonio Cassese, has summarized the totally different conceptions of self-determination and the rights of peoples represented in the United Nations. He writes:[2]

Socialist countries understand self-determination essentially as the liberation of non-self-governing peoples from colonial domination. They have broadened the concept—under pressure from African and Arab countries—to include liberation from racist domination (South Africa and Southern Rhodesia) and from foreign occupation (Arab territories occupied by Israel). Moreover, with the support of Afro-Asian countries (which are worried lest the collapse of colonialism should involve the breaking up of colonial territories), the socialist countries deny that self-determination can legitimate secessions. Thus, to socialist countries, self-determination means only 'external' self-determination and only for peoples subject to colonial or racist rule or to foreign occupation. The achievement of independent status by peoples living in non-racist sovereign States entails the implementation of self-determination. This applies in particular to socialist States: 'only in socialist States and through the sovereignty achieved by them can self-determination be completely realized'. Ultimately, for sovereign and independent States self-determination becomes tantamount to the right to non-intervention. This point is very important and deserves to be particularly stressed. According to socialist countries, self-determination, considered as the right to non-intervention, means the right that foreign States shall not interfere in the life of the community against the will of the government. It does not include the right that a foreign State shall not interfere in the life of the community against the interests of the population but at the request or at any rate with the tacit approval of the government. Western countries have, on many occasions, attacked this outlook for being too restrictive and one-sided. They maintain that the right of peoples oppressed by totalitarian regimes must be recognized and that in any case self-determination must include respect for fundamental freedoms and the basic rights of individuals. The close link between self-determination and individual human rights is one of the main features of the Western doctrine. As was stated in 1972 by the US delegate to the Third Committee of the General Assembly, 'freedom of choice is indispensable to the exercise of the right of self-determination. For this freedom of choice to be meaningful, there must be corresponding freedom of thought, conscience, expression, movement and association. Self-determination entails legitimate, lively dissent and testing at the ballot box with frequent regularity.

A second distinguishing trait of the Western view, according to Professor Cassese, is its emphasis on the universality of self-determination. For Western States the principle of self-determination must be regarded as applying to all peoples, not just to certain specific categories of peoples, those suffering from 'racism' or 'imperialism', where any non-European, non-Western

---

[2] A. Cassese, 'Political Self-Determination—Old Concepts and New Developments' in A. Cassese (ed.), *UN Law/Fundamental Rights: Two Topics in International Law* (Alphen aan den Rijn, 1979) 154-5.

State is automatically and wrongly taken to be incapable of either. The question of indigenous peoples, for example, is certainly treated more sympathetically by prosperous Western States than by Afro-Asian, Islamic or Marxist-Leninist blocs, though no country is fully at ease with the problems involved in recognizing them as nations within a nation, peoples within a people.

The literature on human rights is voluminous and presents us with no sign of general agreement on their nature, their definition or their source, or on the basic moral principle or justification on which they rest. The lists of human rights contained in the Universal Declaration of Human Rights and in the Covenants on Civil and Political, and Economic, Social and Cultural Rights are widely recognized, by philosophers at least, as being conceptually disparate and muddled, containing rhetoric and crucially important conflicts with each other. The rights elevated in the Declaration are the most coherent—but their coherence derives from their close connection with European liberalism and democratic traditions, and they are in fact being safeguarded to a reasonable degree only in countries that have that tradition. Even so, they cannot be and are not presented as uniformly absolute; various escape clauses recognize that they have to be considered in a concrete social context. The social climate and demands furthered by many of their supporters, in Australia as in other democracies, are often destructive of many of these rights and shamelessly selective and biased in elevating some of them and not others. We do not hear much today of the primacy that the Universal Declaration ascribes to the family, or of the UN-endorsed right of parents to choose the kind of education (which includes moral education) they would like their children to have. The right of property guaranteed in the Declaration—and in respect of personal property such guarantee is part of the constitutions of all Communist countries—was simply dropped from the Covenant on Civil and Political Rights; it has not been heard of again. Of direct interest and concern to the philosopher is the failure of the UN documents to distinguish absolute rights ascribed to human beings as a direct consequence of their being simply human (e.g. not to be tortured), and rights ascribed to them in virtue of their entering into specific relationships (e.g. as employees entitled to certain labour conditions etc.), and rights dependent on their capacities or those of the society (e.g. pensions and education). The documents fail to distinguish between rights that are immunities, imposing clear duties of non-interference on all others, and not normally dependent on general social conditions and variations, and rights that are claims to benefits, which are both dependent on social conditions and variations and which, unlike immunities, do not impose duties on a clearly defined addressee. Nor have the proponents of the UN Covenants, as opposed to their critics, been willing to consider seriously the sharp and fundamental clash between civil and political rights, that limit the power of the State, and social, economic, and cultural rights that positively demand ever-increasing State organization of society. The only constitutions I know that successfully but brutally resolve these serious conflicts in the theory of rights are the Communist constitutions which provide, on the model of the constitution and legal codes of the USSR, that all rights granted by the constitution or in the codes shall be exercised only in conformity with the social, economic, and political system of the country and the purposes of building socialism. The United Nations, indeed, and the organizations concerned to promote it, might have been expected to be an arena for discussion, an intellectual battleground, between the very different approaches to human rights and conceptions of their role in social and political life that mark off democratic societies from non-democratic ones. There is no serious engagement between these views in the United Nations or its propaganda organs because democratic representatives there have simply shirked real battle, honestly admitting their shortcomings and exercising restraint in drawing attention to the dishonesty and cynicism of the vast majority of signatories of the Declaration and Covenants and the shameless selectivity they exercise in criticizing other countries. At no UNESCO-organized discussion that I have attended, valuable as they have been in some ways, has the final protocol been discussed properly by the participants or fairly represented the extent of disagreement during the discussions.

The fundamental complexity and danger of incoherence in the elevation and protection from criticism of certain abstract and allegedly fundamental human rights which in fact cover a wide range of social life parallels closely the emergence of the same problems in the history of religion as a doctrine seeking social primacy, authority, and protection. There is the same ready slide from a concept of education to a concept of indoctrination; the same readiness to use means that in fact violate and undermine the moral and intellectual ends being proclaimed; the same attempt to deny rights proclaimed for all to those who are critical of such rights, either openly or by manipulation. Above all, the elevation of indoctrination over education, of results over principles, and the attempt to gloss over incoherence, result in a consistent and deliberate shift of attention to the malleable and impressionable as constituting the most rewarding field of activity. Human rights kits for schools replace serious discussions of human rights and their complexities among adults; UNESCO is not alone in failing to devote sufficient attention to widespread adult discussion of the values, concrete rights, and principles and procedures advocated by the United Nations.

To say all this is not to decry or oppose the values and attitudes to human beings that underlie, in a general way, new trends in international law, the Declaration on Human Rights and most of the proclaimed ideals, as opposed to the practices, of the United Nations and UNESCO. It is to bring out, rather, that conceptions of human rights have value only as exemplifications of more general moral principles and ideals—care and compassion in dealing with other human beings, their dignity and their interests, respect for persons as persons, recognition of the destructive qualities of pain, suffering, and deprivation, a concern for individuality, autonomy, and the development of a person's fruitful potentialities. There are, throughout the world, and there always have been, individual and institutionalized or politicized assaults on these values and principles of the most blatant kind that arouse and indeed demand outrage. Some societies and nations are blatantly worse than others in this regard, and no human or moral value is served by ignoring that point in the interests of a phoney international amity extended beyond the avoidance of physical conflict to the avoidance of moral and intellectual conflict. But a moral system, like a legal system, if it deserves the name, recognises a multiplicity of values and the need to take account of consequences, of inevitable if unintended effects of action, and thus to strike further balances between the good and evil that an action, moral in intent when taken in isolation, may produce. The abstract proclamation of rights, especially if extended over many areas of social life, ignores and militates against this recognition of the complexity of social life, of the need to balance interests and consider consequences. In our own society, it increasingly encourages moral and social insensitivity, a strident self-importance on one's own behalf or on behalf of others who do not need to be consulted, but only protected or spoken for, the elevation of one social problem at the expense of others, and an increasing banishment of serious and complex discussion from politics and social life. Bandwagons—and human rights is becoming a particularly noisy one—provide no space to think in.

The problem, then, is not simply whether the so-called third generation of human rights, the 'rights of peoples', is deducible from or compatible with the first and second generation—with civil and political rights or social, economic, and cultural rights. In strict logic, it conflicts as much with them as they do with each other, though the UN approach to the third generation is even more frankly politicized and opportunist. The point is to recognize any claim made for this third-generation of rights as valid only in so far as it extends, rather than destroys, first generation rights, i.e. the autonomy of individuals and their civil and political liberties. To say this is to insist that second and third generation rights are to be read through, understood in terms of, first-generation rights. For the point is to treat all rights, human or not, as involving balance, care and complexity—an approach that is elevated by law and decried by the strident moralist and all those who come to law, as they often come to the United Nations, only to claim that their needs and rights are more urgent, more important, than anybody else's. The current suspicion of detachment, the elevation beyond what is proper of those affected to be judges of their own cause, on the grounds that they feel it most, compounds the problem.

9

The Rights of 'Peoples' and Individual Rights: Conflict or Harmony?

GILLIAN TRIGGS

The individual whose human rights and fundamental freedoms the United Nations seeks to proclaim and defend is man in his national, cultural, and spiritual environment. Stripped of his environmental, national, and cultural characteristics, spiritually adrift from his past and loosed from his traditional moorings, man loses his essential humanity.[1]

1. Introduction

In 1966 the United Nations General Assembly was unable to agree to include civil and political rights in the same document as economic, social, and cultural rights. The resulting human rights instruments, the International Covenant on Civil and Political Rights (ICCPR) and the International Covenant on Economic, Social and Cultural Rights (ICESR), were each formulated, in the main, in terms of individual rights. At least some civil and political rights now command respect as rights in customary international law, whereas it is doubtful that economic, social, and cultural rights are more than political aspirations. For this reason, among others, attempts have been made, within UNESCO and elsewhere, not only to emphasize fundamental economic, social, and cultural rights but also to reformulate certain individual rights as collective rights or rights of 'peoples'. International law presently affords limited protection to 'peoples': the right to self-determination, the right to physical existence under the Genocide Convention of 1948, the right to 'permanent' sovereignty over natural resources, and the rights of indigenous peoples and of ethnic, religious, and linguistic minorities under Article 27 of the ICCPR have been cited as examples. But it has been argued that there is now a new, 'third' generation of human rights based upon a sense of group solidarity:[2]

[1] Moskowitz, *The Politics and Dynamics of Human Rights* (1968) 169–70.
[2] S. P. Marks, 'Emerging Human Rights: A New Generation for the 1980's?' (1981) 33 *Rutgers LR* 435.

six areas in which these new 'peoples' rights are said to be in the process of development are: rights to a reasonable environment, economic development, international peace and security, the common heritage of mankind, communications, and humanitarian assistance.[3]

One of the justifications given by the United States Department of State for its withdrawal from UNESCO was that:[4]

UNESCO has been pressured, particularly by African States (encouraged by the Soviet Bloc), to give equal or greater attention to 'rights of peoples'. A political 'right of self-determination' has long been recognized and endorsed by the United States, but other purported 'rights of peoples', generally economic in character, such as the 'right to development', are exceedingly vague and ill-defined. This stress on 'collective rights' tends to strengthen the prerogative of a non-democratic State, at the expense of the human rights of individuals.

This comment implies that the debate concerning 'peoples' rights is but one aspect of a wider ideological clash between socialist economic systems, which emphasize the interests of the State, the group, the tribe, or the family, and capitalist economic systems which emphasize the interests of the individual. Fundamental individual rights are threatened, on this view, by the development of collective or peoples' rights, rights which appear to claim a hierarchical superiority to individual rights.[5]

My purpose in this paper is to consider the relationship between peoples' rights and individual rights, and in particular to examine the claim that the international recognition of collective rights would derogate from established individual rights in a manner which is presently not envisaged or permitted by international law. Thus I am not concerned with the question which, if any, of the asserted 'peoples' rights' are presently part of international law and which are mere 'pious hopes unlikely to command adherence within the international community'. No attempt is made to define a 'people' or a minority in international law, nor is there an examination of the substantive content of asserted 'peoples' rights'.

Some preliminary points should be made. The first is that, if peoples' rights are to have any meaning beyond States' rights, they must include the right of a 'people' against its own government.[6] For present purposes it is in the context of 'peoples' rights' asserted against the government of the State to which the people belongs that it is easiest to consider whether individual rights are likely to be prejudiced in favour of the group. There is now a considerable body of jurisprudence developed within national courts which deal with the balance between collective and individual rights,

[3] id., 441.
[4] Executive Summary of the US Department of State's Policy Review of US-UNESCO Relations [1984] *Aust Int Law News* 432.
[5] id., 435.
[6] See J. Crawford's essay in this volume.

especially where indigenous or minority interests are given special recognition or protection by the State.

Such an analysis is, however, carried out within a statist framework. Falk argues that to give effect to the rights of 'peoples' it may be necessary to move outside the physical boundaries of the State, and to jettison the restrictive view that States are the only actors with the legitimate authority to create normative order. He argues that:[7]

it is the underlying legitimacy of peoples, not the transient legitimacy of governments, that constitute the purpose and rationale for the instruments protecting human rights . . .

A strictly statist approach to 'peoples' rights may be artificial and inadequate, but it is difficult to assess the effects of collective rights upon individual rights beyond the framework of the State. Which entity, for example, owes the Hohfeldian duty, whether to a 'people' or the individual? How is the duty justiciable and how is it to be enforced? There are examples, in the practice of the European Commission and Court of Human Rights and the United Nations Human Rights Committee, which suggest how international tribunals might balance individual rights where they appear to conflict with group rights. The development of jurisprudence at the international level depends, however, upon the willingness of States to accord a procedural *locus standi* to individuals or to groups such as minorities or indigenous peoples. In the case of individuals, that willingness so far has been limited; in the case of groups and minorities it has been nearly non-existent. Until peoples and individuals have legal status to pursue their claims before tribunals outside the State of which they are nationals, the interests of the State are likely to predominate.

Secondly, much of the dissatisfaction with the notion of 'peoples' rights' appears to arise from the fear that non-democratic governments will pursue economic and social goals to the prejudice of individual human rights. To the extent that this is already the practice in both non-democratic and democratic States, the formulation of 'peoples' rights' in international law may have the effect of entrenching and legitimizing denials of individual rights. It is difficult to refute these arguments so long as the legal content of peoples' rights has yet to be ascertained. For example, it has been asserted that the right to self-determination (which is relatively well-established and has a relatively certain content) is a precondition for the enjoyment of individual human rights. Empirically this may be true, at least in relation to certain colonized peoples. On the other hand, there is no indication, in authoritative formulations of the asserted 'right to development', that it is to be treated as a precondition to individual rights.[8]

---

[7] See R. Falk's essay in this volume.
[8] See R. Rich's essay in this volume.

Those who argue for 'peoples' rights' emphasize that these rights are intended to supplement, complement and reinforce traditional individual human rights, rather than to detract from them.

Thirdly, the criticism that peoples' rights threaten fundamental individual rights sometimes implies that individual rights are both immutable and absolute. In truth, individual rights are frequently balanced both with other individual rights and with the interests of a democratic society (the latter a collective interest). Rights to freedom of expression, peaceful assembly and freedom of association are, for example, subject to the protection of national security, of public order and of public health and morals.[9] The Universal Declaration of Human Rights of 1948 provides in Article 29 that:

In the exercise of his rights and freedoms, everyone shall be subject only to such limitations as are determined by law solely for the purpose of securing due recognition and respect for the rights and freedoms of others and of meeting the just requirements of morality, public order and the general welfare in the democratic society.

Article 30 provides that the Declaration should not be interpreted as 'implying for any State, group or person, any right to engage in any activity or to perform any act aimed at the destruction of any of the rights and freedoms set forth' in the Declaration. Similarly, most human rights instruments permit derogation from at least some of the rights they define, giving a temporary priority to the State in public emergencies 'threatening the life of the nation'.[10] Certain fundamental rights (such as the right to life, the right not to be subjected to torture or held in slavery, and the right to freedom of thought, conscience, and religion) are not subject to derogation in the interests of the State, but they do remain subject to processes of judicial and legislative interpretation which inevitably take matters of legitimate 'public interest' into account.

Individual rights are thus subject to the just requirements of the general welfare in a democratic society and to the rights and freedoms of others. The ICCPR also guarantees certain collective rights such as the right to manifest one's religion in community with others, the right to self-determination, the right of the family to protection by society and the State, and the right of minorities not to be denied the right, in community with the other members of their group, to enjoy their culture, to profess and practice their own religion, and to use their own language. These rights are guaranteed along with other individual rights, and have not (with the possible exception of self-determination under Article 1, which is given a

[9] See e.g. ICCPR, Arts. 19, 21, and 22.

[10] Cf. European Convention on Human Rights and Fundamental Freedoms, Art. 15. The ICCPR provides for a right of derogation in public emergencies, but prohibits derogations from Arts. 6, 7, 8, 11, 15, 16, & 18. See further Higgins, 'Derogations under Human Rights Treaties' (1976-7) 48 *BYIL* 281.

'Part' of the Covenant to itself) been accorded any special status. The clear implication is that each right is to be interpreted consistently with the others. There is no necessary hierarchy of these rights, except that certain rights cannot be derogated from even in a public emergency.

The fourth point follows from the third. There are many respects in which 'peoples' rights' complement and depend upon individual rights, and to this extent they are not antithetical. This is borne out by the history of the recognition of human rights at the international level since 1919. The United Nations originally chose to avoid the difficulties caused by the minorities' treaties negotiated after the First World War by universalizing the protection of individuals so that all persons would be entitled to certain minimum rights.[11] In a sense, minority rights, which were partly collective, and which certainly recognized the interests of particular groups, came before and helped to generate recognition of individual human rights. That recognition was accompanied by the belief that minority rights needed no further protection: they are barely mentioned, for example, in the Universal Declaration of 1948. By 1966, however, the United Nations Sub-Commission on the Prevention of Discrimination and Protection of Minorities was successful in inserting Article 27 in the International Covenant on Civil and Political Rights. This article recognizes that individual rights may need to be exercised in community with other members of a minority group. The rights of assembly and of association and the enjoyment of cultural, religious and linguistic rights require that the individual be able to act collectively. In this sense, Article 27 implements and strengthens the individual rights guaranteed by other provisions in the Covenant. For example, Article 18, which guarantees freedom of religion, is given practical effect by the guarantee in Article 27 of freedom to practice that religion in community with others.

Thus, while there has been a tendency in the literature to write of minority and individual rights as sharply distinct concepts, they will often be complementary. Minority rights are described as special rights but, as the Permanent Court said in the *Case concerning Minority Schools in Albania*, these rights are intended to ensure real and substantial equality to ethnic, religious, or linguistic groups.[12] The salient point is that, if special rights are not granted to such groups to defend their cultures, the practice of their religion, and the use of their languages, they will be treated unequally and unjustly. Minority rights thus have the purpose of ensuring the effective implementation of fundamental individual human rights.

The decision of the European Court in the *Belgian Linguistics* case demonstrates that some problems of ensuring rights cannot be conceived purely

[11] L. Henkin (ed.), *The International Bill of Rights. The Covenant on Civil and Political Rights* (1981) 275.
[12] PCIJ Ser A/B No 64 (1935) 18.

in individual terms.[13] There may be instances in which no specific individual right is adequate to protect the group interest in question. Here it is arguable that a new group right must be constructed. In such cases 'peoples' rights and individual rights are not only complementary but also interdependent. Each type of right is necessary to preserve minority cultures, for the protection of collective rights will depend, in the first instance, upon the existence of individual rights.[14] Where members of minority groups aim to achieve integration into the general community, individual rights alone may suffice. But where an ethnic minority wishes to retain its integrity and identity, individual rights such as the rights to recognition as a person, to equality before the law, to peaceful assembly, and to freedom of association, though they are a necessary condition, may not be a sufficient one.

Fifthly, while some special interests of 'peoples' may be gaining recognition, there remain significant barriers to the implementation of group rights in international practice. States are often reluctant to recognize or promote group rights. The most important reason is that to concede special treatment to minorities within a State is perceived as detrimental to national unity and stability. The fear is that, once a minority is recognized and grows in strength, it will demand to secede from the host State or, at least, seek some form of autonomous status. The notion of 'peoples' rights' is thus seen as a challenge to the sovereignty of the nation State and to associated precepts of international law. 'Peoples' will often straddle State boundaries, and may give allegiance to the authority of more than one State. As Thornbury points out, some 'peoples' have been politically opportunistic in the aftermath of revolution.[15] In Iran, for example, the Kurds, Turkish speakers of Azerbaijan and the Baluchis have tended to foster their own interests at times of instability in the State. Claims to special group rights thus tend to arouse suspicion and distrust. Another problem is that 'peoples' rights' could be used in an attempt to justify and maintain cultural or religious practices, such as the Hindu caste-system or the subordination of women, which are now generally regarded as intolerable. Some developing States argue that they cannot afford to maintain separate cultural or religious facilities for a minority group, and that the highest priority, and a necessary precondition, must be the economic and social development of the State itself (a development which may well profoundly affect the group in question, for example by eliminating the material basis for their society). Further, it may be difficult to distinguish special rights and protection for community groups from policies of separate development. South Africa's apartheid policy has, for example, been

---

[13] ECHR Ser A vol. 6 (1968).

[14] Thornbury, 'Is there a phoenix in the ashes? International law and minority rights' (1980) 15 *Texas ILJ* 440.

[15] id., 456.

justified in the General Assembly on the grounds that is based on the fact 'that people differ particularly in their group associations, loyalties, cultural outlook, modes of life and standards of development'.[16]

In addition to these, mostly political and self-justifying, objections by States is the argument that rights for minorities and indigenous 'peoples' threaten individual human rights. It is argued, for example, that group rights create invidious distinctions between citizens which are contrary to international law rules prohibiting discrimination on the grounds of race, national origin or religion. Where an individual human right is in question, the individual is the measure of the violation. By contrast, where group rights are involved, the focus is on all the circumstances of the group rather than upon the individual. Questions thus arise whether the advancement and articulation of 'peoples' rights will prejudice individual rights, whether a conflict between them will result and, if so, whether satisfactory principles of interpretation can be found to reconcile these rights.

The following analysis considers a number of attempts by domestic and international tribunals to determine whether legislation protecting or recognizing a group interest violates individual rights to equality or prohibitions against discrimination. There is a danger in drawing conclusions as to the implementation of peoples' rights generally from specific cases. Nevertheless, these decisions suggest methods of judicial approach in cases where it is argued that collective rights prejudice established individual rights.

2. Peoples' Rights and Non-Discrimination: Some Case Studies

Where a State legislates to advance the interests of indigenous peoples or minorities by, for example, recognizing traditional customary law or adopting affirmative employment programs, such measures often attract the criticism that they are discriminatory or that they violate the principle of equality, whether embodied in international instruments such as the ICCPR Art. 26 or Racial Discrimination Convention 1966 Art. 5, or in national laws. It has, however, been accepted by international and domestic tribunals that the concept of equality before the law and the prohibition of certain kinds of discrimination do not require identical treatment. Judge Tanaka in the *South West Africa Cases* (*Second Phase*) recognized that:[17]

the principle of equality before the law does not mean the absolute equality, namely equal treatment of men without regard to individual, concrete circumstances, but it means the relative equality, namely the principle to treat equally what are equal

[16] Van Dyke, 'Self-determination and minority rights' (1969) 13 *Int Studies Q* 223, 241.
[17] ICJ Rep 1966 p6, 305-6.

and unequally what are unequal . . . To treat unequal matters differently according to their inequality is not only permitted but required.

More recently Brennan J of the High Court of Australia said in *Gerhardy* v. *Brown*:[18]

Formal equality before the law is an engine of oppression destructive of human dignity if the law entrenches inequalities 'in the political, economic, social, cultural or any other field of public life'.

The real difficulty lies, not in accepting that some distinctions between people are necessary, but in establishing acceptable limits upon such distinctions to ensure an appropriate balance between the interests of the community at large and individuals and of identifiable groups within that community. A body of jurisprudence and practice has been developed by international and municipal courts, particularly in the United States and Canada, which distinguishes between discriminatory laws on the one hand and protective measures for indigenous inhabitants and minorities on the other. Laws dealing with specific groups must not be arbitrary, invidious, or unjustified; they must have an objective and reasonable justification and pursue a legitimate aim; there must be a reasonable proportion between the aim and the means employed, and, once the object has been achieved, the legislative classification or distinction must be discontinued.[19] The central point for the purposes of the present discussion is that, assuming the existence of rights for minorities and indigenous peoples and an obligation upon States to give domestic effect to these rights, individual rights will necessarily have to be balanced with competing group interests.

(1) The Effect of Special Measures upon Individual Members of the Group

Although these questions are often considered from the perspective of or at the instance of outsiders, a central issue is the effect of special measures on members of the group in question. Are group members entitled to opt out of 'special measures', and what is the effect of any such opting out on their continuing individual rights of association? When considering the validity of special measures enacted under the Land Rights Act in *Gerhardy* v. *Brown*, the High Court examined the effects of the legislation upon individual rights—in this instance, the rights of the Pitjantjatjara. The Pitjantjatjara Land Rights Act 1981 (SA) conferred the right to give permission to enter the land upon the body corporate, Anangu Pitjantjatjaraku (of which all Pitjantjatjaras are members). While Pitjantjatjaras had an

---

[18] (1985) 57 ALR 472, 516.
[19] *Belgian Linguistics Case* ECHR Ser A vol. 6 (1968) 35; see also W. McKean, 'The meaning of discrimination in international and municipal law' (1970) 44 *BYIL* 185, 185-6.

unrestricted right of access to the land they did not individually have the right to invite or permit non-Pitjantjatjaras to come on to the land. Brennan J. recognized that the individual's right to invite or permit to enter one's home was part of the right to freedom of association under Article 20 of the Universal Declaration of Human Rights—a right which, under the Land Rights Act, existed exclusively in the Executive Board of the Pitjantjatjara tribe. He concluded, however, that the Act did not violate individual rights, for:[20]where the enjoyment of the home might be prejudiced if the individual right were not foregone in favour of a collective right, it cannot be said that the human rights and fundamental freedoms of the household's members are impaired by their acceptance of membership on the terms that the rights should be exercised collectively.

The apparently serious impairment of an individual right had not taken place, Brennan J argued, when the reasons for s 19 were considered. These included a fear that individual Pitjantjatjaras would be improperly over-borne by others for socially disruptive purposes, and the need for group control over entry to ensure secrecy during Aboriginal ceremonies. For these reasons, Brennan J. accepted that the absence of an individual power to permit entry did not render s 19 inconsistent with the special measures exception.

It is crucial to this conclusion, and to the notion of a right of 'peoples', that an individual should have accepted membership of the group on the basis that the rights granted by the legislation would be exercised collectively. Brennan J concluded that where an individual Pitjantjatjara had accepted the benefits of membership of the group, 'individual convenience has given way to group protection'.[21] As a corollary to acceptance of group membership, however, it is essential that an individual should be able to opt out of the group and to assert his or her individual rights. That person would not, in opting out, be able to enjoy the benefits of control over the land granted to the Pitjantjatjara 'people', but would be able to exercise individual rights to freedom of movement and residence in relation to any other property lawfully occupied.

Similarly the Australian Law Reform Commission has recognized that an individual must be able to opt out of a group right. In its *Report on the Recognition of Aboriginal Customary Laws* the Commission concluded that measures of recognition of indigenous customary laws, which apply substantially, or even exclusively to a group defined by reference to the race or ethnic origins of its members, would not be discriminatory against the group to which the law applies. This conclusion was subject to the proviso that the measures of recognition:[22]

[20] (1985) 57 ALR 472, 502–5, 518.
[21] id., 507.
[22] Australian Law Reform Commission, Report 31, *The Recognition of Aboriginal Customary Laws* (1986) vol. 1, para. 160.

do not deprive individual members of basic rights (including, in particular, access to the general legal system), are no more restrictive than is necessary to ensure fidelity to the customary law or practices being recognized, and allow for individual members of the group to contest the application of its rules in particular cases.

(2) Equality before the Law and Affirmative Action: United States and Canadian Practice

United States and Canadian courts have also accepted the compatibility of the individual right to equality before the law with legislative measures to protect or advance group interests. Under the Fourteenth Amendment to the United States Constitution citizens may not be denied 'equal protection of the laws'—a right comparable to Article 26 of the ICCPR. The United States Supreme Court has interpreted this right strictly in relation to 'suspect classifications'. In *Regents of the University of California* v. *Bakke* the Supreme Court held that:[23]

racial and ethnic classifications of any sort are inherently suspect and thus call for the most exacting judicial examination.

It is unfortunate that the Court was unable to agree upon the permissible limits to 'reverse discrimination' to achieve equality for minority groups. The medical school of the University of California had a special admissions programme under which only disadvantaged members of certain minority races could be considered for sixteen of the one hundred places in each year's class. Members of any race could qualify for the other eighty-four places. The plaintiff, a white male, failed to gain admission even though applications with lower scores than his gained admission under the special programme. Five members of the Court affirmed that the special programme was unlawful, though for different reasons. Five members of the Court reversed the California Supreme Court judgment which prohibited the Regents from giving any consideration whatever to race in future admissions processes.

The reasoning of Powell J (a member of the majority which concluded that the special programme was unlawful) is particularly interesting. In considering the effect of reverse discrimination upon individuals within the general community, he emphasized that nothing in the Constitution supported the view that individuals should be asked to suffer otherwise impermissible burdens in order to enhance the societal standing of ethnic groups within the community. He also noted that there was a measure of inequity in forcing innocent persons in Bakke's position to bear the burdens

[23]   438 US 265, 291 (1978) (Powell J.).

of redressing grievances not of his making. He warned that to make the principle of equal protection susceptible to 'transitory considerations' would render judicial scrutiny of classifications based on race subject to the 'ebb and flow of political forces', thereby, in his view, fanning racial and ethnic antagonisms.[24] Powell J. argued that an admittedly suspect classification should be permissible only if there was a substantial State purpose or interest, and then only if the classification was necessary to achieve the purpose or safeguard the interest. As none of these requirements had been met the programme was unlawful.

An important implication to be drawn from Powell J's judgment is that, had a legislative or responsible administrative agency found that the University had engaged in a past discriminatory practice which now required remedial efforts, it might have been permissible for the University to take race into account in selecting its medical students. The four members of the minority took a similar position, accepting that the government might take race into account to remedy past disadvantages 'at least when appropriate findings have been made by judicial, or legislative or administrative bodies'.[25] Thus there appears to be a majority for the position that, in appropriate circumstances, some form of reverse discrimination in selection procedures is acceptable. An individual's right to equality before the law may, as a result, be balanced against the properly established need to remedy the effects of past discrimination upon a minority group.

Under the Canadian Bill of Rights, legislative distinctions including those based on race, will be valid where they are directed at a 'valid federal objective'.[26] Under s 15(1) of the Charter of Rights and Freedoms of 1982 affirmative action programmes are specifically permitted, despite the guarantee that 'every individual is equal before and under the law'.

Canadian and United States courts take similar positions with regard to legislative distinctions concerning Indian tribes. In the United States the Supreme Court has consistently relied on the special federal responsibility for Indians. Legislation establishing measures of 'reverse discrimination' will not involve suspect racial classifications. Rather, it will be seen as a political measure founded upon the historically based 'unique obligation' of Congress for Indians.[27] Similarly, the Canadian Parliament may exercise its constitutional responsibility for Indian tribes by enacting special rules with respect to Indians and Indian land provided that they have a legitimate legislative purpose.[28]

These approaches may have significant effects on an individual Indian's right to equality before the law. In *United States* v. *Antelope*[29] Indian

[24] id., 298.
[25] id., 325.
[26] *AG for Canada* v. *Canard* (1975) 52 DLR (3d) 548; see also ALRC 31 vol. 1, para. 138-44.
[27] *Morton* v. *Mancari* 417 US 535, 555 (1974).
[28] *AG for Canada* v. *Canard* (1975) 52 DLR (3d) 548.
[29] 430 US 641 (1977).

defendants were charged with the murder of a non-Indian on a reservation. Federal criminal law applied special rules to the Indian population, including the felony murder rule. Had a non-Indian committed the offence, Idaho law would have applied, and would not have permitted conviction upon a constructive form of *mens rea*. The Supreme Court rejected the argument that the application of federal law violated the equal protection clause, on the ground that federal regulation of Indian affairs 'is not based upon impermissible racial classifications'.[30] Such a categorical refusal to consider Indians as a racial group, denying the protection of the United States Constitution and norms of international law, whatever its historical justification, can clearly have an unjust effect upon individuals. While there is little value in dwelling on the United States' position in relation to Indians from the point of view of discerning international standards, this decision, and others like it, provide clear illustrations of the ways in which the perceived advancement of group interests can prejudice the individual rights of members of the protected group.

The Canadian courts have had particular difficulty in accommodating the individual guarantee of equality before the law with a constitutional power to legislate for 'Indians, and Lands reserved for Indians'.[31] In *Attorney-General for Canada* v. *Canard*[32] the Canadian Supreme Court considered the validity of the Indian Act. This legislation established special laws for Indians on reserves, under which a departmental officer would be appointed as administrator of an estate on intestacy. The wife of an Indian who died intestate claimed the right under general provincial law to be appointed the administrator of her husband's estate, alleging that the Act violated her right to equality before the law. Although the Court rejected her claim, Justices Beetz and Martland adopted a reasonable classification test under which 'legitimate reasons of policy' could justify the apparent inequality. This test of legitimacy has subsequently been adopted by the Canadian Supreme Court, thereby providing a mechanism by which a group interest could be protected.

(3) The United Nations Human Rights Committee

Attempts by national tribunals to resolve conflicts between individual rights and the rights of indigenous 'peoples' are of only limited value in determining the proper approach at the international level to 'peoples' rights'. This is primarily because these courts reflect, to a significant degree, local, historical, political, and economic factors. For these reasons, it is important that the United Nations Human Rights Committee has had the opportunity to consider the relationship between peoples' rights and

---

[30] id., 13.
[31] British North America Act (now Constitution Act) 1867, s 91(24).
[32] (1975) 52 DLR (3d) 548.

individuals rights, in particular in a communication from a Canadian Indian under the Optional Protocol to the ICCPR.

In the Lovelace Case a registered Maliseet Indian married a non-Indian, thereby losing her status as an Indian under the Indian Act 1970 (Can).[33] The legislation would not have applied in this way had a male Indian married a female non-Indian. When the marriage between Lovelace and the non-Indian ended she returned to her reserve, contrary to the Act which limited residence to Indians. Lovelace argued that her rights under Articles 2 and 27 of the ICCPR had been violated. The Committee concluded that the Act violated Article 27 and that Lovelace was entitled, as a member of an ethnic minority, to associate with that group on its reserved land. The Committee took care, however, to emphasize the individual nature of her rights guaranteed under Article 27. In the words of the Capotorti Report, the Committee recognized the potential danger that:[34]

the freedom of each individual member of a minority to choose between voluntary assimilation with the majority and the preservation of his own distinctive characteristics might be disregarded by the organs of the entity formed by the minority group in its concern to preserve the unity and strength of the group.

As there was no question on the facts of any such disregard, the Committee simply drew attention to the limits of Article 27 in the protection of community interests.

Although the Committee did not need to consider the complaint that the Act also violated Article 2, the right not to be discriminated against on the ground of sex constitutes another example of the way in which an individual right can come into conflict with group rights and, indeed, with Article 27 itself. In its submission to the Commission the Canadian government argued that the sexually discriminatory aspect of the Act was necessary, as reserve land was considered to be threatened more by non-Indian men than by non-Indian women. The Committee rejected this argument as a justification for discrimination, on the basis that such a distinction restricting the right to residence of persons belonging to the minority group 'must have both a reasonable and objective justification and be consistent with the other provisions of the Covenant'.[35] Other provisions of the Covenant thought to be relevant by the Committee were Articles 2, 3, 12, 17, 23, and 36. As the Committee did not consider the restriction upon Lovelace to be either 'reasonable, or necessary to preserve the identity of the tribe',[36]

---

[33] Report of the Human Rights Committee, GAOR 36th Sess, Supp. 40 (A/36/40) Annex XVIII, 166–75.

[34] F. Capotorti, 'Study on the Rights of Persons belonging to Ethnic, Religious and Linguistic Minorities' (UN Doc E/CN.4/Sub 2/384/Rev 1 (1979)) 35–6.

[35] GAOR 36th Sess, Supp. 40 (A/36/40) Annex XVIII, 173–4.

[36] Ibid.

there was no need to consider provisions of the Covenant other than Article 27 itself.

The decision is relevant to the question of the relationship between group rights and individual rights because it indicates that the Human Rights Committee, while not denying content to 'group' rights such as Article 27, is likely to read the rights guaranteed by the Covenant so as to avoid any inconsistency and, in particular, to interpret the minority protection afforded by Article 27 in ways which, as far as possible, preserve individual rights.

Lovelace would have raised an even more significant issue had the Committee found that the sexual discrimination was the only effective way to preserve the identity of the tribe.[37] The question would then have been whether the Act was sexually discriminatory and thus contrary to Article 2 or whether it could be justified on the basis that the distinction was reasonably necessary to achieve a legitimate objective. If so, the position would be one in which the individual right not to be discriminated against on the grounds of sex was subordinated to a provision which was admittedly necessary to preserve group interests.

For obvious reasons the Human Rights Committee will be reluctant to consider the hypothesis of a clear collision between rights where none exists on the facts before it. For practical purposes direct collision will be rare, but the potential for collision remains. Some general principles of interpretation are therefore necessary to resolve such conflicts. For example, where an individual right is specific, fundamental, and non-derogable, it is highly unlikely to take precedence over an article, such as Article 27, which is general and imprecise and from which a State may derogate. Moreover, Article 27 affords rights to individual members of minorities and is not a 'group' right as such. Logically, each individual should be free to renounce his rights under Article 27 if he chooses. The Human Rights Committee in Lovelace was concerned that an individual preference to be assimilated in the general population might be hampered in the name of a misconceived group solidarity. Capotorti in his 1979 Study took the position that any such restriction would constitute a violation of the individual's freedom of choice.[38]

(4) Human Rights and the Right to Development

In 1981 the United Nations General Assembly declared that the right to development was an 'inalienable human right'.[39] This emerging concept has been criticized on the ground that, as a collective right, it poses a threat

---

[37] In fact the Committee found that the exclusion of women marrying outside the tribe was not the only way to ensure the integrity of the group.
[38] Capotorti Report, 35–6.
[39] Resolution 36/133 (1981).

to traditional individual rights. The United Nations Secretary General countered this criticism by arguing that the individual and collective dimensions of the right to development are complementary and that 'it is probably unnecessary to pose the issue as one involving the choice of mutually exclusive alternatives'.[40]

The concern that the 'right to development' will involve a conflict between individual and collective rights is met by the Declaration of the Right to Development adopted by the General Assembly on 4 December l986.[41] The Declaration stresses that the 'human person is the central subject of the development process' and that the human being should be the 'main participant and beneficiary of development'. It employs phrases such as 'every human person and all people', 'individually and collectively' and 'entire population and all individuals', emphasizing that both individuals and peoples have the benefit of the right defined. The Declaration also states that all human rights are 'indivisible and interdependent', and that nothing in the Declaration implies a right to act in violation of the rights defined in the Universal Declaration or the International Covenants on Human Rights. Thus the Declaration makes it clear that the right to development cannot detract from individual human rights.

To the extent that the Declaration recognizes a hierarchy of rights it is clear that the individual, as the beneficiary of all human rights, takes the primary position. The Declaration does not, on the other hand, give priority to civil and political rights over economic, social, and cultural rights. It provides that 'equal attention and urgent consideration' should be given to the implementation of civil, political, economic, social, and cultural rights. The promotion of particular human rights cannot justify the denial of other rights.

The Declaration achieved a high level of consensus in the General Assembly, with l46 votes in favour, one against and eight abstentions. This support, coupled with state practice, indicates that the obligation of states to improve the 'well-being' of peoples and to insure their economic, social, cultural, and political development has achieved, or at least is close to achieving, the status of customary international law. But in any event, while the Declaration may be criticized on a number of grounds, it is difficult to sustain the view that it gives any sort of priority to collective rights above traditional individual rights.

4. Conclusion

This paper seeks to address the criticism that to recognize 'peoples' rights would be to jeopardize traditional individual rights. This criticism mis-

[40] UN Doc E/CN 4/l448, para. 89.
[41] Resolution 41/128 (l986).

understands the interdependent relationship between group and individual rights. For example, legislative measures to protect or advance the interests of indigenous peoples or minorities within a State depend upon and complement existing individual rights. International and domestic tribunals have accepted that, in order to achieve actual equality in the enjoyment of human rights, formal inequality or distinctions on otherwise prohibited grounds may be justified, at least where the discrimination is demonstrably reasonable and proportionate to achieve a legitimate objective and where it continues only until its aim has been attained.

While there is, then, no necessary tension between group rights and individual rights, the case law suggests a range of precautionary measures which can be taken to avoid conflict in particular cases or situations. Legislation to advance the interests of indigenous peoples or to protect the interests of minorities may validly institute distinctions affecting others in the community, where it can be demonstrated that they are necessary to achieve genuine equality. But such measures must be demonstrably reasonable and proportionate, and must balance any prejudice to individual equality with the objective to the achieved.

The debate about individual rights versus collective rights becomes sterile once it is accepted that certain individual rights cannot be exercised in isolation from the community. The trade union must be guaranteed certain rights if the individual freedom to join a union is to be exercised; minorities must have the opportunity to protect and develop their cultures if the individual is to enjoy his or her own culture. Certain rights are individual in kind (privacy, the right to fair procedures in criminal trials); others by their nature are collective (economic, social and cultural), even though the individual is the ultimate beneficiary. Some rights have both individual and collective aspects: for example, freedom of association. Thus to focus upon a dichotomy of individual rights and collective rights is to tilt at an imaginary windmill. It also tends to deflect discussion from the central question: that is, which rights should be recognized, and what should their substantive legal content be? The Declaration on the Right to Development adopts a more positive approach to the articulation of peoples' rights by stressing the interrelationship between collective and individual rights, the central role of the individual as the main participant and beneficiary of the right to development, and the protection of traditional human rights defined in the International Covenants.

This analysis has been concerned primarily with the relatively narrow and 'statist' problems of the compatibility of traditional individual freedoms with special measures to protect groups within the State. Further research is required to meet the wider criticism that collective rights strengthen 'the prerogative of a non-democratic State, at the expense of the human rights of individuals'. But that criticism ignores the interdependence of group and individual rights: taken together they provide some guarantee of democracy—a state of affairs itself as much collective as individual!

10

The Rights of Peoples: Some Conclusions

JAMES CRAWFORD

As some of the essays in this volume demonstrate, there is much to criticize in the arguments for a 'third generation' of 'solidarity rights'. One does not have to accept the view that international human rights are a closed category to regard some of the suggestions for the elaboration of 'solidarity rights' as mere novelties, apparently proposed for the sake of finding something new to say. The excessive generality and the disregard for content demonstrated in some of the elaborations of new rights not only raise questions about individual proposals, but reflect badly on the notion of a 'third generation' of rights as such. Their relation to existing human rights is also problematic. If proposals for a right to development can be elaborated and supported without any obvious content first being attributed to that right, how can one be confident of the content of existing rights? If the various peoples' rights elaborated in the African Charter of Human and Peoples' Rights are more likely to be relied on as modifying other rights or rules than as creating new autonomous rights,[1] then peoples rights would seem to be rather a new range of excuses for reducing the scope of other rights—in effect, a new range of State rights in disguise.

Despite these difficulties, there is no doubt that the issues posed in the debate over peoples' rights are important ones. Is the almost exclusive emphasis on individual human rights in international law since 1945 enough? Can the legitimate interests of groups be sufficiently protected by recognition of the individual right to associate? Should individual rights, including the right to opt out of groups or communities, prevail over the interests of those groups or communities? Is development better thought of as a human right, and if so, should that right be treated as an individual or communal one? Even more basic questions are raised. In particular, should international law in the post-colonial period settle back into the established pattern of rights and obligations of a primarily inter-state character? Or is there room for a new category of 'peoples', with rights against their own or other governments?

The debate on peoples' rights is a continuing one. The issues are not yet

[1] As S. C. Neff suggests: 'Human rights in Africa: thoughts on the African Charter of Human and Peoples' Rights in the light of case law from Botswana, Lesotho and Swaziland' (1984) 33 *ICLQ* 331, 332-3.

fully articulated, and State practice itself is changing and in some respects inchoate. Drawing conclusions about such questions is therefore difficult, and may be premature. But one important task is to ensure that the relevant questions are clearly and squarely put, and that conclusions about a third generation of rights are not reached without providing answers to those questions.

1. The Development of 'Peoples' Rights' as a Category

According to the accepted structure of international law in the nineteenth and early twentieth century, only States were subjects of international law. That proposition was, it is true, a dogmatic one rather than a reflection of actual practice. Not all entities with accepted capacities to act in international relations could be fitted within the restricted definition of the fully sovereign State. But these exceptional or 'anomalous' cases did not include individuals and groups: they were regarded as objects rather than as subjects of international law.[2] Thus international law could be thought of as concerned only with States' rights and not with the rights of other entities or persons. In fact it was not usually thought of in that way. It is true that the phrase 'rights and duties of States' was sometimes used, and there were more or less unsuccessful attempts at elaborating lists of 'rights and duties of States'.[3] But one problem with such elaborations was that they were necessarily selective, and that the principle of selection on which they operated was far from clear. If international law was wholly or substantially concerned to confer rights and impose obligations on States, by what principle did one select certain of these rights and obligations for listing in a convention or declaration on the rights and duties of States?[4] The same sort of question could be asked, with even more cogency, about the phrase 'rights of States': rights and duties are connected and in most cases reciprocal. This is especially so in a decentralized society where two of the main generating forces are the principle of equality of States and the notion of reciprocity.[5]

[2] See e.g. *Oppenheim's International Law* (8th edn, H. Lauterpacht (ed.), 1955) vol. 1, 19, 63, 636–9 (as usual, Lauterpacht's modifications should be compared with the 1st edn, 1905).

[3] e.g. the Montevideo Convention on Rights and Duties of States of 1933: (1934) 28 *AJIL Supp.* 75. The International Law Commission also composed a Draft Declaration on Rights and Duties of States, which the General Assembly declined in 1949 to adopt. See H. Kelsen, 'The Draft Declaration on Rights and Duties of States' (1950) 44 *AJIL* 259.

[4] In fact the various instruments and drafts were concerned to identify 'fundamental' rights and duties, according to a now discredited tradition that certain rights of States were 'natural' or 'inherent'. See Oppenheim (8th edn, 1955) vol. 1, 259–61. They were thus concerned more with establishing a hierarchy as between existing States' rights than with their identification or elaboration.

[5] See Kelsen (1950) 266–7, criticizing the ILC's Draft Articles on the basis that in international law duties are prior to rights.

In the century before the First World War, and to an even greater extent in the inter-war period, certain guarantees or protections were developed for groups or communities which did not constitute States. These were mostly formulated under the rubric of 'minority guarantees' or 'minority rights'. The minorities were in many cases minorities within large empires (especially the Ottoman Empire and the Austro-Hungarian Empire), and as a result these guarantees had several distinct purposes. To some extent they aimed to protect the identity of peoples or nations, in the way that the law of self-determination or decolonization would later seek to do. In other contexts, they were more concerned with the religious, cultural, or linguistic rights of groups which were minorities even within the territory they inhabited. Thus the first step towards explicit guarantees for the self-determination of peoples, in the form of the mandate system, was quite closely related in spirit and to some extent in juristic technique to the earlier and contemporary minorities treaties.[6]

None the less, in the period before 1945 both self-determination and minority guarantees were political principles which found legal expression only in specific cases. As a Commission of Jurists advised the League of Nations in the context of the Aaland Islands dispute, they were rules of exception rather than general principles of law.[7] This was one reason why lawyers did not ask whether a new category of 'rights' in international law had been created.

After 1945, a far more thorough-going distinction was drawn between political self-determination and minority rights, one which tended to suppress or ignore the connection between those concepts which had previously existed. Steps were taken, at first faltering but then with increasing stringency, to affirm the principle of self-determination in its application to all peoples under colonial domination.[8] By contrast, minorities guarantees were regarded with great suspicion, and the principle of minority rights, to the extent that it found expression at all, was regarded as a consequence of individual rights rather than of the rights of particular communities or groups. Thus the Universal Declaration of Human Rights of 1948 made no reference whatever to minority rights. The International

[6] See *South West Africa Cases (Second Phase)* ICJ Rep 1966 p6, 374–9 (Judge Jessup, dissenting). See also H. Duncan Hall, *Mandates, Dependencies and Trusteeship* (1948) 9–23.
[7] LNOJ Sp Supp. No 3 (1920) 5–6. See J. Crawford, *The Creation of States in International Law* (1979) 85–7. Similarly on the exceptional character of the minorities guarantees see J. Stone, *International Guarantees of Minority Rights* (1932) 14–15.
[8] The key statement of policy, GA Resolution 1514(XV), the Declaration on the Granting of Independence to Colonial Countries and Peoples of 14 December 1960, referred in its preamble to 'colonialism in all its forms and manifestations', and in its text to 'all peoples', in particular those subject to 'alien subjugation, domination and exploitation'. See also International Covenant on Civil and Political Rights 1966, Art. 1 ('all peoples').

Covenant on Civil and Political Rights of 1966 did so, but in a formulation which hovered uneasily between an individual and a communal right.[9]

The aim of the principle of self-determination was, increasingly, the creation of new States. But in practice various other political forms, which involved neither complete independence nor integration within the population of another State, were accepted as a legitimate form of expressing the will of the 'people' concerned as to their future political status.[10]

Moreover, issues arose concerning the identity and rights of peoples living within self-determination units, before their self-determination was achieved. In both contexts it was possible, and indeed necessary, to talk about the separate legal rights of such entities. Legal protection and the notion of rights were thus connected, more closely than had been the case under the old international dispensation, in which States were regarded as virtually the only entities with rights under international law. In short, the principle of self-determination came to be accepted not only as a 'general principle', but as one which gave rise to rights of the peoples concerned.

A second element after 1945 was the development of the notion of human rights as a matter of international concern, leading, in due course, to the international protection of human rights. Through the United Nations Charter, the Universal Declaration, the various regional human rights instruments and the major multilateral treaties on human rights, the notion of human rights in international law came to be established. No one now objects to the category 'human rights' on the ground that the level of actual protection of those rights in many countries remains problematic, that the machinery for their protection in most cases remains embryonic, or that there are still important areas of uncertainty about the content and application of those rights. These things may be true, but they are taken either as reasons for improving the articulation and enforcement of international human rights standards, or at least as inevitable concomitants, in a diverse, disorganized, and disorderly international community, of recognizing human rights at all.

The category 'human rights' has thus come to be universally accepted in international law. But it is significant that that category does not involve the proposition that individuals are 'subjects' of international law, or that the various human rights are part of international law in the same way that rules about the law of treaties or the law of the sea are. No doubt some aspects of international human rights law do have this status,[11] but others

---

[9] On the background to Art. 27 see UN Sub-Commission on Prevention of Discrimination and Protection of Minorities (Special Rapporteur: F. Capotorti), *Study on the Rights of Persons belonging to Ethnic, Religious and Linguistic Minorities* (UN Doc E/CN 4 Sub 2/384/Rev 1, 1979).

[10] See GA Resolution 1541(XV), Annex, Principle VI; *Western Sahara Opinion* ICJ Rep 1975 p12, 32.

[11] In its well-known dictum in the *Barcelona Traction Case (Second Phase)* ICJ Rep 1970 p3, 32, the Court listed the prohibition of genocide and 'the principles and rules concerning the basic rights of the human person, including protection from slavery and racial discrimination'.

do not. Even where a particular right is accepted as part of general international law, this does not mean that human beings are 'subjects' of
international law in anything other than a very general, and cor-
respondingly unhelpful, sense. For present purposes the point is that the
category 'human rights' was established as a category in international law
with legal consequences of various kinds, without entailing either the incorporation in international law of the whole list of recognized human
rights, or the recognition of the international legal personality of the bearers
of those rights.

The success of this strategy, if it was a strategy—in any event, the success
of the category 'human rights'—inspired imitation. A major concern of the
developing countries, countries which had in most cases recently emerged
as a result of the decolonization movement, countries to whom the principle
of self-determination of peoples was important and which together constituted a substantial majority of all member States of the United Nations,
was economic and social development. Other groups, including what might
be described as a 'third generation' of activist groups and non-
governmental organizations located within Western countries, had a range
of concerns not met by the traditional and individual rights. These concerns
extended to the environment, to peace (seen not merely as the absence of
conflict but as a substantial modification in the inherent tendencies to
conflict of the international system), to cultural rights, and to the rights of
various oppressed groups which did not fall within the orthodox framework
of self-determination. It was from this diverse combination—coalition
would be the wrong word—that the claims to a 'third generation' of
peoples' rights emerged.

2. The Relation of Peoples' Rights to States' Rights and Human Rights

In analysing these claims, it is first necessary to work out the relations
between peoples' rights and the two established categories, that is to say,
between peoples' rights and general human rights, and between peoples'
rights and the general body of international law concerned with the rights
and duties of States. Before doing so, it should be noted that some claims
to 'third generation rights' are essentially individual human rights, devoid
of any group content.[12] Although the phrase 'third generation rights' may
be useful as a description of a range of asserted rights which are thought to
build upon the existing body of human rights, for present purposes the
concern is only with peoples' rights, which may be provisionally defined

---

[12] See for example the candidate rights listed above p. 67 n. 23.

as rights vested in or existing for the benefit of groups, or at least of certain groups ('peoples').

In discussing the relation of peoples' rights to the existing categories of rights in international law, it is helpful to take the right to self-determination as an example, because it was the first and is still the clearest example of a peoples' right. For present purposes, four characteristics of the right to self-determination should be noted. These are independent of such questions as the definition of the 'peoples' who have a right to self-determination, or the ramifications of that right in particular cases. First of all, the right to self-determination, vested in a particular people, is a right against the State which presently administers and controls that people—for example, a right against the colonial government concerned. It is also, no doubt, a right against other governments, which may by assistance to the colonial regime, through acts of intervention on their part or in other ways impede the exercise of the right to self-determination by the people concerned. But the primary impact of that right is against the government of the State in question, and one of its main effects is to internationalize key aspects of the relationship between the people concerned and that State, represented by its government. Indeed it is precisely for that reason that some writers oppose the extension of the principle of self-determination beyond colonial and quasi-colonial situations, since there is no justification in their view for elevating the relationship between the whole population of a State and its government to the international level.[13]

It follows from this first characteristic that the right of self-determination, where it exists, is not vested in any government but is vested in the people concerned. On the other hand, this need not prevent governments from relying on the right of self-determination, vested in a particular people, in certain circumstances. There are many examples of States, although not in any direct sense beneficiaries of the right, in effect taking up the cause of a particular people through diplomatic or other means. A well known example was the *South-West Africa Cases*, where Ethiopia and Liberia sought to vindicate the right of self-determination of the Namibian people implicit in the mandate for South-West Africa.[14] That case failed, notoriously, on technical grounds, but there is no difficulty in principle with a legal system vesting in third parties the right to bring proceedings to vindicate the rights of another, especially where those rights cannot be asserted directly by the other.[15] It is not necessary for present

[13] Cf. C. Tomuschat, 'Rights of Peoples—Some Preliminary Considerations' in Y. Hangartner & S. Trechsel (eds), *Volkerrecht im Dienste des Menschen. Festschrift fur Hans Haug* (1986) 337.

[14] ICJ Rep 1962 p319; ICJ Rep 1966 p6.

[15] In certain circumstances the Human Rights Committee allows third parties to bring claims on behalf of individuals whose rights under the Civil and Political Rights Covenant have been violated, if the individual cannot be expected or is not in a position to bring the

purposes to discuss the extent to which governments can rely upon the principle of self-determination, for example, to legitimize armed intervention in a particular State.[16] The point is that States, including third States, are entitled to act in conformity with the rights of self-determination vested in a people, within whatever limits. But there is a clear distinction between a government's reliance upon the right vested in a people, and the government claiming to exercise that right, or to act as if the right was vested in it.

The fourth characteristic, which underlies the comments made already about the relationship between self-determination and action by governments, is that the right of self-determination, where it exists, is vested in the people in question as a group. It is a genuinely collective right. It was on this basis that the Human Rights Committee has rejected applications brought by individuals claiming a violation of self-determination, although such applications also raised the issue whether the communications procedure under the Optional Protocol to the Civil and Political Rights Covenant extended to violations of Article 1 of the Covenant.[17] It follows from the vesting of the right to self-determination in the people concerned as a group that members of the group forming a minority in relation to a particular decision about self-determination are none the less bound by the result. The position is quite different from the minority rights referred to in Article 27 of the Covenant, which are vested in individual members of minority groups. But it does not follow that there may not be secondary consequences of self-determination for individuals. Although the right of self-determination is vested in a group, it is quite possible for action to be taken with respect to individuals which constitutes a violation of the rights of the group. In certain circumstances it is arguable that those individuals might have a secondary or at least procedural right, on which they can themselves rely notwithstanding that it has its origin in a collective right to self-determination. For example action by a government in detaining or imprisoning the acknowledged leader of a people claiming a right to self-determination could well constitute a violation of that right, and it would seem an unnecessarily rigid insistence on the notion of collective

proceedings: see Human Rights Committee, Rules of Procedure, Art. 90(b) (in M. E. Tardu, *Human Rights. The International Petition System* (1985) vol. 1, Annex Part I, 40). In practice the Committee has applied the rule with great caution: e.g. Communication No 163/1984, *Group of Associations for the Defence of the Rights of Disabled and Handicapped Persons in Italy* v. *Italy*, in *Report of the Human Rights Committee*, GAOR A/39/40 (1984) 198.

[16] For differing views see W. M. Reisman, 'Coercion and Self-Determination: Construing Charter Article 2(4)' (1984) 78 *AJIL* 642; O. Schachter, 'The Legality of Pro-Democratic Invasion' (1984) 78 *AJIL* 645. The International Court in the *Nicaragua Case* (*Merits*) went out of its way to exclude this ground as a basis for intervention, except apparently in cases of decolonization: ICJ Rep 1986 p14, 108–9, and cf. Judge Schwebel (dissenting), id, 351.

[17] Communication No 78/1980, AD on behalf of *Mikmaq Tribal Society* v. Canada, GAOR A/39/40 (1981) 134.

rights to prevent the individual complaining in such circumstances.[18] But this is merely to insist upon a workable and differentiated understanding of group rights: it is not to deny the essential character of self-determination as a collective or group right in the first place.

It is an interesting question when a particular category or concept can be said to be established in a legal system. In particular, how many examples of rules or cases to be included in the category need first to be established? That issue arose with respect to the category '*jus cogens*' at the Vienna Conference the Law of Treaties. It was arguable that, notwithstanding the recognition of the category in the Vienna Convention, no actual example of a rule of *jus cogens*[19] yet existed. That view would not be widely held now, and indeed the recognition of the possibility of peremptory norms of general international law has itself been instrumental in the recognition that certain rules have, or are coming to have, that character. On the other hand it would be generally agreed that there are relatively few peremptory norms of international law falling within the category of *jus cogens*. For present purposes the point is that a category can be established as a legal category if there is some legal point or function in having the category, and if at least some examples of cases which fall within the category can be given.

On that basis, there are good grounds for accepting the category of peoples' rights in international law. There is at least one incontrovertible case of a peoples' right, the right of self-determination. A second example, the principle of permanent sovereignty over natural resources, is also widely recognized. There may be other examples, although most are in the course of development rather than fully fledged rights. In view of the increasingly widespread reference to peoples' rights, in the African Charter of Human and Peoples Rights, in General Assembly resolutions,[20] and also in the literature, the category should be regarded as an established one.

To say this does not imply that the category 'peoples' rights' requires that the term 'peoples' should have the same meaning for the purposes of all rights accepted as falling within the category, that peoples as distinct from individuals are necessarily the bearers of the rights in question, or that peoples are 'subjects' of international law in the orthodox sense, any more than human beings are subjects of international law notwithstanding the recognition that the category 'human rights' is an international law category with a distinct content. But recognition of the category does imply,

---

[18] This issue could conceivably arise under the African Charter, since the African Commission on Human and Peoples' Rights, since under Art. 56 it can consider communications relating to human and peoples rights generally, and there is no requirement that the author of a communication be complaining of a violation of a right vested in him or her personally.

[19] See e.g. J. Sztucki, *Jus Cogens and the Vienna Convention on the Law of Treaties* (1974) 76–89.

[20] e.g. GA Resolution 32/130 (1977) (see Document 14, below); GA Resolution 34/46 (1979) (see Document 16, below).

first, that peoples' rights are distinct from the rights of States or governments, in exactly the way that the right of self-determination is distinct from the right of established governments to act at discretion with respect to matters concerning them, and secondly, that the peoples in whom a particular right is vested are not inherently or necessarily represented by States or by the governments of States for that purpose. In particular cases, governments may be agents through which rights can be vindicated. But they will be acting in a secondary capacity, rather than as the holders of the right. Any insistence that peoples' rights are vested in governments disqualifies the right in question from being regarded as a peoples' right.[21]

It is thus possible to reach a clear understanding of the relationship between peoples' rights and States rights. The relationship between peoples' rights and individual rights is, I would argue, equally clear, and equally a prerequisite for the recognition of peoples' rights as a category. Peoples' rights are concerned with the flourishing of groups, and with individuals who are members of groups. Groups have no ultimate or necessary value, but they are a way in which individuals achieve various ends which are necessary or desirable—in particular the good of community and the fulfillment of certain human capacities and attributes which are best fulfilled in community. Thus peoples rights should be regarded as a sub category of human rights, a conclusion which is reinforced by the fact that many of the characteristics of human rights in international law already identified are also characteristics of peoples' rights.

One expressed concern in the debate over peoples' rights is that they may be used to erode established individual rights. Again it is useful to take the principle of self-determination as an example. That principle is stated in the International Covenant on Civil and Political Rights alongside the other human rights. It is not stated in terms which give it any logical or other priority over those rights. The rights are simply concurrent. It is the case with concurrent rights that in particular circumstances priorities may have to be set and limited resources devoted to fulfilling one right which is at more risk or more significant in the circumstances than another. But this is simply a characteristic of providing for concurrent rights: to give priority of resources to a particular concern does not mean that other rights can be negated or contradicted. In the history of the struggle for self-determination, claims were sometimes made that achieving self-determination was an absolute priority, and that, by implication at least, other rights could be ignored or denied until self-determination was achieved. Similar claims have sometimes been made for economic development, with even less justification. But such claims have not been treated as justifying the denial of other rights, rather than as emphasizing

---

[21] See the differing views summarized in Commission on Human Rights, *Report of the Working Group of Governmental Experts on the Right to Development* (E/CN.4/1985/11) para. 21.

the extent to which denial of self-determination itself can lead to a violation of other individual rights, including freedom of expression, freedom of movement and so on.[22]

The position with respect to minority rights is similar. These are stated in Article 27 as existing alongside other rights, leaving the balance to be struck in particular cases having regard to the basic need for respect for individual rights. This can give rise to difficult questions of implementation: one example frequently referred to in the essays in this volume is the problem of balancing the collective rights of indigenous peoples to land with individual rights of freedom of association and freedom of movement, a conflict exemplified by the Australian case *Gerhardy* v. *Brown*.[23] But these questions of balance or implementation are no different in principle in this area than they are with respect to the coexistences of other rights (e.g. the problem of reconciling the right to freedom of expression and the right to privacy).

A crucial point in this respect is that the Civil and Political Rights Covenant itself sets the balance between the various human rights, and does so with respect to rights or interests not themselves formulated or guaranteed in the Covenant, just as much as with respect to those that are. Certain rights under the International Covenant are expressed to be non-derogable, and are thus fundamental, not able to be modified even in time of public emergency. Thus Article 5(1) of the Covenant itself sets the balance between the rights of the individual and those of groups, as well as the State itself. While there is room for the notion of peoples or collective rights, this can be—and need only be—within the framework of the universally accepted international instruments. Those instruments themselves define the circumstances and considerations relevant to limitation on individual human rights, including limitations in times of public emergency.

3.   Who are Peoples and What Rights do they Have?

If, therefore, the category 'peoples' rights' is a legitimate one, the question is what constitutes a 'people' and what rights do they have? Putting the question in that form is however question-begging. There is no reason to

[22] General Assembly Res 37/200 (1982) para. 1 is emphatic on the point: it affirms that 'protection of one category of rights should never exempt or excuse States from the promotion and protection of the others'. See also preambular para. 11.

[23] (1985) 57 ALR 472, discussed in the articles by Brownlie and Triggs in this volume. The Human Rights Committee acknowledged the problem in the *Lovelace case*, where there was arguably a conflict between Arts. 26 (sexual equality) and 27 (minority rights). In the event the Committee decided that Art. 27 had itself been violated in the circumstances of the case, and did not need to resolve any conflict: see Communication No R6/24, *Sandra Lovelace* v. *Canada*, GAOR A/36/40 (1981) 166.

suppose that what constitutes a 'people' for the purpose of one right necessarily satisfies the requirements of another. In other words, the definition of 'people' could well be—indeed having regard to the breadth of the
claims to peoples' rights, is likely to be—context-dependent. In particular
it is objectionable to insist *a priori*, as some of the sources do, that a people
is nothing but the whole population of existing States. That is only one
possible definition, and by no means the most obvious one.

That the notion of a 'people' is context-dependent appears on the face
of the two human rights treaties incorporating some peoples' rights: the
International Covenant on Civil and Political Rights[24] and the African
Charter. For example Article 1 of the International Covenant proclaims in
paragraph 1 that all peoples have the right of self-determination, without
specifying what constitutes a 'people' for this purpose. Article 1 paragraph
3 refers particularly to States parties 'having responsibility for the administration of Non-Self-Governing and Trust Territories', implying that
the people of such territories in particular have a right of self-
determination. This could be read either as impliedly indicating that the
right of self-determination in Article 1 paragraph 1 is limited to the people
of non-self-governing and trust territories, which is a view often argued
for: on the other hand, it could be read as indicating, *a contrario*, that the
general right enunciated in Article 1 paragraph 1 is not so limited. In either
case, it is clear that Article 1 paragraph 2 adopts a broader meaning of the
term. It states that 'all peoples may, for their own ends, freely dispose of
their natural wealth and resources ... In no case may a people be deprived
of its own means of subsistence.' This is best regarded as a statement of two
distinct rights, the right not to be deprived of one's means of subsistence, an
aspect of the right to existence, and the principle of permanent sovereignty
of natural resources. But it is clear that neither of these is limited to the
people of colonial territories. Either Article 1 paragraphs 1 and 2 consistently use a broad definition of 'peoples' or they use a differential one.
In any event, contextual interpretation is required.

A similar analysis can be applied to the provisions of the African Charter.
Article 20 paragraph 1 states that 'all peoples have the rights to existence.
They shall have the unquestionable and inalienable right to self-
determination.' Paragraph 2 refers to 'colonized or oppressed peoples'
(there is no reason to suggest that the term 'oppressed' is coextensive
with 'colonized'). Those peoples have the rights to free themselves from
domination 'by resorting to any means recognised by the international
community'. Again there is no reason to think that the general right stated
in Article 20 paragraph 1 is limited to 'colonized or oppressed peoples': at
least that limitation is not apparent from the terms of the article. Even if it

[24] Art. 1 is common to the two Covenants of 1966: for convenience, reference will be made
here only to the Civil and Political Rights Covenant.

were, the term 'oppressed' would clearly require contextual interpretation. Article 21 paragraph 1 refers to the right of 'all peoples' to freely dispose of their wealth and natural resources, although the proclamation of this as a right of peoples is diminished by the reference in Article 21 paragraph 4 to the right of 'States parties to the present Charter' to 'exercise the rights to free disposal of their wealth and natural resources'. What was originally treated as a right of peoples is here treated as a right of States, thus casting doubt upon the legitimacy of the assertion that peoples have a right to permanent sovereignty over their natural resources. But for present purposes the point is that it is quite clear from Article 21 that the 'peoples' referred to in paragraph 1 are not limited to colonized or oppressed peoples. In giving effect to the African Charter, the African Commission on Human and Peoples' Rights is required to take into account 'international law on human and peoples' rights' (Article 60), and 'international norms on human and peoples' rights' (Article 61). If general international law recognized a single definition of 'peoples', it could be argued that this was to be read into the African Charter. But it is clear that there is no single international law definition. Indeed there is a growing body of practice to the effect that, even for the purposes of the principle of self-determination, the most categorical and most far-reaching 'peoples' right', the principle is not limited to situations of colonial countries and peoples, although its effect outside the colonial context may well be different.[25]

It follows that peoples' rights embodies a category, not a definition. What constitutes a people may be different for the purposes of different rights. For example the right to existence (incorporating the right not to be subjected to genocide and the right not to be deprived of one's means of subsistence) is plainly applicable to a very broad category of groups, considerably more so than the principle of self-determination, on any view of that principle.

This conclusion conforms with the analogy, already discussed, between peoples' rights and human rights as categories of rights in international law. It is also consistent with the underlying structure of human rights law. In particular, arbitrary definitions of peoples' rights would violate the notion of non-discrimination, both in terms of the peoples themselves but more importantly in terms of the individuals concerned. The principle of non-discrimination, itself one of the cardinal principles of human rights law, thus reinforces the broad view of peoples' rights.[26]

What then is the content of the category 'peoples' rights'? It is too early to be definitive, but three fairly clear examples can be given. The first, the

---

[25] See J. Crawford, 'Self-Determination outside the Colonial Context' in A. Macartney (ed.), *Self-Determination in the Commonwealth* (1987) 1, and references there cited.

[26] This point is made in the UNESCO Declaration on Race and Racial Prejudice (1978) Art. 9: see Document 15, below.

principle of self-determination, has already been discussed in some detail. A second is the right of peoples to existence, which, as I have suggested, incorporates both the right not to be subjected to genocide (a right with respect to which the Genocide Convention adopts the broadest definition of 'group') and the right not to be deprived of one's means of subsistence. It may be that the right to existence may come to generate other particular consequences, given its powerful moral base in the notion of the right of individuals to live in community with each other. The third example is the right of peoples to permanent sovereignty over their natural resources, although as we have seen some of the international texts tend to conflate this with the right of governments, that is to say, of State structures. It may be that at present the notion of permanent sovereignty, which has considerable currency in international relations, is equivocal as between a right of peoples and a right of States.[27] The key criterion of a peoples' right in this respect must be whether the right avails as against decisions of the government of the territory in which the people live: that is to say, whether governmental decisions on the disposal of natural resources are subject to the principle of domestic jurisdiction, or whether they are, on the contrary, subject to international scrutiny on the basis that particular decisions are abusive. But even if, as I suspect, the question of permanent sovereignty in relation to independent States is a right of States rather than peoples, in the context of colonial self-determination it seems clearly to be a peoples' right.

In each case, the criteria for determining whether a particular asserted right is a peoples' right seem to be essentially three: first, whether the right is a right of peoples rather than governments or States; secondly, whether the right has been articulated in such a way that it can been seen to have a certain content, that is, legal consequences of some kind,[28] and thirdly, whether the right, as so articulated, has achieved a sufficient degree of acceptance. These criteria are clearly satisfied for self-determination (within whatever limits) and for the right to existence. They are less clearly satisfied in the case of permanent sovereignty over natural resources, because of the crucial ambiguity of formulations of that right as between a peoples' and a States' right.

Applying these criteria, it is not clear that other claims to peoples' rights have yet achieved a sufficient degree of articulation or recognition. Minority rights, as spelt out in Article 27 of the International Covenant on Civil and Political Rights, are equivocal as between individual and collective rights,

---

[27] Thus General Assembly Res 1803(XVII) expounds the 'right of peoples and nations to permanent sovereignty over their natural resources' (see Document 6, below). By contrast General Assembly Res 3281(XXIX), the Charter of Economic Rights and Duties of States, Art. 2 refers to permanent sovereignty as a right of 'every State'. The point is that it cannot be both.

[28] As indicated already, it does not need to extend to the incorporation of the right in international law or of the right-holder as an international legal person.

although I would argue that they do in fact qualify as peoples' rights.[29] The rights of indigenous peoples, though achieving some degree of recognition in international instruments and in international discourse, at present are only accepted in international law to a very limited degree.[30] So far as claims such as the right to peace or to the environment are concerned, the difficulty is that there is as yet no level of articulation of consequences of those rights, failing which they can only be said to have been accepted as pleasant-sounding formulae.

Perhaps the crucial candidate, and certainly the one which has been the focus of debate, is the right to development. Roland Rich's article in this volume suggests that there are four consequences of the right to development, which warrant its acceptance in international law. These are: (1) an obligation on States in certain circumstances to provide development assistance; (2) general acceptance that special measures to aid developing countries are consistent with the principle of equality of States; (3) the recognition of the category 'developing countries', as a distinct category in international law, and (4) the obligation on all States to ensure that development benefits individuals. The second and third of these are not, expressly or even by implication, included in the General Assembly's Declaration on the Right to Development, as is perhaps not surprising given the emphasis in that Declaration on development as an individual right. They relate rather to the equality of States, an established principle of international law, and are reflected in the special provisions made for developing countries, and in particular for the least developed countries, in instruments such as the United Nations Convention on the Law of the Sea.[31] They have little to do, at least directly, with the notion of a right to development as a human or peoples' right.

The other two suggested consequences do find some reflection in the Declaration, but only to a limited degree. This is particularly true of the notion of an obligation to provide development assistance, which is expressed in qualified terms in Article 4(1) of the Declaration:

States have the duty to take steps, individually and collectively, to formulate international development policies with a view to facilitating the full realization of the right to development.

[29] Although Art. 27 of the Civil and Political Rights Covenant refers to the rights of individual members of minority groups, this could be explained on the basis that minorities of minorities must equally be accorded rights with respect to the various matters listed. If article 27 is an individual right only, why was it necessary to confine it to members of minority groups in those countries in which such groups exist?

[30] Compare the very limited provisions of ILO Convention 107 of 1957 (Document 3, below) with formulations by indigenous groups and non-governmental organizations (e.g. Documents 18 and 19 below). See also Nettheim's essay in this volume. On the other hand see e.g. R. L. Barsh, 'Indigenous Peoples: An Emerging Object of International Law' (1986) 80 *AJIL* 369.

[31] (1982) 21 ILM 1261. See W. D. Werway, 'The Recognition of the Developing Countries as Special Subjects of International Law beyond the Sphere of United Nations Resolutions' in R. J. Dupuy (ed.), *Hague Academy of International Law and United Nations University Workshop* (1980) 30.

Clearly this does not take us very far. Moreover the notion of an obligation to provide development assistance only contributes to a right to development if that obligation is to provide development assistance to those who will benefit, that is to say the individuals and groups in need of development, rather than to the State apparatus. This result could no doubt be achieved directly or indirectly. One way would be through asserting a right to provide development assistance, and in extreme cases even famine relief, directly to peoples or groups in need rather than through the machinery of the territorial government. There have been examples of such claims, but they are highly controversial, and it is clear that States do not generally accept the right of other States to provide even food and medical aid in this way. On the other hand, there are traces of this approach in the *Nicaragua Case*,[32] and it would be extraordinary if international law accepted the right to humanitarian intervention by the use of force,[33] but did not accept that right in respect of 'peaceful measures'.

A second method of establishing a right to development would be by asserting that States, including the territorial sovereign, are under an obligation to ensure that development benefits individuals. Article 1 paragraph 1 of the General Assembly Declaration states that the right to development is 'an alienable human right', and, that 'the human person is the central subject of development' (Article 2). On the other hand States have 'the primary responsibility for the creation of a national and international conditions favourable to the realization of the right to development' (Article 3), and should undertake 'all necessary measures for the realization of the right to development' (Article 8). There is very little here in the way of an entitlement on the part of individuals to raise the development policies of their own governments at the international level. This reticence is combined with the deliberate avoidance, in Article 1, of the idea that the right to development is a peoples' right. Article 1 says only that 'the right to development is an alienable human right by virtue of which every human person and all peoples are entitled to participate in ... development'. The contrast with earlier versions of Article 1 makes it clear that all that is proclaimed here is development as an individual right[34] and apparently without much in the way of international consequences.

One can only conclude that, quite apart from the failure of the General Assembly Declaration to be adopted by consensus, there is so far no sufficient acceptance or articulation of the right to development as a peoples'

---

[32] Judge Schwebel (dissenting) stated that 'it is lawful for a foreign State or movement to give to a people struggling for self-determination moral, political and humanitarian assistance ...': *Nicaragua Case (Merits)* ICJ Rep 1986 p14, 351. It seems likely that the majority would agree: cf. id, 108–9.

[33] For an examination of whether coercive humanitarian intervention is now lawful see N. Ronzitti, *Rescuing Nationals Abroad through Military Coercion and Intervention on Grounds of Humanity* (1985).

[34] For the travaux of the Declaration on this point see e.g. Commission on Human Rights, *Report of the Working Group of Governmental Experts on the Right to Development* (E/CN.4/1985/11) para. 20, and Annex II, Art. 1.

right for it to qualify as such. On the other hand, some elements of modern State practice, in particular in the area of intervention by 'peaceful means', suggests that some elements which might go to make a right to development may be evolving.

It would be unfair to regard the debate on peoples' rights as another case where the mountains have divided to produce only a mouse. The principle of self-determination, the clearest example of a peoples' right, was a major instrument in one of the most significant reformations of the geography of the world. Some of the other claims—in particular the right to existence of groups and to certain minimum rights of subsistence and, perhaps, sociality involved in the existence of human groups—are capable of having significant results, at least over the longer term. If the more exaggerated claims of the proponents of a 'third generation' of rights cannot be justified, none the less the debate remains a significant one, both in terms of outcomes and implications.

4. Broader Perspectives

So far the discussion has focused on the place the category 'rights of peoples' presently occupies, or may come to occupy, in the established system of interstate relations and international law. International law is predominantly if not overwhelmingly a system of interstate relations, expressed through the relations between the governments of States and the organizations they create. The acceptance of a category of human rights in international law qualifies this position only to a limited extent, as we have seen. But one view, expressed for example by Richard Falk in his essay in this volume, is that peoples' rights, and indeed the whole third generation of 'solidarity rights', are part of a developing normative order substantially independent of the State system. Falk describes this as an expression of a developing international civil community, one in which individuals and groups combine to express values, independent of their acceptance by States, but rather relying on the inherent rights and common conscience of mankind. This view finds perhaps its clearest expression in the Universal Declaration of the Rights of Peoples, the Algiers Declaration of 1976.[35] The Universal Declaration is no sense an interstate or international instrument: it is not open to accession or ratification by States, but provides a normative basis for the work of several related non-governmental organizations, including the Permanent Peoples' Tribunal.[36] Falk argues that:[37]

[35] For the text of the Declaration see Document 13, below.
[36] E. Jouve (ed.), *Un Tribunal pour les Peuples* (1983) contains a summary of various projects undertaken by the Tribunal. See also Permanent Peoples' Tribunal, *A Crime of Silence. The Armenian Genocide* (1985); M. Dixon, *On Trial. Reagan's War against Nicaragua. Testimony of the Permanent Peoples' Tribunal* (1985).
[37] 'The Algiers Declaration of the Rights of People' in R. Falk, *Human Rights and State Sovereignty* (1981) 184, 192-3.

The Algiers Declaration codifies the popular claims of competence asserted on a more *ad hoc* basis by the Russell Tribunal. It extends the scope of such competence to the various spheres of human rights, including those connected with the existence of a people; economic, political, cultural, and environmental rights are claimed, as well as rights for minority peoples within a state.

It is thus 'as assertion of popular sovereignty, asserting that it is the peoples of the world that are the fundamental source of authority with respect to the governing process'.[38]

Assessing the 'international civil community' thesis is difficult, especially since, as Falk concedes, the various developments on which he relies are partial and incomplete. Indeed in view of its genesis and aims, it may be for others than international lawyers to assess the validity and usefulness of the idea. But it would a mistake to admit a rigid distinction in international law between 'reality' and 'idealism', between the demands of the interstate system and the humanitarian ideals to which any system of law worthy of the name should aspire. One of the historical roots of international law was the assumption that 'the law of nature and of nations' were interrelated, and something like that idea, however submerged and overlaid by positivist theory and the manifest body of State practice, still underlies the notion of the 'international community' as a generating concept in international law. Moreover these theoretical underpinnings are accompanied by many activities on the part of individuals and non-governmental organizations in the interests of an international order which is none the less recognizably also an interstate order. While the international system reflects, only too emphatically, the power relations between States (as well as strongly entrenched nationalistic attitudes on the part of the people of most States) it has, as a result of its history and intellectual tradition, a broader orientation. Here as elsewhere the flexibility of international law can be a strength as well as a source of weakness. For example many non-governmental organizations work within or partly within the established international framework, relying on international instruments and their acceptance by States. The International Committee of the Red Cross is only the oldest example.

In any event, the notion of rights of peoples, as embodied for example in the African Charter of Human and Peoples' Rights, is firmly entrenched within the interstate framework. As with human rights generally, the task for international lawyers is to understand the framework, to explain it— both its strengths and weaknesses—to those seeking to rely on it, and to make it work, if possible in the interests of individuals and their communities, as well as in the interests of the governments whose primary domain it continues to be.

[38] id., 192.

Selected Treaties, Resolutions, and Other Documents on the Rights of Peoples

NOTE: The debate over the 'rights of peoples' involves a range of documents of widely differing status, provenance, and availability. They range from major international treaties and United Nations declarations, to instruments prepared by non-governmental groups or organizations which have no official status, but which may none the less be influential in shaping public, legal, and official opinion. Set out here chronologically is a selection of the major documents in the field, with a note about their status, provenance, and (in the case of certain documents not generally available) their English text. Documents listed are as follows:

1. Universal Declaration of Human Rights, 10 December 1948
2. Convention on the Prevention and Punishment of the Crime of Genocide, 9 December 1948
3. International Labour Organization Convention 107 concerning the Protection and Integration of Indigenous and other Tribal and Semi-Tribal Populations in Independent Countries, 26 June 1957
4. Declaration on the Granting of Independence to Colonial Countries and Peoples, 14 December 1960
5. General Assembly Resolution on Permanent Sovereignty over Natural Resources, 14 December 1962
6. Declaration on the Elimination of All Forms of Racial Discrimination, 20 November 1963
7. International Convention on the Elimination of All Forms of Racial Discrimination, 21 December 1965
8. International Covenant on Economic, Social and Cultural Rights, 16 December 1966
9. International Covenant on Civil and Political Rights, 16 December 1966
10. UNESCO Declaration of the Principles of International Cultural Co-operation, 4 November 1966*
11. Convention for the Protection of the World Cultural and Natural Heritage, 15 November 1972
12. International Convention on the Suppression and Punishment of the Crime of Apartheid, 30 November 1974
13. Universal Declaration of the Rights of Peoples, Algiers, 4 July 1976*
14. Resolution on Alternative Approaches and Ways and Means within the United Nations System for Improving the Effective Enjoyment of Human Rights and Fundamental Freedoms, 16 December 1977*
15. UNESCO Declaration on Race and Racial Prejudice, 27 November 1978*
16. Resolution on Alternative Approaches and Ways and Means within the United Nations System for Improving the Effective Enjoyment of Human Rights and Fundamental Freedoms, 23 November 1979*

17. African Charter on Human and Peoples' Rights, Nairobi, June 1981*
18. UNESCO Latin-American Conference, Declaration of San José, 11 December 1981*
19. World Conference of Indigenous Peoples, Declaration of Principles of Indigenous Rights, Panama, September 1984*
20. Declaration on the Right to Development, 4 December 1986*

* indicates that a document is reproduced in whole or part. Documents not reproduced are available in the official version cited below, and most are also reprinted in one or more of the following collections:

I. Brownlie, *Basic Documents on Human Rights* (2nd edn, Clarendon Press, Oxford, 1981)
J. A. Joyce, *Human Rights: International Documents* (Sijthoff & Noordhoff, Alphen aan der Rijn, 1978)
W. Laqueur & B. Rubin, *The Human Rights Reader* (Temple UP, Philadelphia, 1979)
Council of Europe, *Human Rights in International Law. Basic Texts* (Directorate of Human Rights, Strasbourg, 1985)

DOCUMENT 1: Universal Declaration of Human Rights, 10 December 1948.

Official Source: United Nations General Assembly Resolution 217A(III); UN Doc A/811.

Secondary Sources: Brownlie, 21-7; Laqueur & Rubin, 197-201; Joyce I, 10-26; Council of Europe, 7-14.

Status: Resolution adopted by the UN General Assembly (48-0:8), pursuant to Art. 13(1)(b) & 55(c) of the UN Charter.

Comment: An influential document, though merely recommendatory. Emphasis strongly on individual rights, but Art. 28 states right to 'a social and economic order' in which basic human rights can be achieved.

DOCUMENT 2: Convention on the Prevention and Punishment of the Crime of Genocide, 9 December 1948.

Official Source: 78 UNTS 277.

Secondary Sources: Brownlie, 31-4; Laqueur & Rubin, 201-2; Joyce I, 50-3.

Status: Multilateral treaty (in force: 12.1.1951). 100 States parties (as at 31.12.1985).

Comment: The basic international instrument defining genocide as 'a crime under international law', in terms of certain acts 'committed with intent to destroy, in whole or in part, a national, ethnical, racial or religious group, as such'.

DOCUMENT 3: International Labour Organization Convention 107 concerning the Protection and Integration of Indigenous and other Tribal and Semi-Tribal Populations in Independent Countries, 26 June 1957.

Official Source: 328 UNTS 247.

Secondary Sources: International Labour Organization, *Conventions and Recommendations* (Geneva, 1966) 901–8.

Status: Multilateral treaty (in force: 2 June 1959). 26 States parties (as at 1.1.1986).

Comment: Historically significant ILO standard-setting instrument dealing with 'tribal and semi-tribal populations in independent countries', concerned with 'protection' of those groups, but with a view to their eventual 'integration' in the wider community of the State in question. Not widely ratified, and in recent years rejected by some States and by indigenous groups as assimilationist in tendency. The ILO has begun work on revision of the Convention. See also the accompanying Recommendation 104.

DOCUMENT 4: Declaration on the Granting of Independence to Colonial Countries and Peoples, 14 December 1960.

Official Source: United Nations General Assembly Resolution 1514 (XV).

Secondary Sources: Brownlie, 28–30; Joyce I, 29.

Status: General Assembly resolution (adopted 89-0:9); recommendatory *vis-à-vis* member States.

Comment: Principal and very influential statement of rights of colonial peoples to self-determination in context of decolonization under Chapters XI and XII of UN Charter.

DOCUMENT 5: General Assembly Resolution on Permanent Sovereignty over Natural Resources, 14 December 1962.

Official Source: United Nations General Assembly Resolution 1803 (XVII).

Secondary Sources: I. Brownlie, *Basic Documents on International Law* (3rd edn, Oxford, 1983) 230–4.

Status: General Assembly resolution (adopted 87-2:12); recommendatory *vis-à-vis* member States.

Comment: Basic United Nations resolution expounding 'the right of peoples and nations to permanent sovereignty over their natural wealth and resources', described as 'a basic constituent of the right to self-determination'. It refers *inter alia* to 'appropriate compensation, in accordance with . . . international law' for expropriation of property. In both respects Res 1803 (XVII) contrasts with GA Res 3281(XXIX), the Charter of Economic Rights and Duties of States, adopted on 12 December 1974 (120–6: 10): see Art. 2(1), which refers to permanent sovereignty as a right of 'every State', & Art. 2(c).

DOCUMENT 6: Declaration on the Elimination of All Forms of Racial Discrimination, 20 November 1963.

Official Source: United Nations General Assembly Resolution 1904 (XVIII).

Secondary Sources: Laqueur & Rubin, 204–8.

Status: General Assembly resolution (adopted unanimously); re-commendatory *vis-à-vis* member States.

Comment: Precursor to Document 7, which, while not defining 'discrimination', provided expressly for 'special measures' to restore equality to disadvantaged groups (Art. 2).

DOCUMENT 7: International Convention on the Elimination of All Forms of Racial Discrimination, 21 December 1965.

Official Source: 660 UNTS 195.

Secondary Sources: Brownlie, 150–63; Laqueur & Rubin, 228–32; Joyce I, 32–8; Council of Europe, 54–69.

Status: Multilateral treaty (in force: 4.1.1969). 131 States parties (as at 31.12.1985).

Comment: Basic and widely accepted international instrument on the elimination of racial discrimination (defined broadly in Art. 1(1) to include discrimination on grounds of 'race, colour, descent or national or ethnic origin'). Very influential, despite interpretative difficulties due in part to rushed drafting. Arts 1(4), 2(2) specifically provide for 'special measures' for disadvantaged groups.

DOCUMENT 8: International Covenant on Economic, Social and Cultural Rights, 16 December 1966.

Official Source: 993 UNTS 3.

Secondary Sources: Brownlie, 118–27; Laqueur & Rubin, 208–16; Joyce I, 12–16; Council of Europe, 14–26.

Status: Multilateral treaty (in force: 3.1.1976). 94 States parties (as at 31.12.1985).

Comment: One of two major universal human rights treaties. Despite focus of economic, social and cultural rights, the emphasis is on individual rights, except for Arts 1(1) (self-determination), 1 (2) (right of peoples to freely dispose of their natural resources); although Arts 11 (right to food), 12 (health), 13 (education) & 15 (science & culture) touch on issues of 'group' rights.

DOCUMENT 9: International Covenant on Civil and Political Rights, 16 December 1966.

Official Source: 999 UNTS 171.

Secondary Sources: Brownlie, 128–45; Laqueur & Rubin, 216–24; Joyce I, 16–24; Council of Europe, 26–49.

Status: Multilateral treaty (in force: 23.3.1976). 92 States parties (as at 31.12.1985).

Comment: One of two major universal human rights treaties. Emphasis generally on individual rights, except for Arts 1(1) (self-determination), 1 (2) (right of peoples to freely dispose of their natural resources), 27 (right of members of ethnic, religious & linguistic minorities).

DOCUMENT 10: UNESCO Declaration of the Principles of International Cultural Cooperation, 4 November 1966.

Official Source: UNESCO Doc 14C/8.1.

Secondary Sources: Joyce I, 112–13.

Status: Resolution of UNESCO General Conference with recommendatory force.

Comment: Proclaims right of each people to develop its culture and to engage in cultural co-operation, with 'due regard for human rights and fundamental freedoms' (Arts 1, 5, 11).

Text:

Declaration of the Principles of International Cultural Co-operation.

The General Conference of the United Nations Educational, Scientific and Cultural Organization, met in Paris for its fourteenth session, this fourth day of November 1966, being the twentieth anniversary of the foundation of the Organization.

Recalling that the Constitution of the Organization declares that "since wars begin in the minds of men, it is in the minds of men that the defences of peace must be constructed" and that the peace must be founded, if it is not to fail, upon the intellectual and moral solidarity of mankind.

Recalling that the Constitution also states that the wide diffusion of culture and the education of humanity for justice and liberty and peace are indispensable to the dignity of man and constitute a sacred duty which all the nations must fulfill in a spirit of mutual assistance and concern.

Considering that the Organization's Member States believing in the pursuit of truth and the free exchange of ideas and knowledge, have agreed and determined to develop and to increase the means of communication between their peoples.

Considering that, despite the technical advances which facilitate the development and dissemination of knowledge and ideas, ignorance of the way of life and customs of peoples still presents an obstacle to friendship among the nations, to peaceful co-operation and to the progress of mankind.

Taking account of the Universal Declaration of Human Rights, the Declaration of the Rights of the Child, the Declaration on the Granting of Independence to Colonial Countries and Peoples, the United Nations Declaration on the Elimination of all Forms of Racial Discrimination, the Declaration on the Promotion among Youth of the Ideals of Peace, and the Declaration on the Inadmissibility of Intervention in the Domestic Affairs of States and the Protection of their Independence and Sovereignty, proclaimed successively by the General Assembly of the United Nations.

Convinced by the experience of the Organization's first twenty years that, if international cultural co-operation is to be strengthened, its principles require to be affirmed.

Proclaims this Declaration of the principles of international cultural co--operation, to the end that governments, authorities, organizations, associations and institutions responsible for cultural activities may constantly be guided by these principles; and for the purpose, as set out in the Constitution of the Organization of advancing, through the educational, scientific and cultural relations of the peoples of the world, the objectives of peace and welfare that are defined in the Charter of the United Nations.

Article I

1. Each culture has a dignity and value which must be respected and preserved.
2. Every people has the right and the duty to develop in culture.
3. In their rich variety and diversity, and in the reciprocal influences they exert on one another, all cultures form part of the common heritage belonging to all mankind.

Article II

Nations shall endeavour to develop the various branches of culture side by side and, as far as possible, simultaneously, so as to establish a harmonious balance between technical progress and the intellectual and moral advancement of mankind.

Article III

International cultural co-operation shall cover all aspects of intellectual and creative activities relating to education, science and culture.

Article IV

The aims of international cultural co-operation in its various forms, bilateral or multilateral, regional or universal, shall be:

1. To spread knowledge, to stimulate talent and to enrich cultures;
2. To develop peaceful relations and friendship among the peoples and bring about a better understanding of each other's way of life;
3. To contribute to the application of the principles set out in the United Nations Declarations that are recalled in the Preamble to this Declaration;
4. To enable everyone to have access to knowledge, to enjoy the arts and literature of all peoples, to share in advances made in science in all parts of the world and in the resulting benefits, and to contribute to the enrichment of cultural life;
5. To raise the level of the spiritual and material life of man in all parts of the world.

Article V

Cultural co-operation is a right and a duty for all peoples and all nations, which should share with one another their knowledge and skills.

Article VI

International co-operation, while promoting the enrichment of all cultures through its beneficent action, shall respect the distinctive character of each.

Article VII

1. Broad dissemination of ideas and knowledge, based on the freest exchange and discussion, is essential to creative activity, the pursuit of truth and the development of the personality.
2. In cultural co-operation, stress shall be laid on ideas and values conducive to the creation of a climate of friendship and peace. Any mark of hostility in attitudes and in expression of opinion shall be avoided. Every effort shall be made, in presenting and disseminating information, to ensure its authenticity.

Article VIII

1. Cultural co-operation shall be carried on for the mutual benefit of all the nations practicing it. Exchanges to which it gives rise shall be arranged in a spirit of broad reciprocity.

Article IX

Cultural co-operation shall be carried on for the mutual benefit of all the nations practicing it. Exchanges to which it gives rise shall be arranged in a spirit of broad reciprocity.

Article X

Cultural co-operation shall be specially concerned with the moral and intellectual education of young people in a spirit of friendship, international understanding and peace and shall foster awareness among States of the need to stimulate talent and promote the training of the rising generations in the most varied sectors.

Article XI

1. In their cultural relations, States shall bear in mind the principles of the United Nations. In seeking to achieve international co-operation, they shall respect the sovereign equality of States and shall refrain from intervention in matters which are essentially within the domestic jurisdiction of any State.
2. The principles of this Declaration shall be applied with due regard for human rights and fundamental freedoms.

DOCUMENT 11: Convention for the Protection of the World Cultural and Natural Heritage, 15 November 1972.

Official Source: UNESCO Doc 17C/106 (1972).

Secondary Sources: (1972) 11 ILM 1358-66.

Status: Multilateral treaty (in force: 17.7.1975). 83 States parties as at 31 October 1984.

Comment: Major instrument extending protection to certain monuments, sites and other heritage items 'of outstanding universal value'; these items declared to be a 'world heritage', whose preservation requires international co-operation.

DOCUMENT 12: International Convention on the Suppression and Punishment of the Crime of Apartheid, 30 November 1974.

Official Source: 1015 UNTS 244.

Secondary Sources: (1974) 13 ILM 50-7; Brownlie, 164-70.

Status: Multilateral treaty (in force: 18.7.1976). 87 States parties (as at 31.12.1985).

Comment: Declares that *apartheid*, defined as certain violations of human rights 'committed for the purpose of establishing and maintaining domination by one racial group of persons over any other racial group of persons and systematically oppressing them', is a crime against humanity. Text partly modelled on the Genocide Convention (Document 2).

DOCUMENT 13: Universal Declaration of the Rights of Peoples, Algiers, 4 July 1976.

Official Source: International Lelio Basso Foundation for the Rights and Liberation of Peoples, *Universal Declaration of the Rights of Peoples* (Paris, François Maspero, 1977).

Secondary Sources: A. Cassese, *UN Law/Fundamental Rights* (Sijthoff & Noordhoff, Alphen aan der Rijn, 1979) 219.

Status: Unofficial declaration of scholars and publicists; basis for activities of Permanent Peoples' Tribunal, a private foundation.

Comment: Emphasizes right of 'peoples', without definition and without specific reference to individual human rights.

Text:

Article 1

Every people has the right to existence.

Article 2

Every people has the right to the respect of its national and cultural identity.

Article 3

Every people has the right to retain peaceful possession of its territory and to return to it if it is expelled.

Article 4

No one shall be subjected, because of his national or cultural identity, to massacre, torture, persecution, deportation, expulsion or living conditions such as may compromise the identity or integrity of the people to which he belongs.

Article 5

Every people has an imprescriptible and unalienable right to self-determination. It shall determine its political status freely and without any foreign interference.

Article 6

Every people has the right to break free from any colonial or foreign domination, whether direct or indirect, and from any racist regime.

Article 7

Every people has the right to have a democratic government representing all the citizens without distinction as to race, sex, belief or colour, and capable of ensuring effective respect for the human rights and fundamental freedoms for all.

Article 8

Every people has an exclusive right over its natural wealth and resources. It has the right to recover them if they have been despoiled, as well as any unjustly paid indemnities.

Article 9

Scientific and technical progress being part of the common heritage of mankind, every people has the right to participate in it.

Article 10

Every people has the right to a fair evaluation of its labour and to equal and just terms in international trade.

Article 11

Every people has the right to choose its own economic and social system and pursue its own path to economic development freely and without any foreign interference.

Article 12

The economic rights set forth above shall be exercised in a spirit of solidarity amongst the peoples of the world and with due regard for their respective interests.

Article 13

Every people has the right to speak its own language and preserve and develop its own culture, thereby contributing to the enrichment of the culture of mankind

Article 14

Every people has the right to its artistic, historical and cultural wealth.

Article 15

Every people has the right not to have an alien culture imposed upon it.

Article 16

Every people has the right to the conservation, protection and improvement of its environment.

Article 17

Every people has the right to make use of the common heritage of mankind, such as the high seas, the seabed, and outer space.

Article 18

In the exercise of the preceding rights every people shall take account of the necessity for coordinating the requirements of its economic development with solidarity amongst all the peoples of the world.

DOCUMENT 14: Resolution on Alternative Approaches and Ways and Means within the United Nations System for Improving the Effective Enjoyment of Human Rights and Fundamental Freedoms, 16 December 1977.

Official Source: United Nations General Assembly Resolution 32/130.

Secondary Sources: (1977) 31 *UN Ybk* 734.

Status: General Assembly resolution (adopted 123-0:15); recommendatory *vis-à-vis* member States.

Comment: Emphasizes relationship between civil and political and economic, social and cultural rights; recognition of people's rights limited to self-determination.

Text: The following is the text of operative para. 1:

1. Decides that the approach to the future work within the United Nations system with respect to human rights questions should take into account the following concept:
   (*a*) All human rights and fundamental freedoms are individual and interdependent; equal attention and urgent consideration should be given to the implementation, promotion and protection of both civil and political, and economic, social and cultural rights;
   (*b*) The full realization of civil and political rights without the enjoyment of economic, social and cultural rights is impossible, the achievement of lasting progress in the implementation of human rights is dependent upon sound and effective national and international policies of economic and social development.
   (*c*) All human rights and fundamental freedoms of the human person and of peoples are inalienable;
   (*d*) Consequently, human rights questions should be examined globally taking into account both the overall context of the various societies in which they present themselves, as well as the need for the promotion of the full dignity of the human person and the development and well-being of the society;
   (*e*) In approaching human rights questions within the United Nations system, the international community should accord, or continue

to accord, priority to the search for solutions to the mass and flagrant violations of human rights of peoples and persons affected by situations such as those resulting from apartheid from all forms of racial discrimination, from colonialism, from foreign domination and occupation, from aggression and threats against national sovereignty, national unity and territorial integrity, as well as from the refusal to recognize the fundamental rights of peoples to self-determination and of every nation to the exercise of full sovereignty over its wealth and natural resources;

(f) The realization of the new international economic order is an essential element for the effective promotion of human rights and fundamental freedoms and should be accorded priority;

(g) It is of paramount importance for the promotion of human rights and fundamental freedoms that Member States undertake specific obligations through accession to or ratification of international instruments in this field of human rights and the universal acceptance and implementation of the relevant international instruments should be encouraged;

(h) The experience and contributions of both developed and developing countries should be taken into account by all organs of the United Nations system in their work related to human rights and fundamental freedoms

DOCUMENT 15: UNESCO Declaration on Race and Racial Prejudice, 27 November 1978.

Official Source: UNESCO Doc 20C/3/1.1/2.

Secondary Sources:—

Status: Resolution of UNESCO General Conference (adopted unanimously) with recommendatory force.

Comment: Distinguishes between the right of individuals and groups to be different and to maintain their cultural identity, on the one hand, and practices of racial discrimination and domination on the other. Emphasizes equality of all human beings and all peoples.

Text: Relevant articles of the Declaration are as follows:

Article 1

1. All human beings belong to a single species and are descended from a common stock. They are born equal in dignity and rights and all form an integral part of humanity.

2. All individuals and groups have the right to be different, to consider themselves as different and to be regarded as such. However, the diversity of life styles and the right to be different may not, in any circumstances, serve as a pretext for racial prejudice; they may not

justify either in law or in fact any discriminatory practice whatsoever, nor provide a ground for the policy of apartheid, which is the extreme form of racism.

3. Identity of origin in no way affects the fact that human beings can and may live differently, nor does it preclude the existence of differences based on cultural, environmental and historical diversity nor the right to maintain cultural identity.

4. All people of the world possess equal faculties for attaining the highest level in intellectual, technical, social, economic, cultural and political development.

5. The differences between the achievements of the different peoples are entirely attributable to geographical, historical, political, economic, social and cultural factors. Such differences can in no case serve as a pretext for any rank-ordered classification of nations for peoples.

Article 2

1. Any theory which involves the claim that racial or ethnic groups are inherently superior or inferior, thus implying that some would be entitled to dominate or eliminate others, presumed to be inferior, or which bases value judgements on racial differentiation, has no scientific foundation and is contrary to the moral and ethical principles of humanity.

2. Racism includes racist ideologies, prejudiced attitudes, discriminatory behaviour, structural arrangements and institutionalized practices resulting in racial inequality as well as the fallacious notion that discriminatory relations between groups are morally and scientifically justifiable; it is reflected in discriminatory provisions in legislation or regulations and discriminatory practices as well as in anti-social beliefs and acts; it hinders the development of its victims, perverts those who practice it, divides nations internally, impedes international co-operation and gives rise to political tensions between peoples; it is contrary to the fundamental principles of international law and, consequently, seriously disturbs international peace and security.

3. Racial prejudice, historically linked with inequalities in power, reinforced by economic and social differences between individuals and groups, and still seeking today to justify such inequalities, is totally without justification.

Article 3

Any distinction, exclusion, restriction or preference based on race, colour, ethnic or national origin or religious intolerance motivated by racist considerations, which destroys or compromises the sovereign equality of States and the right of peoples to self-determination, or which limits in an arbitrary or discriminatory manner the right of every human being and group to full development is incompatible with the requirements of an international order which is just and guarantees respect for human rights; the right to full development implies equal access to the means of personal and collective advancement and fulfillment in a climate of respect for the values of civilizations and cultures, both national and world-wide.

Article 9

1. The principle of the equality in dignity and rights of all human beings and all peoples, irrespective of race, colour and origin, is a generally accepted and recognized principle of international law. Consequently any form of racial discrimination practiced by a State constitutes a violation of international law giving rise to its international responsibility.

2. Special measures must be taken to ensure equality in dignity and rights for individuals and groups wherever necessary, while ensuring that they are not such as to appear racially discriminatory. In this respect, particular attention should be paid to racial or ethnic groups which are socially or economically disadvantaged, so as to afford them, on a completely equal footing and without discrimination or restriction, the protection of the laws and regulations and the advantages of the social measures in force, in particular in regard to housing, employment and health; to respect the authenticity of their culture and values; and to facilitate their social and occupational advancement, especially through education.

3. Population groups of foreign origin, particularly migrant workers and their families who contribute to the development of the host country, should benefit from appropriate measures designed to afford them security and respect for their dignity and cultural values and to facilitate their adaptation to the host environment and their professional advancement with a view to their subsequent reintegration in their country of origin and their contribution to its development; steps should be taken to make it possible for their children to be taught their mother tongue.

4. Existing disequilibria in international economic relations contribute to the exacerbation of racism and racial prejudice; all States should consequently endeavour to contribute to the restructuring of the international economy on a more equitable basis.

DOCUMENT 16: Resolution on Alternative Approaches and Ways and Means within the United Nations System for Improving the Effective Enjoyment of Human Rights and Fundamental Freedoms, 23 November 1979.

Official Source: United Nations General Assembly Resolution 34/46.

Secondary Sources: (1979) 33 *UN Ybk* 865.

Status: General Assembly resolution (adopted 136–1:7); recommendatory *vis-à-vis* member States.

Comment: Reiterates Resolution 32/130 (see Document 15), but with increased emphasis on the right to development as a human right.

Text: The following is the text of operative paragraphs 6–8:

6. *Emphasizes* the need to create conditions at the national and international levels for the full promotion and protection of the human rights of individuals and peoples;
7. *Recognizes* that, in order fully to guarantee human rights and complete personal dignity, it is necessary to guarantee the right to work, participation of workers in management, and the right to education, health and proper nourishment, though the adoption of measures at the national and international levels, including the establishment of the new international economic order;
8. *Emphasizes* that the right to development is human right and that equality of opportunity for development is as much a prerogative of nations as of individuals within nations . . .

DOCUMENT 17: African Charter on Human and Peoples' Rights, Nairobi, June 1981.

Official Source: Doc CAB/LEG/67/3/Rev 5 (1981).

Secondary Sources: (1982) 21 ILM 59–68; Council of Europe, 207–225.

Status: Regional human rights treaty adopted by the Assembly of Heads of State and Government of the Organization of African Unity in Nairobi in June 1981, after the text had been concluded at an OAU Ministerial Meeting on the African Charter on Human and Peoples' Rights, 7–19 January 1981, in Banjul, The Gambia. The Charter entered into force on 21 October 1986, at which time 30 African States were parties.

Comment: Sometimes referred to as the Banjul Charter. Only human rights treaty (universal or regional) to deal specifically with peoples' rights in general. Also guarantees individual rights, although without expressly addressing the relationship between human and peoples' rights.

Text:

African Charter on
Human and Peoples' Rights

PREAMBLE

The African States members of the Organization of African Unity, parties to the present convention entitled African Charter on Human and Peoples' Rights.

Recalling Decision 115 (XVI) of the Assembly of Heads of State and Government at its Sixteenth Ordinary Session held in Monrovia, Liberia, from 17 to 20 July 1979 on the preparation of 'a preliminary draft of an African Charter on Human and Peoples' Rights providing inter alia for the establishment of bodies to promote and protect human and peoples' rights';

Considering the Charter of the Organization of African Unity, which stipulates that 'freedom, equality, justice and legitimate aspirations of the African peoples';

Reaffirming the pledge they solemnly made in Article 2 of the said Charter to eradicate all forms of colonialism from Africa, to co-ordinate and intensify their co-operation and efforts to achieve a better life for the peoples of Africa and to promote international co-operation having due regard to the Charter of the United Nations and the Universal Declaration of Human Rights;

Taking into consideration the virtues of their historical tradition and the values of African civilization which should inspire and characterize their reflection on the concept of human and peoples' rights;

Recognizing on the one hand, that fundamental human rights stem from the attributes of human beings, which justifies their international protection and on the other hand that the reality and respect of peoples' rights should necessarily guarantee human rights;

Considering that the enjoyment of rights and freedoms also implies the performance of duties on the part of everyone;

Convinced that it is henceforth essential to pay a particular attention to the right to development and that civil and political rights cannot be dissociated from economic, social and cultural rights in their conception as well as universality and that the satisfaction of economic, social and cultural rights is a guarantee for the enjoyment of civil and political rights;

Conscious of their duty to achieve the total liberation of Africa, the peoples of which are still struggling for their dignity and genuine independence, and undertaking to eliminate colonialism, neo-colonialism, apartheid, zionism and to dismantle aggressive foreign military bases and all forms of discrimination, language, religion or political opinions;

Reaffirming their adherence to the principles of human and peoples' rights and freedoms contained in the declarations, conventions and other instruments adopted by the Organization of African Unity, the Movement of Non-Aligned Countries and the United Nations;

Firmly convinced of their duty to promote and protect human and peoples' rights and freedoms taking into account the importance traditionally attached to these rights and freedoms in Africa;

Have agreed as follows:

Part I—Rights and Duties

Chapter I—Human and Peoples' Rights

Article 1

The Member States of the Organization of African Unity parties to the present Charter shall recognize the rights, duties and freedoms enshrined in this Charter and shall undertake to adopt legislative or other measures to give effect to them.

Article 2

Every individual shall be entitled to the enjoyment of the rights and freedoms recognized and guaranteed in the present Charter without distinction of any kind such as race, ethnic group, colour, sex, language, religion, political or any other opinion, national and social origin, fortune, birth or other status.

Article 3

1. Every individual shall be equal before the law.
2. Every individual shall be entitled to equal protection of the law.

Article 4

Human beings are inviolable. Every human being shall be entitled to respect for his life and the integrity of his person. No one may be arbitrarily deprived of this right.

Article 5

Every individual shall have the right to the respect of the dignity inherent in a human being and to the recognition of his legal status. All forms of exploitation and degrading punishment and treatment shall be prohibited.

Article 6

Every individual shall have the right to liberty and to the security of his person. No one may be deprived of his freedom except for reasons and conditions previously laid down by law. In particular, no one may be arbitrarily arrested or detained.

Article 7

1. Every individual shall have the right to have his cause heard. This comprises:
   a. The right to an appeal to competent national organs against acts

violating his fundamental rights as recognized and guaranteed by conventions, laws, regulations and customs in force;

  b. The right to be presumed innocent until proved guilty by a competent court or tribunal;

  c. the right to defence, including the right to be defended by counsel of his choice;

  d. the right to be tried within a reasonable time by an impartial court or tribunal.

2. No one may be condemned for an act or omission which did not constitute a legally punishable offence at the time it was committed. No penalty may be inflicted for an offence for which no provision was made at the time it was committed. Punishment is personal and can be imposed only on the offender.

Article 8

Freedom of conscience, the profession and free practice of religion shall be guaranteed. No one may, subject to law and order, be submitted to measures restricting the exercise of these freedoms.

Article 9

1. Every individual shall have the right to receive information.
2. Every individual shall have the right to express and disseminate his opinions within the law.

Article 10

1. Every individual shall have the right to free association provided that he abides by the law.
2. Subject to the obligation of solidarity provided for in Article 29 no one may be compelled to join an association.

Article 11

Every individual shall have the right to assemble freely with others. The exercise of this right shall be subject only to necessary restrictions provided for by law in particular those enacted in the interest of national security, the safety, health, ethics and rights and freedoms of others.

Article 12

1. Every individual shall have the right to freedom of movement and residence within the borders of a State provided he abides by the law.
2. Every individual shall have the right to leave any country including his own, and to return to his country. This right may only be subject to restrictions, provided for by law for the protection of national security, law and order, public health or morality.

3. Every individual shall have the right, when persecuted, to seek and obtain asylum in other countries in accordance with the law of those countries and international conventions.

4. A non-national legally admitted in a territory of a State Party to the present Charter, may only be expelled from it by virtue of a decision taken in accordance with the law.

5. The mass expulsion of non-nationals shall be prohibited. Mass expulsion shall be that which is aimed at national, racial, ethnic or religious groups.

Article 13

1. Every citizen shall have the right to participate freely in the government of his country, either directly or through freely chosen representatives in accordance with the provisions of the law.

2. Every citizen shall have the right of equal access to the public service of his country.

3. Every individual shall have the right of access to public property and services in strict equality of all persons before the law.

Article 14

The right to property shall be guaranteed. It may only be encroached upon in the interest of public need or in the general interest of the community and in accordance with the provisions of appropriate laws.

Article 15

Every individual shall have the right to work under equitable and satisfactory conditions, and shall receive equal pay for equal work.

Article 16

1. Every individual shall have the right to enjoy the best attainable state of physical and mental health.

2. States Parties to the present Charter shall take the necessary measures to protect the health of their people and to ensure that they receive medical attention when they are sick.

Article 17

1. Every individual shall have the right to education.

2. Every individual may freely take part in the cultural life of his community.

Article 18

1. The family shall be the natural unit and basis of society. It shall be protected by the State.

2. The State shall have the duty to assist the family which is the cus-
todian of morals and traditional values recognized by the community.
3. The State shall ensure the elimination of every discrimination against
women and also ensure the protection of the rights of the woman and
the child as stipulated in international declarations and conventions.
4. The aged and the disabled shall also have the right to special measures
of protection in keeping with their physical or moral needs.

Article 19

All people shall be equal; they shall enjoy the same respect and shall
have the same rights. Nothing shall justify the domination of a people
by another.

Article 20

1. All peoples shall have right to existence. They shall have the unquestionable and inalienable right to self-determination. They shall
freely determine their political status and shall pursue their economic
and social development according to the policy they have freely
chosen.
2. Colonized or oppressed peoples shall have the right to free themselves
from the bonds of domination by resorting to any means recognized
by the international community.

Article 21

1. All peoples shall freely dispose of their wealth and natural resources.
The right shall be exercised in the exclusive interest of the people. In
no case shall a people be deprived of it.
2. In case of spoliation the dispossessed people shall have the right to the
lawful recovery of its property as well as to an adequate compensation.
3. The free disposal of wealth and natural resources shall be exercised
without prejudice to the obligation of promoting international economic co-operation based on mutual respect, equitable exchange and
the principles of international law.
4. States parties to the present Charter shall individually and collectively
exercise the right to free disposal of their wealth and natural resources
with a view to strengthening African unity and solidarity.
5. States parties to the present Charter shall undertake to eliminate all
forms of foreign economic exploitation particularly that practiced by
international monopolies so as to enable their peoples to fully benefit
from the advantages derived from their national resources.

Article 22

1. All peoples shall have the right to their economic, social and cultural

development with due regard to their freedom and identity and in the equal enjoyment of the common heritage of mankind.

2. States shall have the duty, individually or collectively to ensure the exercise of the right to development.

Article 23

1. All peoples shall have the right to national and international peace and security. The principles of solidarity and friendly relations implicitly affirmed by the Charter of the United Nations and reaffirmed by that of the Organization of African Unity shall govern relations between States.

2. For the purpose of strengthening peace, solidarity and friendly relations, States parties to the present Charter shall ensure that:

   a. any individual enjoying the right of asylum under Article 12 of the present Charter shall not engage in subversive activities against his country of origin or any other State party to the present Charter.

   b. their territories shall not be used as bases for subversive or terrorist activities against the people of any other State party to the present Charter.

Article 24

All peoples shall have the right to a general satisfactory environment favourable to their development.

Article 25

States parties to the present Charter shall have the duty to promote and ensure through teaching, education and publication, the respect of the rights and freedoms and rights as well as corresponding obligations and duties are understood.

Article 26

States parties to the present Charter shall have the duty to guarantee the independence of the Courts and shall allow the establishment and improvement of appropriate national institutions entrusted with the promotion and protection of the rights and freedoms guaranteed by the present Charter.

Chapter II—Duties

Article 27

1. Every individual shall have duties towards his family and society, the State and other legally recognized communities and the international community.

2. The rights and freedoms of each individual shall be exercised with due regard to the rights of others, collective security, morality and common interest.

Article 28

Every individual shall have the duty to respect and consider his fellow beings without discrimination, and to maintain relations aimed at promoting, safeguarding and reinforcing mutual respect and tolerance.

Article 29

The individual shall also have the duty:
1. To preserve the harmonious development of the family and to work for the cohesion and respect of the family; to respect his parents at all times, to maintain them in case of need;
2. To serve his national community by placing his physical and intellectual abilities at its service;
3. Not to compromise the security of the State whose national or resident he is;
4. To preserve and strengthen social and national solidarity, particularly when the latter is threatened;
5. To preserve and strengthen the national independence and the territorial integrity of his country and to contribute to its defence in accordance with the law;
6. To work to the best of his abilities and competence, and to pay taxes imposed by law in the interest of the society;
7. To preserve and strengthen positive African cultural values in his relations with other members of the society, in the spirit of tolerance, dialogue and consultation and, in general, to contribute to the promotion of the moral well-being of society.
8. To contribute to the best of his abilities, at all times and at all levels, to the promotion and achievement of African unity.

Part II Measures of Safeguard

Chapter I—Establishment and organization of the African Commission on Human and Peoples' Rights

Article 30

An African Commission on Human and Peoples' Rights, hereinafter called 'the Commission', shall be established within the Organization of African Unity to promote human and peoples' rights and ensure their protection in Africa.

[*Articles 30–54 not reproduced*]

Other communications

Article 55

1. Before each Session, the Secretary of the Commission shall make a list of the Communications other than those of States parties to the present Charter and transmit them to the Members of the Commission, who shall indicate which communications should be considered by the Commission.
2. A communication shall be considered by the Commission if a simple majority of its members so decide.

Article 56

Communication relating to human and peoples' rights referred to in Article 55 received by the Commission, shall be considered if they:

1. indicate their authors even if the latter request anonymity,
2. are compatible with the Charter of the Organization of African Unity or with the present Charter,
3. are not written in disparaging or insulting language directed against the State concerned and its institutions or to the Organization of African Unity,
4. are not based exclusively on news disseminated through the mass media,
5. are sent after exhausting local remedies, if any, unless it is obvious that this procedure is unduly prolonged,
6. are submitted within a reasonable period from the time local remedies are exhausted or from the date the Commission is seized with the matter, and
7. do not deal with cases which have been settled by these States involved in accordance with the principles of the Charter of the United Nations, or the Charter of the Organization of African Unity or the provisions of the present Charter.

[*Articles 57–9 not reproduced*]

Chapter IV—Applicable principles

Article 60

The Commission shall draw inspiration from international law on human and peoples' rights, particularly from the provisions of various African instruments on human and peoples' rights, the Charter of the United Nations, the Charter of the Organization of African Unity, the Universal Declaration of Human Rights, other instruments adopted by the United

Nations and by African countries in the field of human and peoples' rights as well as from the provisions of various instruments adopted within the Specialized Agencies of the United Nations of which the parties to the present Charter are members.

Article 61

The Commission shall also take into consideration, as subsidiary measures to determine the principles of law, other general or special international conventions, laying down rules expressly recognized by member States of the Organization of African Unity, African practices consistent with international norms on human and peoples' rights, customs generally accepted as law, general principles of law recognized by African States as well as legal precedents and doctrine.

[Articles 57-9 not reproduced]

DOCUMENT 18: UNESCO Latin-American Conference, Declaration of San José, 11 December 1981.

Official Source: UNESCO Doc FS 82/WF.32 (1982).

Secondary Sources:—.

Status: Resolution of a Meeting of Experts on Ethno-Development and Ethnocide in Latin America, held in Costa Rica under UNESCO auspices. No formal status.

Comment: In context of 'loss of cultural identity among the Indian populations of Latin America', seeks to develop the idea that 'ethnocide' is equivalent to genocide.

Text:

For the past few years, increasing concern has been expressed at various international forums over the problems of the loss of cultural identity among the Indian populations of Latin America. This complex process, which has historical, social, political and economic roots, has been termed *ethnocide.*

Ethnocide means that an ethnic group is denied the right to enjoy, develop and transmit its own culture and its own language, whether collectively or individually. This involves an extreme form of massive violation of human rights and, in particular, the right of ethnic groups to respect for their cultural identity, as established by numerous declarations, covenants and agreements of the United Nations and its Specialized Agencies, as well as various regional intergovernmental bodies and numerous non-government organizations.

In response to this demand, UNESCO organized an international meeting on ethnocide and ethno-development in Latin America, in collaboration with FLACSO, which was held in December 1981 in San José, Costa Rica.

The participants in the meeting, Indian and other experts, made the following Declaration:

1. We declare that ethnocide, that is, cultural genocide, is a violation of international law equivalent to genocide, which was condemned by the United Nations Convention on the Prevention and Punishment of the Crime of Genocide of 1948.

2. We affirm that ethno-development is an inalienable right of Indian groups.

3. By ethno-development we mean the extension and consideration of the elements of its own culture, through strengthening the independent decision-making capacity of a culturally distinct society to direct its own development and exercise self-determination, at whatever level, which implies an equitable and independent share of power. This means that the ethnic group is a political and administrative unit, with authority over its own territory and decision-making powers within the confines of its development project, in a process of increasing autonomy and self-management.

4. Since the European invasion, the Indian peoples of America have seen their history denied or distorted, despite their great contributions to the progress of mankind, which has led to the negation of their very existence. We reject this unacceptable misrepresentation.

5. As creators, bearers and propagators of a civilizing dimension of their own, as unique and specific facets of the heritage of mankind, the Indian peoples, nations and ethnic groups of America are entitled, collectively and individually, to all civil, political, economic, social and cultural rights now threatened. We, the participants in this meeting, demand universal recognition of all these rights.

6. For the Indian peoples, the land is not only an object of possession and production. It forms the basis of their existence, both physical and spiritual, as an independent entity. Territorial space is the foundation and source of their relationship with the universe and the mainstay of their view of the world.

7. The Indian peoples have a natural and inalienable right to the territories they possess as well as the right to recover the land taken away from them. This implies the right to the natural and cultural heritage that this territory contains and the right to determine freely how it will be used and exploited.

8. An essential part of the cultural heritage of these peoples is their philosophy of life and their experience, knowledge and achievements accumulated throughout history in the cultural, social, political, legal, scientific and technological sphere. They therefore have a right to access to and use, dissemination and transmission of this entire heritage.

9. Respect for the forms of autonomy required by the Indian peoples is an essential condition for guaranteeing and implementing these rights.

10. Furthermore, the Indian peoples' own forms of internal organization are part of their cultural and legal heritage which has contributed to their cohesion and to maintaining their socio-cultural traditions.

11. Disregard for these principles constitutes a gross violation of the right of all individuals and peoples to be different, to consider themselves as different and to be regarded as such, a right recognized in the Declaration on Race and Racial Prejudice adopted by the UNESCO General Conference in 1978, and should therefore be condemned, especially when it creates a risk of ethnocide.

12. In addition, disregard for these principles creates disequilibrium and lack of harmony within society and may incite the Indian peoples to the ultimate resort of rebellion against tyranny and oppression, thereby endangering world peace. It therefore contravenes the United Nations Charter and the Constitution of UNESCO.

As a result of their reflections, the participants appeal to the United Nations, UNESCO, the ILO, WHO and FAO, as well as to the Organizations of American States and the Inter-American Indian Institute, to take the necessary steps to apply these principles in full.

The participants address their appeal to Member States of the United Nations and the above-mentioned Specialized Agencies, requesting them to give special attention to the application of these principles, and also to collaborate with international, intergovernmental and non-governmental organizations, both universal and regional including, in particular, Indian organizations, in order to ensure observance of the fundamental rights of the Indian peoples of America.

This appeal is also addressed to officials in the legislative, executive, administrative and legal branches, and to all public servants concerned in the countries of America, with the request that in the course of their daily duties they will always act in conformity with the above principles.

The participants appeal to the conscience of the scientific community, and the individuals comprising it, who have the moral responsibility for ensuring that their research, studies and practices, as well as the conclusions they draw, cannot be used as a pretext for misrepresentation or interpretations which could harm Indian nations, peoples and ethnic groups.

Finally, the participants draw attention to the need to provide for due participation by genuine representatives of Indian nations, peoples and ethnic groups in any activity that might affect their future.

DOCUMENT 19: World Conference of Indigenous Peoples, Declaration of Principles of Indigenous Rights, Panama, September 1984.

Official Source: E/CN.4/Sub 2/1985/22, Annex II.

Secondary Sources: (1984) 40 *IWGIA Newsletter* 129.

Status: Declaration adopted at the Fourth Assembly of the World Council of Indigenous Peoples, a non-governmental organization.

Comment: The WCIP is a confederation of indigenous organizations from various countries. The declaration represents a statement by the World Council of the common views of its member associations and groups, and thus, indirectly, a statement of the aspirations and claims of those peoples, in particular to self-determination.

Text:

Declaration of Principles of Indigenous Rights

Principle 1

All indigenous peoples have the right of self-determination. By virtue of this right they may freely determine their political status and freely pursue their economic, social, religious and cultural development.

Principle 2

All states within which an indigenous people lives shall recognize the population, territory and institutions of the indigenous people.

Principle 3

The cultures of the indigenous peoples are part of the cultural heritage of mankind.

Principle 4

The tradition and customs of indigenous people must be respected by the states, and recognized as a fundamental source of law.

Principle 5

All indigenous peoples have the right to determine the person or groups of persons who are included within its population.

Principle 6

Each indigenous people has the right to determine the form, structure and authority of its institutions.

Principle 7

The institutions of indigenous peoples and their decisions, like those of states, must be in conformity with internationally accepted human rights both collective and individual.

Principle 8

Indigenous peoples and their members are entitled to participate in the political life of the state.

Principle 9

Indigenous people shall have exclusive rights to their traditional lands and its resources: Where the lands and resources of the indigenous peoples have been taken away without their free and informed consent such lands and resources shall be returned.

Principle 10

The land rights of an indigenous people include surface and subsurface rights, full rights and interior and coastal waters and rights to adequate and exclusive coastal economic zones within the limits of international law.

Principle 11

All indigenous peoples may, for their own needs, freely use their natural wealth and resources in accordance with Principles 9 and 10.

Principle 12

No action or course of conduct may be undertaken which, directly or indirectly, may result in the destruction of land, air, water, sea ice, wildlife, habitat or natural resources without the free and informed consent of the indigenous peoples affected.

Principle 13

The original rights to their material culture, including archaeological sites, artifacts, designs, technology and works of art lie with the indigenous people.

Principle 14

The indigenous peoples have the right to receive education in their own language or to establish their own educational institutions. The languages of the indigenous peoples are to be respected by the states in all dealings between the indigenous people and the state on the basis of equality and non-discrimination.

Principle 15

The indigenous peoples and their authorities have the right to be previously consulted and to authorize the realization of all technological and scientific investigations to be conducted within their territories and to be informed and have full access to the results of the investigation.

Principle 16

Indigenous peoples have the right, in accordance with their traditions, to move freely and conduct traditional activities and maintain kinship relationships across international boundaries.

Principle 17

Treaties between indigenous nations or peoples and representatives of states freely entered into, shall be given full effect under national and international law.

DOCUMENT 20: Declaration on the Right to Development, 4 December 1986

Official Source: United Nations General Assembly Resolution 41/128

Secondary Sources:

Status: Declaration annexed to General Assembly resolution (adopted 146–1:8); recommendatory *vis-à-vis* member States

Comment: Adopted after lengthy gestation, but without avoiding a vote. Proclaims the 'right to development' as 'an inalienable human right by virtue of which every human person and all peoples are entitled to participate in, contribute to and enjoy economic, social, cultural and political development', with the human person as the central subject, active participant and beneficiary of the right to development. Avoids specific reference to certain issues, such as 'increased concessional assistance to developing countries', and to earlier resolutions such as the Charter of Economic Rights and Duties of States: these were incorporated in a separate resolution, Res 41/133, The Right to Development, also adopted on 4 December 1986 by a vote of 133–11:12.

Text:

The General Assembly.
Having considered the question of the right to development,
  1. Decides to adopt the Declaration on the Right to Development, the text of which is annexed to the present resolution.

Annex Declaration on the Right to Development

Bearing in mind the purposes and principles of the Charter of the United Nations relating to the achievement of international co-operation in solving international problems of an economic, social, cultural or humanitarian nature, and in promoting and encouraging respect for human rights and fundamental freedoms for all without distinction as to race, sex, language or religion.

Recognizing that development is a comprehensive economic, social, cultural and political process, which aims at the constant improvement of the well-being of the entire population and of all individuals on the basis of their active, free and meaningful participation in development and in the fair distribution of benefits resulting therefrom.

Considering that under the provisions of the Universal Declaration of Human Rights everyone is entitled to a social and international order in which the rights and freedoms set forth in that Declaration can be fully realized.

Recalling the provisions of the International Covenant on Economic, Social and Cultural Rights and the International Covenant on Civil and Political Rights.

Recalling further the relevant agreements, conventions, resolutions, recommendations and other instruments of the United Nations and its specialized agencies concerning the integral development of the human being, economic and social progress and development of all peoples, including those instruments concerning decolonization, the prevention of discrimination, respect for, and observance of, human rights and fundamental freedoms, the maintenance of international peace and security and the further promotion of friendly relations and co-operation among States in accordance with the Charter.

Recalling the right of peoples to self-determination, by virtue of which they have the right freely to determine their political status and to pursue their economic, social and cultural development.

Recalling further the right of peoples to exercise, subject to relevant provisions of both International Covenants on Human Rights, their full and complete sovereignty over all their natural wealth and resources.

Mindful of the obligation of States under the Charter to promote universal respect for, and observance of, human rights and fundamental freedoms for all without distinction of any kind such as race, colour, sex, language, religion, political or other opinion, national or social origin, property, birth or other status.

Considering that the elimination of the massive and flagrant violations of the human rights of the peoples and individuals affected by situations such as those resulting from colonialism, neo-colonialism, apartheid, all forms of racism and racial discrimination, foreign domination and occupation, aggression and threats against national sovereignty, national unity and territorial integrity and threats of war would contribute to the establishment of circumstances propitious to the development of a great part of mankind.

Concerned at the existence of serious obstacles to development, as well as to the complete fulfillment of human beings and of peoples, constituted, *inter alia*, by the denial of civil, political, economic, social and cultural rights, and considering that all human rights and fundamental freedoms are indivisible and interdependent and that, in order to promote development, equal attention and urgent consideration should be given to the implementation, promotion and protection of civil, political, economic, social and cultural rights and that, accordingly, the promotion of, respect for, and enjoyment of certain human rights and fundamental freedoms cannot justify the denial of other human rights and fundamental freedoms.

Considering that international peace and security are essential elements for the realization of the right to development.

Reaffirming that there is a close relationship between disarmament and development and that progress in the field of disarmament would considerably promote progress in the field of development and that resources released through disarmament measures should be devoted to the economic and social development and well-being of all peoples and, in particular, those of the developing countries.

Recognizing that the human person is the central subject of the development process and that development process and that development policy should therefore make the human being the main participant and beneficiary of development.

Recognizing that the creation of conditions favourable to the development of peoples and individuals is the primary responsibility of their States.

Aware that efforts to promote and protect human rights at the international level should be accompanied by efforts to establish a new international economic order.

Confirming that the right to development is an inalienable human right and that equality of opportunity for development is a prerogative both of nations and of individuals who make up nations.

Proclaims the following Declaration on the right to development:

Article 1

1. The right to development is an inalienable human right by virtue of which every human person and all peoples are entitled to participate in, contribute to and enjoy economic, social, cultural and political development, in which all human rights and fundamental freedoms can be fully realized.

2. The human right to development also implies the full realization of the right of peoples to self-determination, which includes, subject to relevant provisions of both International Covenants on Human Rights, the exercise of their inalienable right to full sovereignty over all their natural wealth and resources.

Article 2

1. The human person is the central subject of development and should be the active participant and beneficiary of the right to development,

2. All human beings have a responsibility for development, individually and collectively, taking into account the need for full respect of their

human rights and fundamental freedoms as well as their duties to the community, which alone can ensure the free and complete fulfillment of the human being, and they should therefore promote and protect an appropriate political, social and economic order for development.

3. States have the right and the duty to formulate appropriate national development policies that aim at the constant improvement of the well-being of the entire population and of all individuals, on the basis of their active, free and meaningful participation in development and in the fair distribution of the benefits resulting therefrom.

Article 3

1. States have the primary responsibility for the creation of national and international conditions favourable to the realization of the right to development.

2. The realization of the right to development requires full respect for the principles of international law concerning friendly relations and co-operation among States in accordance with the Charter of the United Nations.

3. States have the duty to co-operate with each other in ensuring development and eliminating obstacles to development. States should fulfill their rights and duties in such a manner as to promote a new international economic order based on sovereign equality, interdependence, mutual interest and co-operation among all States, as well as to encourage the observance and realization of human rights.

Article 4

1. States have the duty to take steps, individually and collectively, to formulate international development policies with a view to facilitating the full realization of the right to development.

2. Sustained action is required to promote more rapid development of developing countries. As a complement to the efforts of developing countries effective international co-operation is essential in providing these countries with appropriate means and facilities to foster their comprehensive development.

Article 5

States shall take resolute steps to eliminate the massive and flagrant violations of the human rights of peoples and human beings affected by situations such as those resulting from *apartheid*, all forms of racism and racial discrimination, colonialism, foreign domination and occupation, aggression, foreign interference and threats against national sovereignty, national unity and territorial integrity, threats of war and refusal to recognize the fundamental right of peoples to self-determination.

Article 6

1. All States should co-operate with a view to promoting, encouraging and strengthening universal respect for and observance of all human rights and fundamental freedoms for all without any distinction as to race, sex, language and religion.
2. All human rights and fundamental freedoms are indivisible and interdependent; equal protection of civil, political, economic, social and cultural rights.
3. States should take steps to eliminate obstacles to development resulting from failure to observe civil and political rights as well as economic, social and cultural rights.

Article 7

All States should promote the establishment, maintenance and strengthening of international peace and security and, to that end, should do their utmost to achieve general and complete disarmament under effective international control as well as to ensure that the resources released by effective disarmament measures are used for comprehensive development, in particular that of the developing countries.

Article 8

1. States should undertake, at the national level, all necessary measures for the realization of the right to development and shall ensure, *inter alia*, equality of opportunity for all in their access to basic resources, education, health services, food, housing, employment and the fair distribution of income. Effective measures should be undertaken to ensure that women have an active role in the development process. Appropriate economic and social reforms should be made with a view to eradicating all social injustices.
2. States should encourage popular participation in all spheres as an important factor in development and in the full realization of all human rights.

Article 9

1. All the aspects of the right to development set forth in this Declaration are indivisible and interdependent and each of them should be considered in the context of the whole.
2. Nothing in this Declaration shall be construed as being contrary to the purposes and principles of the United Nations, or as implying that any State, group or person has a right to engage in any activity or to perform any act aimed at the violation of the rights set forth in the Universal Declaration of Human Rights and in the International Covenants on Human Rights.

Article 10

Steps should be taken to ensure the full exercise and progressive enhancement of the right to development, including the formulation, adoption and implementation of policy, legislative and other measures at the national and international levels.

Select Bibliography

Note: The Select Bibliography lists items under the following categories:

1. General and Miscellaneous
2. African Charter on Human and Peoples' Rights
3. Communication, Right to
4. Cultural and Linguistic Rights
5. Development, Right to
6. Environment, Rights to
7. Existence, Right to
8. Indigenous Peoples, Rights of
9. International Peace, Right to
10. Minorities, Rights of
11. Natural Resources, Permanent Sovereignty over
12. Self-Determination, Right to

This bibliography makes no attempt to cover the general human rights literature, except so far as it is relevant to the debate over peoples' rights. For a recent survey and bibliography see AE.-S. Tay, *Human Rights for Australia* (Human Rights Commission, Monograph Series No 1, Australian Government Publishing Service, Canberra, 1986).

1. General and Miscellaneous

ALSTON, P., 'A third generation of solidarity rights: progressive development or obfuscation of international human rights law?' (1982) 29 *Neth Int L Rev* 307.

—— 'Conjuring up new human rights: a proposal for quality control' (1984) 78 *AJIL* 607.

BASTID, S., 'Les droits des peuples dans le plan à moyen terms (1984–1989) de l'UNESCO' in *Mélanges offerts à Charles Chaumont* (Paris, A Pedone, 1984) 11.

BATAILLER-DEMICHEL, F., 'Droits de l'homme et droit des peuples dans l'ordre international' in *Mélanges offerts à Charles Chaumont* (Paris, A Pedone, 1984) 23.

CASSESE, A. & JOUVE, E. (eds), *Pour un Droit des Peuples. Essais sur la Déclaration d'Alger* (Berger Levrault, Paris, 1978).

Colloque International des Experts . . . , *Droits de Solidarité; Droits des Peuples* (San Marino, 1982).

DINSTEIN, Y., 'Collective human rights of peoples and minorities' (1976) 25 *ICLQ* 102.

FALK, R., 'The Algiers Declaration of the Rights of People' in R. Falk, *Human Rights and State Sovereignty* (1981) 184.

FENET, A. (ed.), *Droits de l'Homme, Droits des Peuples* (Paris, Presses Universitaires de France, 1982).

HASSAN, F., 'The right to be different: an exploratory proposal for the creation of a new human right' (1982) 5 *Loyola of LA Int & Comp LJ* 67.

KISS, C. A., 'Le concept d'égalité: définition et expérience' (1986) 27 *C de D* 145.

LILLICH, R. B., 'The Paris Minumum Standards of Human Rights Norms in a State of Emergency' (1985) 79 *AJIL* 1072.

McKEAN, W. A., 'The meaning of discrimination in international and municipal law' (1970) 44 *BYIL* 185.

—— *Equality and Discrimination under International Law* (Clarendon Press, Oxford, 1983).

MARKS, S., 'Emerging human rights: a new generation for the 1980s' (1981) 33 *Rutgers L Rev* 435.

MATARASSO, L., 'A propos d'initiatives de caractère non étatique en faveur du droit des peuples' in *Mélanges offerts à Charles Chaumont* (Paris, A Pedone, 1984) 397.

MERON, T., 'On the inadequate reach of humanitarian and human rights and the need for a new instrument' (1983) 77 *AJIL* 589.

—— 'On a hierarchy of international human rights' (1986) 80 *AJIL* 1.

Note, 'The American Convention of Human Rights: Toward uniform interpretation of human rights law' (1982/3) 6 *Fordham International LJ* 610.

PANICHAS, G. E., 'The structure of basic human rights' (1985) 4 *Law & Phil* 343.

PAUST, J. J., 'Authority: From a human rights perspective' (1983) 28 *Am J Juris* 44.

—— 'Aggression against authority: the crime of oppression, politicide and other crimes against human rights' (1986) 18 *Case W Res J Int L* 283.

POLLIS, A. & SCHWAB, P., 'Human rights; a western construct of limited applicability', in A. Pollis and P. Schwab (eds), *Human Rights. Cultural and Ideological Perspectives* (Praeger, New York, 1980) 1.

RHOODIE, E., *Discrimination in the Constitutions of the World. A Study of the Group Rights Problem* (Brentwood, Columbus, 1984).

ROUSSEAU, C., 'Droits de l'homme et droits des gens' *René Cassin Amicorum Discipulorumque Liber* (Paris, A Pedone, 1969) IV, 69.

RUILOBA SANTANA, E., 'Nueva categoria en el panorama de la subjetividad internacional: el concepto de pueblo' in *Estudios de Derecho Internacional: Homenaje al Professor Miaja de la Muela* (Editorial Tecnos, Madrid, 1979) 303.

SCHACHTER, O., 'Human dignity as a normative concept' (1983) 77 *AJIL* 848.

TESON, F. R. 'International human rights and cultural relativism' (1985) 54 *Va JIL* 869.

TOMUSCHAT, C. J., 'Rights of Peoples.—Some Preliminary Considerations' in Y. Hangartner & S. Trechsel (eds), *Volkerrecht im Dienste des Menschen. Festschrift fur Hans Haug* (1986) 337.

URIBE VARGAS, D., *La Troisième Génération des Droits de l'Homme et de la Paix* (Paris, CIEM, 1986).

WATSON, J. S., 'Normativity and reality in international human rights law' (1984) 13 *Stetson L Rev* 221.

WEISSBRODT, D., 'Strategies for the pursuit of international human rights objectives' (1981) 8 *Yale St Wld Pub Ord* 62.

2. African Charter on Human and Peoples' Rights

BALANDA, M. L., 'African Charter on Human and Peoples' Rights' in K. Ginther & W. Benedek (eds), *New Perspectives and Conceptions of International Law* (Springer Verlag, Vienna, 1983) 134.

BENEDEK, W., 'Human rights in a multi-cultural perspective: The African Charter and the human right to development' in K. Ginther & W. Benedek (eds), *New Perspectives and Conceptions of International Law* (Springer Verlag, Vienna, 1983) 147.

D'SA, R. M., 'Human and peoples' rights: distinctive aspects of the African Charter' (1985) 29 *J Af L* 72.

GITTLEMAN, R., 'The African Charter on Human and Peoples' Rights: a legal analysis' (1982) 22 *Va JIL* 667.

HAILE, M., 'Human rights, stability and development in Africa: Some observations on concept and reality' (1984) 24 *Va JIL* 575.

—— 'Human rights in Africa: observations on the implications of economic priority' (1986) 19 *Vanderbilt JTL* 299.

KUNIG, P., 'The role of "peoples" rights' in the African Charter on Human and Peoples' Rights' in K. Ginther and W. Benedek (eds), *New Perspectives and Conceptions of International Law* (Springer Verlag, Vienna, 1983) 147.

NEFF, S. C., 'Human rights in Africa: thoughts on the African Charter on Human and Peoples' Rights in the light of case law from Botswana, Lesotho and Swaziland' (1984) 33 *ICLQ* 331.

Note, 'Regional human rights models in Europe and Africa: a comparison' (1983) 10 *Syracuse J Int L & Com* 135.

OBINNA OKERE, B., 'The protection of human rights in Africa and the African Charter: a comparative analysis of European and American systems' (1984) 6 *Human Rights Q* 141.

SHIVJI, I. G., 'Law in independent Africa: some reflections in the role of legal ideology' (1985) 46 *Ohio St LJ* 489.

TURACK, D. C., 'The African Charter on Human and Peoples' Rights: some preliminary thoughts' (1984) 17 *Akron L Rev* 365.

UMOZURIKE, O. U., 'The African Charter on Human and Peoples' Rights' (1983) 77 *AJIL* 902.

3. Communication, Right to

ANAWALT, H. C., 'The right to communicate' (1985) 13 *Denver JILP* 219.

ANDROUNAS, E. & ZASSOURSKY, Y., 'Protecting the sovereignty of information' (1979) 29 *J Com* 186.

CHEN, L.-C., 'Human rights and the free flow of information' (1982) 4 *NYL Sch J Int & Comp L* 37.

International Commission for the Study of Communication Problems, *Report by the International Commission for the Study of Communications Problems, Many Voices, One World: Communication and Society Today and Tomorrow. Towards a New more just and more efficient World Information and Communication Order* (McBride Report) (Kogan Page, London, 1980).

KATSH, M. E., 'Communications revolutions and legal revolutions: the new media and the future of law' (1984) 8 *Nov LJ* 631.

LEHMANN, R. A., 'The human right of communication' (1982) 4 *NYLSJ Int & Comp L* 83.

MASMOUDI, M., 'The New World Information Order' (1979) 29 *J Com* 172.

NORDENSTRENG, K., 'Behind the semantics—a strategic design' (1979) 29 *J Com* 195.

Note, 'The New International Information Order: the developing world and the free flow of information controversy' (1982) 8 *Syracuse JILC* 249.

—— 'The human right of communication' (1982) 4 *NYL Sch J Int Comp L* 83.

—— 'The New World Information Order: a legal framework for debate' (1982) 14 *Case W Res JIL* 387.

—— 'The New World Information and Communication Order: is the international program for the development of communication the answer?' (1983) 5 *NW J Int L & Bus* 953.

—— 'Analysis of the legal authority for the establishment of private international communications satellite systems' (1984) 18 *Geo Wash J Int L & Econ* 355.

—— 'Jamming and law of international communications' [1984] *Mich YB Int L Stud* 391.

—— 'Jamming the stations: is there an international free flow of information?' (1984) 14 *Col W Int LJ* 501.

—— 'Politics among the airwaves: an analysis of Soviet and Western perspectives on international broadcasting and the right to exchange ideas and information regardless of Frontiers' (1985) 7 *Houston J Int Law* 237.

—— 'The New World Information and Communication Order and international human rights law' (1986) 9 *Brooklyn College Int & Comp L Rev* 107.

O'BRIEN, R. C. & HELLEINER, G. K., 'The political economy of information in a changing international economic order' (1980) 34 *Int Org* 445.

PASCALL, D. B. & SCHMIDT, V. M., 'United States international communications and information policy: a crisis in the making?' (1983) 5 *NW J Int L & Bus* 486.

POWERS, S., 'Reciprocity of international telecommunications trade: a new trade barrier?' [1984] *Mich YB Int L Stud* 169.

RIGHTER, R., 'Who won?' [A comment on the 1978 UNESCO Declaration Concerning the Mass Media] (1979) 29 *J Com* 192.

SMITH, A., *The Geopolitics of Information: How Western Culture Dominates the World* (Oxford University Press, New York, 1980).

TRUDEL, P., 'Réflexion pour une approche critique de la notion de droit à l'information en droit international' (1982) 23 *C de D* 847.

4. Cultural and Linguistic Rights

AGRAWALA, S. K., 'Jawaharlal Nehru and the language problem' (1977) 19 *Journal of the Indian Law Institute* 44.

ANDREWS, J. A. & HENSHAW, L. G., 'The Irish and Welsh Languages in the courts: a comparative study' (1983) 18 *Ir Jur* 1.

Avila, J. G., 'Equal educational opportunities for language minority children' (1984) 55 *U Colo L Rev* 339.

Bartole, S., 'Tutela della minoranza linguistica slovena ed esecuzione del trattato di Osimo' (1977) 60 *Rivista di Diritto Internazionale* 507.

Bilodeau, R., 'La langue, l'éducation et les minorités: avant et depuis la Charte Canadienne des Droits et Libertés' (1983) 13 *Man LJ* 371.

—— 'La judiciarisation des conflits linguistiques au Canada' (1986) 27 *C de D* 215.

Bossuyt, M., 'Droits linguistiques: une perspective européenne' (1983) 13 *Man LJ* (Special Issue) 663.

Boutros-Ghali, B., 'Droit à la culture et la Déclaration Universelle des Droits de l'Homme' (1968) 24 *Revue Egyptienne de Droit International* 67.

Brandt, G. J., 'Parties and participants in constitutional litigation: the minority language rights issue in Quebec and Manitoba' (1986) 35 *UNBLJ* 201.

Carignan, P., 'De la notion de droit collectif et de son application en matière scolaire au Québec' (1984) 18 *RJT* 1.

Colin, J.-P. & Lang, J., 'La culture entre les peuples et les états: vers un nouveau droit international' in *Mélanges offerts à Charles Chaumont* (Paris, A Pedone, 1984) 179.

Conklin, W. C., 'Constitutional ideology, language rights and political disunity in Canada' (1979) 28 *New Brunswick LJ* 39.

Davis, W. E., 'Language and the justice system: problems and issues' (1985) 10 *Just Sys J* 353.

Forget, M. A., 'Quebec Charter of the French Language—recent developments' (1980) 70 *Trademark Rep* 339.

Fortier, D., 'Les droits linguistiques canadiens en évolution' (1986) 27 *C de D* 227.

Garcia Martinez, A. L., 'Language policy in Puerto Rico 1898–1930' (1981) 42 *Rev C Abo PR* 87.

Garant, L., 'La Charte de la Langue Française' (1982) 23 *C de D* 263.

Lange, D. J., 'Constitutional jurisprudence, politics and minority language rights' (1980) 11 *Man LJ* 33.

Lebel, M., 'L'individu et la protection des valeurs culturelles' (1979) 17 *UW Ont L Rev* 253.

Lindsay, E. H., 'Linguistic minority educational rights in Canada: an international and comparative perspective' (1983) 13 *Ga J Int & Comp L* 515.

McDougal, M., Lasswell, H., & Chen, L. C., 'Freedom from discrimination in choice of language and international human rights (1976) *So Ill ULJ* 151.

Magnet, J. E., 'Language rights: myth and reality' (1981) 12 *Rev Gen de Droit* 261.

—— 'The future of official language minorities' (1986) 27 *C de D* 189.

Maroy, P., 'Lois et décrets sur l'emploi des langues dans les entreprises' (1978) 93 *Journal des Tribunaux* 269, 289.

Marks, S., 'UNESCO and Human Rights: The Implementation of Rights relating to Education, Science, Culture and Communication' (1977) 13 *Texas ILJ* 35.

Munday, R., 'Legislating in Defence of the French Language' (1985) 44 *Cambridge LJ* 218.

Niec, H., 'Human right to culture' (1979) 44 *Yearbook of the AAA* 109.

Note, 'Egalité juridique des langues' (1983) 24 *C de D* 9.

—— 'Minority language education rights' (1985) 43 *U Toronto L Rev* 45.

PARADIS, J. B., 'Language rights in multicultural states: a comparative study' (1970) 48 *Can B Rev* 651.

PETRELLA, R., 'Langues et société' (1976) 24 *European Yearbook* 72.

PIATT, B., 'Toward domestic recognition of a human right to language' (1986) 23 *Houst L Rev* 885.

PROTT, L. & O'KEEFE, P., *Law and the Cultural Heritage. vol. I: Discovery and Excavation* (Professional Books, Abingdon, 1984)

PROUBT, D., 'La précarité des droits linguistiques scolaires ou les singulières difficultés de mise en œuvre de l'article 23 de la Charte Canadienne des Droits et Libertés' (1983) 14 *Rev Gen de Droit* 335.

SAVREN, C., 'Language rights and Quebec Bill 101' (1978) 10 *Case Wes Res JIL* 543.

SHORT, D. E., 'Restrictions on access to English language schools in Quebec: an international human rights analysis' (1981) 4 *Can-US LJ* 1.

SZABO, I., *Cultural Rights* (Sijthoff, Leiden, 1974).

TETLEY, W., 'Language and education rights in Quebec and Canada (a legal, historical and personal political diary)' (1982) 45 *Law & Contemp Prob* 177.

TREMBLAY, A., 'Droits linguistiques—instruction dans la langue de la minorité' (1983) 41 *Can B Rev* 407.

—— 'L'interprétation des dispositions constitutionelles relatives aux droits linguistiques' (1983) 13 *Man LJ* 65.

TURI, J. G., 'Quelques considérations sur le droit linguistique' (1986) 27 *C de D* 463.

UDINA, M., 'Sull'attuazione dell'arte 6 della constituzione per la tutela delle minoranze linguistiche' (1974) 19 *Giurisprudenza Constitutionale* 3602.

UNESCO, *Cultural Rights as Human Rights* (UNESCO, Studies and Documents on Cultural Policies, Paris, 1970).

WOEHRLING, J., 'Minority cultural and linguistic rights and equality rights in the Canadian Charter of Rights and Freedoms' (1985) 31 *McGill LJ* 50.

—— 'L'article 15(1) de la Charte Canadienne des Droits et Libertés et la langue' (1985) 30 *McGill LJ* 266.

ZAPHIRIOU, G. A., 'Cultural and ideological pluralism and contemporary public international law' (1986) 34 *AJCL (Supp)* 341.

5. Development, Right to

AGUILAR NAVARRO, M., *Ensayo de Delimitacion del Derecho Internacional Economico* (University of Madrid, Faculty of Law, Madrid, 1972).

ALSTON, P., 'Development and the rule of law: prevention versus cure as a human rights strategy', in *Development, Human Rights and the Rule of Law, Report of a Conference held in The Hague on 27 April–1 May 1981* (Pergamon Press, Oxford, 1981) 31.

—— 'The shortcoming of a "Garfield the Cat" approach to the right to development' (1985) 15 *Calif WILJ* 510.

BEDJAOUI, M., *Towards a New International Economic Order* (UNESCO, Paris, 1979).

BENEDEK, W., 'Human rights in a multi-cultural perspective: the African Charter and the human right to development' in K. Ginther & W. Benedek (eds), *New Perspectives and Conceptions of International Law* (Springer Verlag, Vienna, 1983) 147.

BOVEN, T. C. VAN, 'Right to development and human rights' (1982) *Review of the International Commission of Jurists* No 28, 49.

BRIETZKE, P. H., 'Consorting with the chameleon, or realizing the right to development' (1985) 15 *Calif WILJ* 560.

BURG, E. M., 'Law and development: a review of the literature: a critique of scholars in self-estrangement' (1977) 25 *AJ Comp L* 492.

CARILLO SALCEDO, J. A., 'El derecho al desarrollo como un derecho humano' (1972) 25 *Revista Española de Derecho Internacional* 119.

CLARK, R., 'A World Food Bank: integrating will and idealism' (1985) 15 *Calif WILJ* 461.

Commission on Human Rights, *Report of the Working Group of Governmental Experts on the Right to Development* (E/CN.4/1985/11).

Commission on International Development (Chairman: LB Pearson), *Partners in Development: Report of the Commission on International Development* (Praeger, New York, 1969).

CUADRA, H., 'Reflexiones sobre el derecho economico' in H. Cuadra (ed.), *Estudios de Derecho Economico* (Universidad Nacional Autonoma de Mexico, Mexico, 1977) I, 11.

DOMENACH, J., *Our Moral Involvement in Development* (Centre for Economic and Social Information, Executive Briefing Paper 4, United Nations, New York, 1971).

DONNELLY, J., 'In search of the unicorn: the jurisprudence and politics of the right to development' (1985) 15 *Calif WILJ* 473.

DUPUY, R.-J. (ed.), *The Right to Development at the International Level* (Sijthoff and Noordhoff, Alphen aan den Rijn, 1980).

—— 'Thème et variations sur le droit au développement' in *Mélanges offerts à Charles Chaumont* (Paris, A Pedone, 1984) 433.

FERGUSON, C. C., 'Redressing global injustices: the role of the law' (1981) 33 *Rutgers L Rev* 410.

FLORY, M., *Droit International du Développement* (Presses Universitaires de France, Paris, 1977).

—— 'Inégalité économique du droit international' in Société Française Pour le Droit International, Colloque d'Aix-en-Provence, *Pays en Voie de Développement et Transformations du Droit International* (Actes du VIIe Colloque d'Aix-en-Provence) (A Pedone, Paris, 1974).

FRIEDMANN, W., 'The relevance of international law to the processes of economic and social development' in R. Falk and C. Black (eds), *The Future of the International Legal Order, Wealth and Resources* (Princeton UP, Princeton, 1970) II, 3.

GROS ESPIELL, H., *Derecho Internacional del Desarrollo* (2nd edn, 1977).

—— 'The right to development as a human right' (1981) 16 *Tex ILJ* 189.

HAZARD, J. N., 'Development and "new law" ' (1977/8) 45 *U Chi L Rev* 637.

HOWARD, R. E., 'Law and economic rights in Commonwealth Africa' (1985) 15 *Calif WILJ* 607.

ISRAEL, J. J., 'Droit au développement' (1983) 87 *RGDIP* 5.

JACKSON, J., 'Measuring human rights and development by one yardstick' (1985) 15 *Calif WILJ* 453.

KASSAHUN, Y., 'The food questions within the prism of the international law of development' (1985) 38 *Oklahoma LR* 863.

M'BAYE, K., 'Le Droit au développement comme un droit de l'homme' (1972) 5 *Human Rights J* 505.

—— *Emergence du Droit au Développement en tant que Droit de L'Homme dans le Contexte du Nouvel Ordre Économique International* (1978).

—— 'Le Droit au développement en droit international' in J. Makarczyk (ed.), *Essays in International Law in Honour of Judge Manfred Lachs* (Martinus Nijhoff, The Hague, 1984) 163.

MENEZES, J., 'Law and absolute poverty' (1981) 15 *Val UL Rev* 343.

MESTDAGH, K. DE V., 'The right to development' (1981) 28 *Neth Int L Rev* 30.

—— 'The right to development', in *Development, Human Rights and the Rule of Law* (Pergamon Press, Oxford, 1981) 143.

MUTHARIKA, A. P. (ed.), *The International Law of Development, Basic Documents* (Oceana, Dobbs Ferry, 1978).

NANDA, V. P., 'Development as an emerging human right under international law' (1985) 13 *Denver J Int L & Pol* 141.

—— 'The right to development under international law—challenges ahead' (1985) 15 *Calif WILJ* 431.

Note, 'Economic development and human rights' (1973) 67 *ASIL Proc* 198.

—— 'Innocents abroad: infant food technology at the law's frontier' (1980) 20 *Va JIL* 617.

—— 'International legal obligation to assist in the energy development arises from the Charter of Economic Rights and Duties of States' (1982) 12 *Ga JIL* 401.

PANEL, 'Demand for economic justice' (1981) 75 *ASIL Proc* 120.

PELLET, A., *Le Droit International du Développement* (Presses Universitaires de France, Paris, 1978).

REDCLIFT, M., *Development and the Environmental Crisis: Red or Green Alternatives?* (Methuen, London, 1984).

RICH, R., 'The right to development as an emerging human right' (1983) 23 *Va JIL* 287.

SCHACHTER, O., 'The evolving international law of development' (1976) 15 *Colum J Transnat L* 1.

Société Française Pour le Droit International, Colloque d'Aix-en-Provence, *Pays en Voie de Développement et Transformations du Droit International* (Actes du VIIe Colloque d'Aix-en-Provence) (A Pedone, Paris, 1974).

SNYDER, F. G., 'Law and development in the light of the dependency theory' (1980) 14 *Law & Soc Rev* 723.

THEBERGE, L. J., 'Law and economic development' (1980) 9 *Denver J Int & Pol* 231.

UMOZORIKE, U. O., 'Freedom from hunger—a third world view' (1985) 70 *Iowa L Rev* 1329.

United Nations, Report of the Secretary-General, *The International Dimensions of the Right to Development as a Human Right, in Relation with Other Human Rights Based on International Cooperation, Including the Right to Peace, Taking into Account the Requirements of the New International Economic Order and the Fundamental Human Needs* (1979).

United Nations, Commission on Human Rights, *Report of the Working Group of Governmental Experts on the Right to Development* (E/CN.4/1985/11, 24 January 1985).

VERWAY, W. D., 'The recognition of the developing countries as special subjects of international law beyond the sphere of United Nations resolutions', in R. J. Dupuy (ed.), *The Right to Development at the International Level* (Sijthoff & Noordhoff, Alphen aan den Rijn, 1980) 30.

VIRALLY, M., 'Le deuxième décennie des Nations Unies pour le développement' (1970) 16 *AFDI* 9.

—— 'Vers un droit international du développement' (1965) 11 *AFDI* 3.

WEIL, P., 'Le droit international économique: mythe ou réalité?' in Société Française Pour le Droit International, Colloque d'Orléans, *Aspects du droit international économique* (Actes du VIe Colloque d'Orléans) (A Pedone, Paris, 1972) 1.

YOUNG, A., 'Human right or necessity?' (1985) 15 *Calif WILJ* 441.

6. Environment, Rights to

DUPUY, P. M., 'Le Droit à la santé et la protection de l'environnement' in R. J. Dupuy (ed.), *The Right to Health as a Human Right* (Sijthoff and Noordhoff, Alphen aan den Rijn, 1979) 340.

DUPUY, R.-J., *L'Avenir du Droit International de l'Environnement. Colloque de l'Académie de Droit International de La Haye* (Martinus Nijhoff, Dordrecht, 1985).

EDMOND, D. P., 'Co-operation in nature: a new foundation for environmental law' (1984) 22 *Osgoode Hall LJ* 323.

ELDER, P. S., 'Legal rights for nature—the wrong answer to the right(s) question' (1984) 22 *Osgoode Hall LJ* 285.

GORMLEY, W. P., *Human Rights and Environment; The Need for International Cooperation* (Sijthoff, Leyden, 1976).

HONDIUS, F. W., 'The environment and human rights' (1971) 41 *Yearbook of the AAA* 68.

International Colloquium, *An Individual Right or an Obligation of the State? International Colloquium on the Right to a Humane Environment* (E. Schmidt, Berlin, 1976).

JOHNSON, D. M., 'Systemic environmental damage: the challenge to international law and organisation' (1985) 12 *Syracuse J Int L & Com* 185.

NANDA, V. P. & others, 'Ten years after Stockholm—International environmental law' (1985) 79 *Proc ASIL* 411.

PATTI, S., 'Environmental protection in Italy: the emerging concept of a right to a healthful environment' (1984) 24 *Natural Resources J* 535.

SMITH, G. P., 'The United Nations and the environment: sometimes a great notion?' (1984) 19 *Texas Int LJ* 335.

STEVENSON, C. P., 'A new perspective on environmental rights after the Charter' (1983) 21 *Osgoode Hall LJ* 390.

Symposium, 'Environmental law and policy in developing countries' (1985) 12 *Ecology LQ* 907.
—— 'Global environmental problems: a legal perspective' (1985) 12 *Syracuse JILC* 185.
WOOD Jr, H. W., 'The United Nations World Charter for Nature: the developing nations' initiative to establish protections for the environment' (1985) 12 *Ecology LQ* 675.

7. Existence, Right to

ALSTON, P. & TOMASKEVI, K. (eds), *The Right to Food* (Martinus Nijhoff, The Hague, 1984).
ARENS, R. (ed.), *Genocide in Paraguay* (Temple UP, Philadelphia, 1976).
BASSIOUNI, M. C., 'International law and the holocaust' (1979) 9 *Calif WILJ* 201.
BEDAU, H. A., 'Genocide in Vietnam' (1973) 53 *BUL Rev* 574; also in Held & ors (eds), *Philosophy, Morality and International Affairs* (Oxford UP, New York, 1974) 46.
BITKER, B. V., 'Genocide revisited' (1970) 56 *ABAJ* 71.
BOREL, R. L., 'The right to food' (1985) 70 *Iowa L Rev* 1279.
BRYANT, B., 'Substantive scope of the Convention' (1975) 16 *Harv Int LJ* 686.
CHAUDHURI, K., *Genocide in Bangladesh* (Orient-Longman, Bombay, 1972).
CHRISTENSON, C. & HANRAHAN, L., 'African food crises: short, medium and long-term responses' (1985) 70 *Iowa L Rev* 1293.
DAES, E.-IA. 'Protection of minorities under the International Bill of Human Rights and the Genocide Convention', in *Xenion. Festschrift für Pan J Zepos* (Katsikalis Verlag, Athens, 1973) II, 35.
DAVIS, S., *Victims of the Miracle: Development and the Indians of Brazil* (Cambridge UP, Cambridge, 1977).
DUFFET, J. (ed.), *Against the Crime of Silence: Proceedings of the International War Crimes Tribunal* (Simon & Schuster, New York, 1970).
GALES, R. P., 'Genocide: Israeli law' (1966) 42 *NDL Rev* 418.
GOLDBERG, A. J., 'Crimes against humanity' (1970) 10 *Western Ont L Rev* 1.
KENNEDY, E. M., *et al*, 'Biafra, Bengal and beyond: international responsibility and genocidal conflict' (1972) 66 *ASIL Proc* 89.
KUPER, L., *The Prevention of Genocide* (New Haven, Yale UP, 1985).
KUTNER, L., 'A world genocide tribunal—rampart against future genocide: proposal for planetary preventative measures supplementing a genocide early warning system' (1984) 18 *Val UL Rev* 373.
LANE, E., 'Mass killings by governments: lawful in the world legal order?' (1979) 12 *NYUJ Int L & Pol* 239.
LE BLANC, L. J., 'The intent to destroy groups in the Genocide Convention' (1984) 78 *AJIL* 369.
LIPPMAN, M., 'The drafting of the 1948 Convention on the Prevention and Punishment of the Crime of Genocide' (1985) 3 *Boston U Int LJ* 1.
MELADY, T., *Burundi, The Tragic Years* (Orbis, NY, 1974).
Note, 'Genocide: a commentary on the convention' (1948-9) 58 *Yale LJ* 1142.

—— 'The United States and the 1948 Genocide Convention'(1975) 16 *Harv Int LJ* 683.

—— 'Genocide and international law: is there a cause of action?' (1984) 8 *ASILS Int LJ* 1.

PEARLMAN, P. B., 'The Genocide Convention' (1951) 30 *Neb L Rev* 1.

PHILLIPS, O. L., 'The Genocide Convention: its effects on our legal system' (1949) 35 *ABAJ* 623.

—— & DEUTSCH, F. P., 'Pitfalls of the Genocide Convention' (1970) 56 *ABAJ* 641.

PORTER, J. N. (ed.), *Genocide and Human Rights. A Global Anthology* (University Press of America, Washington, 1982).

RAMCHARAN, B. G., *The Right to Life in International Law* (Martinus Nijhoff, The Hague, 1985).

RAYMOND, J. M., 'Genocide: an unconstitutional human rights convention' (1972) 12 *Santa Clara L* 294.

ROSENTHAL, J., 'Legal and political considerations of the United States' ratification of the Genocide Convention' (1985) 3 *Antioch LJ* 117.

SCHILLER, B. M., 'Life in a symbolic universe: comments on the Genocide Convention and international law' (1977) 9 *SWUL Rev* 47.

SHEPHERD, G. W., 'The denial of the right to food: Development and intervention in Africa'(1985) 15 *Calif WILJ* 528.

SHUE, H., *Basic Rights: Subsistence, Affluence and US Foreign Policy* (Princeton, Princeton UP, 1980).

STRICKLAND, P., 'Genocide at law: an historic and contemporary view of the native American experience' (1986) 34 *U Kansas LR* 713.

Symposium, 'International law and world hunger' (1985) 70 *Iowa LR* 1183.

TOMASEVSKI, K., 'Human rights: the right to food' (1985) 70 *Iowa L Rev* 1321.

Genocide: see Existence, Right to;

8. Indigenous Peoples, Rights of

ALFREDSSON, G., 'International law, international organizations and indigenous peoples' (1982) 36 *J Int Aff* 113.

—— 'Fourth Session of the Working Group on Indigenous Populations' (1986) 55 *Nordik J Int L* 22.

ANDERSON, E., 'The indigenous people of Saskatchewan: their rights under international law' (1981) 7 *American Indian Jnl* No 1, 4; No 2, 2.

ANDRESS, J. L. & FALOWSKI, J. E., 'Self-determination: Indians and the United Nations—the anomalous status of America's "domestic dependent nations" ' (1980) 8 *American Indian LR* 97.

Australia, Senate Standing Committee on Constitutional and Legal Affairs, *Two Hundred Years Later . . . Report on the Feasibility of a Compact or 'Makarrata' between the Commonwealth and Aboriginal People* (Australian Government Publishing Service, Canberra, 1983).

Australian Law Reform Commission, *The Recognition of Aboriginal Customary Laws* (Australian Government Publishing Service, Canberra, 1986, 2 vols & Summary).

BARSH, R., 'Indigenous peoples: an emerging object of international law' (1986) 80 *AJIL* 369.

BARSH, R. & HENDERSON, Y., 'Tribal administration of natural resource development' (1975) 52 *NDL Rev* 307.

———— 'Betrayal. Oliphant v. Suquamish Indian Tribe (98 Sup Ct 1011) and the hunting of the snark' (1979) 63 *Minn L Rev* 609.

BAYEFSKY, A. F., 'The Human Rights Committee and the case of Sandra Lovelace' (1982) 20 *Can YB Int L* 244.

BENNETT, G., *Aboriginal Rights in International Law* (London, 1978: Royal Anthropological Institute, Occasional Paper No 37).

BENNETT, G. I., 'ILO Convention on Indigenous and Tribal Populations—the resolution of a problem of vires' (1972-3) 46 *BYIL* 382.

—— 'Developing law of aboriginal rights' (1979) 22 *Review of the International Commission of Jurists* 37.

BERGER, T. R., 'Native rights and self-determination: an address to the Conference on the Voice of Native People, September 25, 1983' (1984) 22 *U W Ont L Rev* 1.

BOLDT, M., LONG, J. A., & LITTLE BEAR, L. (eds), *The Quest for Justice: Aboriginal Peoples and Aboriginal Rights* (Toronto, Toronto UP, 1985).

BRØSTED, J. & ORS (eds), *Native Power. The Quest for Autonomy and Nationhood of Indigenous Peoples* (Universitetsførlaget AS, Oslo, 1985).

BRYAN, D., 'Cultural relativism—power in service of interests: the particular case of native American education' (1983) 32 *Buffalo L Rev* 643.

Canada, House of Commons, Special Committee on Indian Self-Government (Chairman: K. Penner MP), *Indian Self-Government in Canada* (Ottawa, Government Printer, 1983).

CLINEBELL, J. H. & THOMSON, J., 'Sovereignty and self-determination: the rights of native Americans under international law' (1978) 27 *Buffalo L Rev* 669.

CUMMING, P. A. *et al*, 'Rights of indigenous peoples: a comparative analysis' (1974) 68 *ASIL Proc* 265.

DAES, E.-I., 'Native people's rights' (1986) 27 *C de D* 123.

EGGLESTON, E., 'Prospects for United Nations protection of the human rights of indigenous minorities' (1970-73) 5 *Aust YBIL* 68.

EIDE, A., 'Indigenous populations and human rights: the United Nations efforts at midway' in J. Brøsted & ORS (eds), *Native Power. The Quest for Autonomy and Nationhood of Indigenous Peoples* (Universitetsførlaget AS, Oslo, 1985) 196.

GALEY, M. F., 'Indigenous peoples, international consciousness raising and the development of international law on human rights' (1975) 8 *Revue des Droits de l'Homme, Droit International et Droit Comparé* 21.

GAYIM, E., 'United Nations law on self-determination of indigenous peoples' (1982) 51 *Nordisk Tidsskrift* 53.

GREEN, L. C., 'Canada's Indians: federal policy, international and constitutional law' (1970) 4 *Ottawa L Rev* 101.

HAWKES, D. C., *Aboriginal Self-Government: What Does It Mean?* (Discussion Paper, Institute of Intergovernmental Relations, Queen's University, Kingston, 1985).

HENDERSON, J. Y., 'Unravelling the riddle of aboriginal title' (1977) 5 *Am Indian L Rev* 75.

HODGSON, D. C., 'Aboriginal Australians and the World Court. Sovereignty by conquest. The advisory jurisdiction of the World Court' [1985] *NZLJ* 33, 64.

LUCAS, E., 'Towards an International Declaration on Land Rights' (1984) 33 *Review of the International Commission of Jurists* 61.

LYSYK, K. 'Human rights and the native peoples of Canada' (1968) 46 *Can B Rev* 695.

McCOY, R. G., 'Doctrine of tribal sovereignty: accommodating tribal, state and federal interests' (1978) 13 *Harv Civil Rights L Rev* 357.

McHUGH, P., 'Aboriginal rights and sovereignty: Commonwealth developments' [1986] *NZLJ* 57.

MACKINNON, V. S., 'Booze, religion, Indians and the Canadian Bill of Rights' [1973] *Pub Law* 295.

MANDELL, L., 'Indian nations: not minorities' (1986) 27 *C de D* 101.

MARTINEZ COBO, J. R., *Study of the Problem of Discrimination against Indigenous Populations* (E/CN 4/Sub 2/476 & Add 1-6; E/CN 4/Sub 2/1982/2 & Add 1-7l E/CN 4/Sub 2/1983/21 & Add 1-8, 1982).

MARTONE, F. J., 'American Indian tribal self government in the federal system: inherent right or Congressional licence?' (1976) 51 *Notre Dame L Rev* 600.

MASON, M. D., 'Canadian and United States approaches to Indian sovereignty' (1983) 21 *Osgoode Hall LJ* 422.

METTLER, E., 'Unified theory of Indian tribal sovereignty' (1978) 30 *Hastings LJ* 89.

MORSE, B. W., *Aboriginal Self-Government in Australia and Canada* (Background Paper No 4, Institute of Intergovernmental Relations, Queen's University, Kingston, 1984).

MUSKRAT, J., 'The Constitution and the American Indian: past and prologue' (1976) 3 *Hastings Const LQ* 657.

NETTHEIM, G. (ed.), *Human Rights for Aboriginal People in the 1980s* (Legal Books, Sydney, 1983).

—— 'Justice and indigenous minorities: a new province for international and national law' in A. R. Blackshield (ed.), *Legal Change. Essays in Honour of Julius Stone* (Butterworths, Sydney, 1983) 257.

Note, 'Federal Indian policy: a violation of international treaty law' (1977) 4 *West St U L Rev* 229.

—— 'Sovereignty under restriction: American Indian tribal sovereignty in law and practice' (1983) 4 *N YL Sch J Int & Comp L* 589.

—— 'Eagles and Indians: the law and the survival of a species' (1984) 5 *Pub Land L Rev* 100.

—— 'A constitutional right of Indian self-government' (1985) 43 *U Toronto Fac L Rev* 72.

—— 'The quest of the Six Nations Confederacy for self-determination' (1986) 44 *U Toronto Fac LR* 1.

PARTLETT, D., 'Benign racial discrimination: equality and Aborigines' (1979) 10 *FLR* 238.

SANDERS, D. E., 'The Indian Act and the Bill of Rights' (1974) 6 *Ottawa LR* 397.

—— *The Formation of the World Council of Indigenous Peoples* (International Work Group for Indigenous Affairs, Doc 29, Copenhagen, 1977).

—— 'Aboriginal peoples and the Constitution' (1981) 19 *Alberta LR* 410.

—— 'The Re-Emergence of Indigenous Questions in International Law' (1983) 1 *Canadian Human Rights Yearbook* 3.

SLATTERY, B., 'The constitutional guarantee of aboriginal and treaty rights' (1983) 8 *Queens LJ* 232.

—— 'The hidden Constitution: Aboriginal rights in Canada' (1984) 32 *Am J Comp L* 361.

SWAN, G. S., 'Self-determination Pretoria-style: The case of the Transkei' (1981) 3 *Whittier L Rev* 475.

SWEPSTON, L., 'Latin American approaches to the "Indian problem"' (1978) 117 *Int Labour Review* 179.

United Nations, *Analytical Compilation of Existing Legal Instruments and Proposed Draft Standards relating to Indigenous Rights, Prepared by the Secetariat in Accordance with Sub-Commission Resolution 1985/22* (M/HR/86/36, GE.86-15907/3954E (1986)).

WASSER, M. B. & GRUMET, L. 'Indian rights: the reality of symbolism' (1978) 50 *NYSBJ* 482.

WERHAM, K. M., 'Sovereignty of Indian tribes: a reaffirmation and strengthening in the 1970s' (1978) 54 *Notre Dame LR* 5.

WHITLAM, E. G., 'Australian's international obligations on Aborigines' (1981) 53 *Aust Q* 433.

See also: Minorities, Rights of

9. International Peace, Right to

BILDER, R., 'The individual and the right to peace: the right to conscientious dissent' (1980) 11 *Bull Peace Proposals* 387.

CONAN, T., 'Why the international law defence is no. defence for nuclear war protesters' (1986) 12 *Syracuse JILC* 473.

DAWES, C. E., 'The right to peace' (1986) 60 *Australian LJ* 156.

DEWAR, J., *Nuclear Weapons, the Peace Movement and the Law* (Macmillan, Basingstoke, 1986).

ESEN, B. N., 'Réflexions sur le droit de vivre en paix' in *Miscellanea WG Ganshof van der Meersch* (Etablissements Emile Bruylant, Bruxelles, 1972) I, 487.

LIPPMAN, M., 'Nuclear weapons and international law: towards a Declaration on the Prevention and Punishment of the Crime of Nuclear Humancide' (1986) 8 *Loyola LA ICLJ* 183.

NANDA, V. P., 'Nuclear weapons and the right to live in peace under international law' (1983) 9 *Brooklyn J Int L* 283.

ROSTOW, E. V., 'Peace as a human right' (1983) 4 *NYL Sch J Int & Comp L* 215.

SAJOO, A. B., 'Human rights perspectives on the arms race' (1982-3) 28 *McGill LJ* 628.

TOTH, J., 'Human Rights and world peace' in *Cassin Collection* (1969) 362.

United Nations, *Report of the Secretary-General, The International Dimensions of the Right to Development as a Human Right, in Relation with Other Human Rights Based on International Cooperation, Including the Right to Peace, Taking into Account the Requirements of the New International Economic Order and the Fundamental Human Needs* (1979).

10. Minorities, Rights of

BILINSKI, A., 'Neue historiche Katagorie—Sowjetvolk' (1977) 21 *Recht in Ostend West* 213.

BREUGEL, J. W., 'A neglected field: the protection of minorities (1971) 4 *Revue des Droits de l'Homme* 413.

CAPOTORTI, F., *Study on the Rights of Persons Belonging to Ethnic, Religious and Linguistic Minorities* (UN Doc E/CN 4 Sub 2/384 Rev 1, 1979).

—— 'Diritti dei membri di minoranze: verso una dichiarazione delle Nazioni Unite?' (1981) 64 *Rivista di Diritto Internazionale* 30.

—— 'Les développements possibles de la protection internationale des minorités' (1986) 27 *C de D* 239.

CLAUDE, I., *National Minorities. An International Problem* (Harvard UP, Harvard, 1955).

CLAYDON, J., 'Transnational protection of ethnic minorities: a tentative framework for inquiry' (1975) 13 *Can YIL* 25.

—— 'Internationally uprooted people and the transnational protection of minority culture' (1978) 24 *N YLS L Rev* 125.

Colloquium, 'Tensions between religious or ethnic communities and the larger society' (1984) 41 *Wash & Lee L Rev* 31.

DAES, E.-IA., 'Protection of minorities under the International Bill of Human Rights and the Genocide Convention', in *Xenion. Festschrift für Pan J Zepos* (Katsikalis Verlag, Athens, 1973) II, 35.

DESCHNES, J. 'Qu'est-ce qu'une minorité?' (1986) 27 *C de D* 255.

ERMACORA, F., 'Volkengruppeausgleich in Osterreich' (1977) 37 *ZaöRV* 276.

FAIRWEATHER, G., 'The rights of religious minorities' (1986) 27 *C de D* 89.

FELDBRUGGE, F. J. M., 'Criminal law and traditional society: the role of Soviet law in the integration of non-slavic peoples' (1977) 3 *Review of Socialist Law* 3.

FEINBERG, N., 'The legal validity of the undertakings concerning minorities and the clausula rebus sic stantibus' in *Studies in International Law* (1979) 17.

FISCHER, E., *Minorities and Minority Problems* (Vantage Press, New York, 1980).

FRICKEY, P. P., 'Majority rule, minority rights and the right to vote: reflections upon a reading of minority vote dilution' (1985) 3 *Law & Inequality* 209.

GARBER, L. & O'CONNOR, L. M., 'The 1984 UN Sub-Commission on Prevention of Discrimination and Protection of Minorities' (1985) 79 *AJIL* 168.

GARDINIERS, T., HANNUM, H. & KRUGER, J., '1981 session of the United Nations Sub-Commission on the Prevention of Discrimination and the Protection of Minorities' (1982) 76 *AJIL* 405.

GLAZER, N. & YOUNG, K. (eds), *Ethnic Pluralism and Public Policy. Achieving Equality in the United States and Britain* (Heinemann, London, 1983).

HAKSAR, V., *Minority Protection and the International Bill of Human Rights* (Allied Publishers, Bombay, 1974).

HANNUM, H., 'Thirty-third session of the UN Sub-Commission on Prevention of Discrimination and Protection of Minorities' (1981) 75 *AJIL* 172.

HANTKE, J., '1982 session of the United Nations Sub-Commission on the Prevention of Discrimination and the Protection of Minorities' (1983) 77 *AJIL* 651.

HAUSER, R., 'International protection of minorities and the right of self-determination' (1971) 1 *Israel YB on Human Rights* 92.

HAVER, P., 'United Nations Sub-Commission on the Prevention of Discrimination and the protection of minorities' (1982) 21 *Colum J Transnat L* 103.

HONDIUS, F., 'Minorities in international law' (1964) 34 *Yearbook of the AAA* 196.

HUMPHREY, J., 'United Nations Sub-Commission on the Prevention of Discrimination and the protection of minorities' (1968) 62 *AJIL* 869.

HUMPHREY, J. P., 'Preventing discrimination and positive protection for minorities: aspects of international law' (1986) 27 *C de D* 23.

KELLY, J. B., 'National minorities in international law' (1973) 3 *Denver J Int & Pol* 253.

KRISHNA IYER, V. P., 'Mass expulsion as a violation of human rights' (1973) 13 *Indian JIL* 169.

KUNZ, J. L., 'The present status of international law for the protection of minorities' (1954) 48 *AJIL* 282.

LADOR-LEDERER, J. J., *International Group Protection* (Sijthoff, Leyden, 1968).

LANNUNG, H., 'Rights of Minorities' in *Mélanges offerts à Polys Modinos. Problèmes des Droits de l'Homme et de l'Unification Européenne* (Paris, Pedone, 1968) 181.

LEIBHOLZ, G., 'Some remarks on the protection of racial and linguistic minorities in Europe during the nineteenth century' (1979) *Internationales Recht und Diplomatie* 119.

MAGNET, J. E., 'Collective rights, cultural autonomy and the Canadian state' (1986) 32 *McGill LJ* 170.

MAJUL, C. A., 'Problems in the implementation of Sharia personal laws in Muslim minority countries in the far east' (1978) 8 *J of Islamic and Comp L* 107.

MARSHALL, B., 'A Comment on the non-discrimination principle in a "nation of minorities" ' (1984) 93 *Yale LJ* 1006.

MODEEN, T., *The International Protection of National Minorities in Europe* (Acta Academiae Aboensis, Ser A Vol 37 No l, 1969)).

MONACO, R. 'Minorités nationales et la protection internationale des droits de l'homme' in *René Cassin Amicorum Discipulorumque Liber* (Paris, A Pedone, 1969) 175.

de MONTIGNY, Y., 'L'ONU et la protection internationale des minorités depuis 1945' (1978) 13 *RJT* 389.

NARIMAN, F. S., 'Minority Rights' [1984] *NZLJ* 211.

Note, 'Ethnic minority groups and self-determination: the case of the Basques' (1986) 20 *Colum J L & Soc Probs* 55.

—— 'Japan's denationalisation of the Korean minority' (1982) 29 *Review of the International Commission of Jurists* 28.

—— 'Situation of the Finland-Swedish population in the light of international, constitutional and administrative law' (1970) 16 *McGill LJ* 121.

de NOVA, R., 'International protection of national minorities and human rights' (1965) 11 *How LJ* 275.

PALLEY, C., 'The role of law in relation to minority groups' in A. E. Alcock, B. K. Taylor & J. M. Welton (eds), *The Future of Cultural Minorities* (St Martin's Press, London, 1979) 120.

PETRIC, E., 'Helsinki Conference and the national minorities'(1977) 24 *Jugoslovenska Revija za Medunarodno. Pravo* 146.

—— 'Quelques aperçus de droit international sur les minorités dans les accords d'Osimo' (1978) 25 *Jugoslovenska Revija za Medunarodno Pravo* 201.

RABINOWICZ, A. M. K., 'Classical international law and the Jewish question' (1977) 24 *Neth Int L Rev* 205.

RECHETOV, Y. M., 'Minority rights in contemporary international law' (1978) 31 *Revue Héllenique de Droit International* 154.

ROBINSON, J., 'International protection of minorities: a global view' (1971) 1 *Israel YB on Hum Rights* 61.

ROSTING, H., 'Protection of minorities by the League of Nations' (1923) 17 *AJIL* 641.

SAMUELS, A., 'Legal recognition and protection of minority customs in a plural society in England' (1981) 10 *Anglo-Am L Rev* 241.

SOHN, L. B., 'The rights of minorities' in L. Henkin (ed.), *The International Bill of Rights. The Covenant on Civil and Political Rights* (Columbia UP, New York, 1981) 270.

'Symposium: Minority rights' (1975) 63 *Calif L Rev* 597.

SZABO, Z., 'Minorités et les droits de l'homme' (1981) Acta Juridica Acadamiae Scientarium Hungaricae 1.

SZEPESSY, T., 'Democratic institutional framework for the participation of the coinhabiting nationalities in the management, organisation and performance of a country's overall economic, social, political cultural and artistic activities' (1979) 23 *Revue Roumaine de Sciences Sociales, Série de Sciences Juridiques* 15.

THORNBERRY, P., 'Is there a phoenix in the ashes? International law and minority rights' (1981) 15 *Tex Int LJ* 421.

TOMUSCHAT, C., 'Protection of minorities under Art. 27 of the International Covenant on Civil and Political Rights' in R. Bernhardt, W. K. Geck, G. Jaenicke & H. Steinberger (eds), *Festschrift für Hermann Mosler* (Springer Verlag, Berlin, 1983) 949.

TURK, D., 'Outline of the international legal regulation ofthe protection of minorities within the United Nations' (1976) 23 *Jugoslovenska Revija za Medunarodno. Pravo* 61.

UIBOPUU, H.-J., 'International legal status of Soviet minorities today' (1976) 2 *Review of Socialist Law* 217.

VIERDAG, E. W., *The Concept of Discrimination in International Law* (Sijthoff, The Hague, 1973).

VUKAS, B., 'General international law and the protection of minorities' (1975) 8 *Revue des Droits de l'Homme* 41.

WHITAKER, B. (ed.), *Minorities. A Question of Human Rights?* (Pergamon Press, Oxford, 1984).

WOEHRLING, J., 'Minority cultural and linguistic rights in the Canadian Charter of Rights and Freedoms' (1985) 31 *McGill LJ* 50.

WOOLRIDGE, F. & SHARMA, V. D., 'International law and the expulsion of Ugandan Asians' (1975) 9 *Int Law* 30.

See also: Cultural and Linguistic Rights; Indigeneous Peoples, Rights of.

11. Natural Resources, Permanent Sovereignty over

BANERJEE, S. K., 'The concept of permanent sovereignty over natural resources: an analysis' (1968) 8 *Indian JIL* 515.

BARSCH, R. & HENDERSON, J. Y., 'Tribal administration of natural resource development' (1975) 52 *NDL Rev* 307.

ELIAN, G., 'Le principe de la souveraineté sur les ressources nationales et ses incidences juridiques sur le commerce international' (1976) 149 *Hague Receuil* 1.

FISCHER, G., 'La souveraineté sur les ressouces naturelles' [1962] *Annuaire Française de DI* 516.

GAINER, G., 'Nationalization: the dichotomy between western and Third World perspectives in international law' (1983) 26 *Howard LJ* 1547.

GESS, K. N., 'Permanent sovereignty over natural resources: an analytical review of the United Nations resolution and its genesis' (1964) 13 *ICLQ* 398.

HALPERIN, M., 'Human rights and natural resources' (1968) 9 *Wm and Mary L Rev* 770.

HIGGINS, R., 'Taking of property by the state: recent developments in international law' (1982) 176 *Hague Receuil* 259.

HOSSAIN, K. & CHOWDHURY, S. R. (eds), *Permanent Sovereignty over Natural Resources in International Law. Principle and Practice* (Frances Pinter, London, 1984).

HYDE, C. C., 'Permanent sovereignty over natural wealth and resources' (1956) 50 *AJIL* 854.

JOYNER, C. C., 'Legal implications of the concept of the common heritage of mankind' (1986) 35 *ICLQ* 190.

Note, 'The New International Economic Order and General Assembly resolutions: the debate over the legal effects of General Assembly resolutions revisited' (1985) 15 *Calif WILJ* 647.

van THEMMAAT, P. V., *The Changing Structure of International Economic Law* (Martinus Nijhoff, The Hague, 1981).

de WAART, P. J., 'Permanent sovereignty over natural resources as a cornerstone for international economic rights and duties' in H. Meijers and E. W. Vierdag (eds), *Essays on international law and relations in honour of A. J. P. Tammes* (Sijthoff, Leyden, 1977) 304.

WESTON, B. H., 'The Charter of Economic Rights and Duties of States and the deprivation of foreign-owned wealth' (1981) 75 *AJIL* 437.

ZAKARIYA, H. S., 'Sovereignty over natural resources and the search for a new international economic order' in K. Hossain (ed.), *Legal Aspects of the New International Economic Order* (Frances Pinter, London, 1980) 208.

12. Self-Determination, Right to

BENNETT, T. W. & PEART, N. S., 'The Ingwavuma land deal: a case study of self-determination' (1986) 4 *BC Third World LJ* 23.

BERGER, T., 'Native rights and self-determination: an address to the Conference on the Voices of Native Peoples, Sept 25, 1983' (1984) 22 *UW Ont L Rev* 1.

BLAY, S. K. N., 'Self-determination versus territorial integrity in decolonization' (1986) 18 *NYL J Int L & Pol* 441.

BLUMENWITZ, D., 'Selbstbestimmung und Menschenrechte im geteilten Deutschland' (1974) 17 *Jahrbuch für Internationales Recht* 11.

BROSSARD, J., 'Le droit du peuple québécois de disposer de lui-même au regard du droit international' (1977) *Can YBIL* 84.

CASSESE, A., 'Political self-determination—old concepts and new developments', in A. Cassese (ed.), *UN Law/Fundamental Rights: Two Topics in International Law* (Sijthoff & Noordhoff, Alphen aan den Rijn, 1979).

CHARPENTIER, J., 'Autodétermination et décolonisation' in *Mélanges offerts à Charles Chaumont* (Paris, A Pedone, 1984) 117.

CHEN, L. *et al.*, 'Self-determination: an important dimension in the demand for freedom' (1981) 75 *ASIL Proc* 88.

COLLINS, J. A., 'Self-determination in international law: the Palestinians' (1980) 12 *Case Wes Res JIL* 137.

CRAWFORD, J., *The Creation of States in International Law* (*Clarendon Press, Oxford*, *1979*).

—— 'Self-determination outside the colonial context' in A. Macartney (ed.), *Self-Expression and Self-Determination in the Commonwealth Context* (1987) 1.

CRISTESCU, A., *The Right to Self-Determination. Historical and Current Development on the Basis of United Nations Instruments* (UN Doc E/CN.4/Sub 2/404/Rev 1, 1981).

EMERSON, P., 'Self-determination' (1971) 65 *AJIL* 459.

FRIEDLANDER, R. A., 'Self-determination: a legal and political enquiry' (1975) *Det Col L Rev* 71.

GAUTIER MAYORA, C., 'La elevacion del caso de Puerto Rico ante la Asamblea General de las Naciones Unidas en la década actual' (1984) 45 *Rev Col Ab PR* 69.

GREEN, L. C., 'Self-determination and the settlement of the Arab-Israeli conflict' (1971) 65 *AJIL* 40.

GROS ESPIELL, H., *The Right to Self-Determination: Implementation of United Nations Resolutions* (United Nations, New York, Doc E/EN.4/Sub.2/405/Rev 1, 1980).

—— 'Los derechos humanos y el derecho a la libre determinacion de los pueblos' in *Estudios en honor de Manuel Garcia Pelayo* (1980) II, 576.

GUILHAUDIS, J.-F., *Le Droit des Peuples à Disposer d'eux-mêmes* (Presses Universitaires de Grenoble, Grenoble, 1976).

HIGGINS, R., 'Territorial claims as a limitation to the right of self-determination in the context of the Falkland Islands dispute' (1982/83) 4 *Fordham Int LJ* 443.

—— 'Judge Dillard and the right to self-determination' (1983) 23 *Va J Int L* 387.

MAGUIRE, J. R., 'Decolonisation of Belize: self determination v. territorial integrity' (1982) 22 *Va JIL* 849.

NAYAR, M.-GK., 'Self-determination beyond the colonial context: Biafra in retrospect' (1975) 10 *Tex Int LJ* 321.

N'KOLOMBUA, A., 'L'ambivalence des relations entre le droit des peuples à disposer d'eux-mêmes et l'integrité territoriale des états en droit international contemporain' in *Mélanges offerts à Charles Chaumont* (Paris, A Pedone, 1984) 433.

Note, 'Ethnic minority groups and self-determination: the case of the Basques' (1986) 20 *Colum J L & Soc Probs* 55.

—— 'Legal aspects of membership in the Organisation of African Unity: the case of the Western Sahara' (1985) 17 *Case W Res J Int L* 123.

—— 'Logic of secession' (1980) 89 *Yale LJ* 802.

—— 'Self-determination for the people of Taiwan' (1984) 14 *Cal W Int LJ* 471.

—— 'Self-determination in Hong Kong: a new challenge to an old doctrine' (1985) 22 *San Diego L Rev* 839.

POMERANCE, M. 'The United States and self-determination: perspectives on the Wilsonian conception' (1976) 70 *AJIL* 1.

—— *Self-Determination in Law and Practice. The New Doctrine in the United Nations* (Martinus Nijhoff, The Hague, 1982).

REISMAN, W. M., 'Coercion and self-determination: construing Charter article 2(4)' (1984) 78 *AJIL* 642.

RICHARDSON, H. J., 'Constitutive questions for Namibian independence' (1984) 78 *AJIL* 76.

SCHACHTER, O., 'The legality of pro-democratic invasion' (1984) 78 *AJIL* 645.

SHAW, M., 'The international status of national liberation movements' (1983) 5 *Liverpool L Rev* 19.

SINHA, S. P., 'Is self-determination passé?' (1973) 12 *Colum J Transnat L* 260.

SUZUKI, E., 'Self-determination and world public order: community response to territorial separation' (1976) 16 *Va JIL* 779.

SWAN, G. S., 'Self-determination Pretoria-style: the case of the Transkei' (1981) 3 *Whittier L Rev* 475.

TURP, D., 'Le droit de sécession en droit international public' (1982) 20 *Can YBIL* 24.

UMOZURIKE, U. O., *Self-Determination in International Law* (Archon Books, Hamden, 1972).

van DYKE, J., 'Self-determination and minority rights' (1969) 13 *Int Studies Q* 223.

WHITE, R. C. A., 'Self determination: a time for reassessment?' (1981) 28 *Neth Int L Rev* 147.

See also: Indigenous peoples, Rights of

Index